CHESTER GOULD

To my grandchildren,
Megan and Elizabeth,

in memory of my father's words,
"Life goes on."

CHESTER GOULD

A Daughter's Biography of the Creator of *Dick Tracy*

JEAN GOULD O'CONNELL

Foreword by Dick Locher
Introduction by Garyn G. Roberts

McFarland & Company, Inc., Publishers
Jefferson, North Carolina, and London

LIBRARY OF CONGRESS CATALOGUING-IN-PUBLICATION DATA

O'Connell, Jean Gould, 1927–
Chester Gould : a daughter's biography of
the creator of Dick Tracy / Jean Gould O'Connell ;
foreword by Dick Locher ; introduction by Garyn G. Roberts.
p.   cm.
Includes index.

ISBN-13: 978-0-7864-2825-0
(illustrated case binding : 50# alkaline paper) ∞

1. Gould, Chester.   2. Cartoonists— United States—Biography.
3. Dick Tracy (Comic strip).   I. Title.
PN6727.G667Z65   2007
741.5092 — dc22   2006036270
[B]

British Library cataloguing data are available

On the cover: Chester Gould with his creation, Dick Tracy
(Photograph courtesy of Richard Pietrzyk)

Manufactured in the United States of America

McFarland & Company, Inc., Publishers
Box 611, Jefferson, North Carolina 28640
www.mcfarlandpub.com

Contents

Acknowledgments

I am so overwhelmed with gratitude that it is hard for me to put into words my appreciation to my dear friend and advisor, Dr. Garyn Roberts. His encouragement and guidance were an inspiration to me when I doubted my ability to write this book. His faith in me brought me through to this wonderful day when I can proudly share this book and the private years of a man I so dearly loved, my father.

It wasn't until the 1990s that I wanted to write and had some hours to spend at it. Dick, my husband, had previously suffered a severe stroke; that was in 1981. Together we fought this crippling and disabling disease for twenty years. I lost Dick on January 3, 2002, after forty-six years of marriage, and I miss him.

If ever there was a man whose personality and optimistic view of life were in tune with my father, it is Dick Locher. Dick worked with Dad on the strip from 1957 to 1958 and went on to become a Pulitzer Prize–winning editorial cartoonist for the *Chicago Tribune*. Although Dick still submits editorial cartoons to the paper from time to time, he took over the artwork for *Dick Tracy* in 1983; today he is both author and artist of the strip. I felt he was the perfect person to write the foreword for my book. Dick, I thank you, my friend.

I sincerely thank Shel Dorf, Richard Pietrzyk and Matt Masterson, all longtime personal friends of Dad's, who have added their delightful stories about discovering *Dick Tracy* as children, as well as some memories of Dad. Being professionals in the comic strip world and artists themselves, they offer an especially educated perspective on Chester Gould, his art and his unique storytelling ability. You will be charmed by what they have to say.

Richard Pietrzyk renewed the look of several pieces of Dad's pre–*Dick Tracy* newspaper artwork that were torn. I don't know how he did it, but I am most grateful. Matt Masterson, from his wonderful collection of *Dick Tracy* comic strips, sent me seven of the Mrs. Pruneface and nine of the Coffyhead story strips as examples of Dad's work and storytelling. Thank you so much, Matt.

Last but not least, I thank my dear family: my late husband for his patience, and my two children, Sue and Tracy, their spouses, Brett and Cynthia, and my two grandchildren, Megan and Elizabeth, for encouraging me. Their belief in me made it my priority to leave them with what turned out to be a wonderful story of their grandfather and great-grandfather. After writing this book, I found the story too important to share with just my family. It is an inspiring story for all ages. I hope that you will feel the same.

Foreword
by Dick Locher

Nourishing a friendship between two people, especially of different occupational attitudes, is not always simple. A spark must fly from person to person and cut across the accidents of time and place: thus is born a new bond.

This spark was handed to me in 1957 when Chester Gould hired me as his new assistant. Many creative people would be envious of the lifetime I had with my exceptional friend Chet Gould and his *Dick Tracy*. I was charged from the very beginning with an aura of working

Chester Gould and Dick Locher lunching at the Tavern Club in Chicago, circa 1980.

1

with a true comic pioneer. He inspired me; he urged my talents and challenged me with his awareness of God, human folly and laughter. He added that we can do much with the latter but not with the first two. That I was selected to work on his strip when so much talent prevailed enhances the association I was so privileged to be part of.

I was handed a legend from a legend, and I exult today on the accident of time and place that I was assigned. I admire Chester Gould, who was an effective revolutionary in the comic industry. He invented a genre and an icon. I sat at his table and as his descendent, my cup runneth over.

Dick Locher, current artist and author of *Dick Tracy*.

Dick Locher, a Pulitzer Prize–winning editorial cartoonist, carries Gould's Dick Tracy *forward as its current artist and author.*

Preface

My father was Chester Gould, creator of the comic strip *Dick Tracy*.

Two years before my father died, I asked him if he would reminisce with me, recalling his childhood, his teenage years and his adult life. Though his body was failing, his mind was sharp. We both found that this was an experience filled with great love and emotion, sometimes spilling over with tears, sometimes with laughter.

Words alone cannot describe those hours we sat together in his studio with the tape recorder between us. It turned out to be a wonderful kind of therapy for both of us. For my father, it fulfilled a need to remember, to feel the closeness to those he had so loved in the past and present, and to recall his challenges and accomplishments. For me, this provided a part of my father I would always have — his memories, and the examples he had set forth during his life that would be an inspiration throughout my lifetime and the lives of my children and their children.

What started out as an oral biography of my father turned out to be a remarkable story filled with goals, disappointments, determination, accomplishments, and above all, a love for his family. Though I am not a professional writer, I knew I wanted to share this man's story in his words and in my own, relating his thoughts as he carefully expressed them to me. At eighty-three years of age, his memory was clear, as you will see as you read through these pages. The strong will of this man is filled with compassion, self-esteem and a sense of humor.

Being a personal glimpse into my father's life, this book will show you a side of him that very few people have known. Dad was a private person in the public eye. He paced himself carefully, setting aside time to collect his thoughts in keeping his imagination fertile in creativity. His sole objective was to keep his Tracy on his toes — to keep his readers guessing from one week to the next. This technique meant he needed a time to think and not lose his concentration. Never knowing where his story would take him from week to week was a challenge, but that's what he liked. Dad also needed time to relax and to enjoy his family, and, of course, take care of personal responsibilities. He loved his fans, reading every piece of fan mail that arrived and answering all that he could personally. That is what kept him in business.

As we talked together, taping his memories on those days in 1983, there were a few subjects I failed to cover with him. For information on those times I resorted to some interviews Dad gave to Matt Masterson, Max Collins, Shel Dorf and several others. But in most cases, we did pretty well on our own. Dad thoroughly enjoyed recalling his past, as Mother and I, along with his nurse, sat in the studio and listened to him. He had to chuckle at some recollections, and then at other times, he was overcome recalling the effort that he had laid out only to see it rejected.

I consider those tapes a most precious gift that Dad gave to his family. I hope that you will consider this book my gift to you.

Introduction
by Garyn G. Roberts

"Chester was a brilliant man, highly motivated by a great power that helped him attain his goals."

— Mrs. Chester (Edna) Gould

The stories and memories you are about to read here are real. These are inspiring tales of one extraordinary man, his extended family and friends, and humble beginnings that define the American character of the twentieth century. These stories are provided by the man himself, and are lovingly detailed and related by his beautiful daughter, Jean Gould O'Connell.

Chester Gould (pronounced "Goold" though he made his life "gold"; November 20, 1900 to May 11, 1985) was the descendant of Oklahoma Territory pioneers, and the son of a newspaper man. During his childhood and adolescence, Gould lived in Pawnee, Oklahoma, the frontier town whose residents and frequent visitors at the time included entertainers Buffalo Bill and Pawnee Bill, Tom Mix, Iron Tail (whose image is found on the Indian Head/Buffalo nickel started in 1913), major league ball player Moses Yellowhorse and others from African American, American Indian, and European American communities. Chet was an accomplished artist at an early age, publishing his drawings in local newspapers and painting his art for hire on the sides of local buildings.

From 1919 to 1921, Gould attended Oklahoma A&M (Agricultural and Mechanical — later renamed Oklahoma State University) in Stillwater. In 1921, with $50 in his pocket, he boarded a train and moved to Chicago to pursue a career as an illustrator and newspaper comic strip writer. In 1923, he earned a degree in Commerce and Marketing from Northwestern University. Over a period of ten years, Chester Gould worked for all the major newspapers in Chicago.

His big break came in 1931 when he landed a contract with the *Chicago Tribune–New York News* syndicate to write and draw a comic strip originally titled *Plainclothes Tracy* (later *Dick Tracy*). William Randolph Hearst, Marshall Field (known more for his department stores than his newspaper syndicate), and J. Edgar Hoover would later, unsuccessfully, each try to buy Gould away from the *Tribune–News* Syndicate.

5

Responding to the culture of gangsterism and crime he found in Depression-era Chicago, Gould symbolically brought frontier justice to urban rogues of Dick Tracy's not-so-fictional world. Developing and employing a story formula where documented police procedures and sciences were conventions (Gould worked closely with Chicago area police forces and forensic scientists), and physically and morally grotesque villains were inventions, Chester Gould provided a morality play and articulated a mythology in *Dick Tracy* that captivated audiences internationally. In the process, he predicted and foresaw a number of significant technological advances including wrist radios and wrist televisions, and advances in crime detection, transportation, medical procedures, and more. Having completed forty-six years, eleven weeks, and six days—16,886 nonstop days counting twelve leap years—of *Dick Tracy* continuity, Gould retired as the writer and artist of his famous strip on Christmas Day, 1977. When he retired, newspaper comic strips were more than eighty years old. They would never be the same again.

No newspaper comic strip was as important a cultural document, relating a message of high morality, family life, and patriotism, than Chester Gould's *Dick Tracy*. None ever has been, through the present day.

Cultural Significance

In *The Power of Myth* (New York: Doubleday, 1988), Joseph Campbell wrote, "The moral objective is that of saving a people, or saving a person or supporting an idea. The hero sacrifices himself for something—that's the morality of it." Chester Gould and Dick Tracy were and are heroes who support and defend the highest moral code.

Numerous methods of communicating an idea exist, or have existed, in American society, and now in the world community. Various messages can be conveyed, and the media employed to disseminate these messages are improved upon daily. Through the media, American culture is widely recorded and popularized. The Great Depression (Gould called it the "Big Depression") provided the circumstances for the development of significant, enduring sociohistoric events and advances; among these was the emergence or further development of a variety of popular media. Motion pictures, pulp magazines, story radio, Big Little Books, and comic strips enjoyed their respective golden ages during this time. In the fact and fantasy of the 1930s, a vast array of heroes arose to protect the social paradigm.

In October of 1931, a comic strip was born which chronicled the popular culture of the day, and which focused its content on the then socially prescribed "War on Crime." Its story lines, protagonists, and antagonists were intentional exaggerations of actual historical events and people. Ever conscious of newly documented police procedures, the strip's producer selected and effectively exploited a unique mass medium where he could convey a message of high morality. The man was Chester Gould; the strip was *Dick Tracy*.

The Confines of the Medium and the Art

What constitutes Art with a capital "A" must be defined by the opportunities afforded by the medium. In other words, the aesthetics or value judgments levied on the work must include the form's potential and limitations.

In Chester Gould's weekday (i.e. Monday through Saturday) *Dick Tracy* newspaper comic strip, the medium or form consisted of white Bristol board and (preceded by pencil and art gum eraser) black India ink. For all practical purposes, that medium was two-dimensional, and confined to black and white space. Any extension of these parameters (for example, perspectives, angles, atmospheres, and related details) was the responsibility and challenge of the newspaper comic strip artist. With this in mind, Chester Gould's storytelling and drawing in each of his five decades on *Dick Tracy* achieved moments of Art with a capital "A." Scrutiny of his more than forty-six years of *Tracy* dailies bears this out.

The medium or form in which Gould's *Dick Tracy* Sunday pages appeared — and they were most often full pages, even in 1977 — had an added potential. This was color. The result was that Gould's Sunday pages not only summarized a week of preceding daily strips, predicted the story line of the next week's dailies, and expanded upon the same; they told a different kind of story and provided a different kind of art. And they required yet another kind of dexterity from their artist and his assistants. Taken out of the context of the larger daily continuity, these, by necessity, were individual stories which stood by themselves. With these considerations in mind, then, Gould's *Dick Tracy* (dailies and Sundays) often achieved the status of Art.

Formulas for Success

Never underestimate the power of vision, high goals, drive, work ethic, and persistence. These are still today vital ingredients for success. Chester Gould knew this, and followed a formula rooted in these precepts.

In crime and mystery fiction, Edgar Allan Poe's C. Auguste Dupin and Arthur Conan Doyle's Sherlock Holmes are prototypes or archetypes, with Holmes the more readily recognized of the two. In some ways, Chester Gould considered Dick Tracy a logical, contemporary extension of Poe's and Doyle's creations. Over time, Tracy achieved similar international status. Today, Dick Tracy ranks with Sherlock Holmes as one of the most recognized fictional detectives of all time.

Here in his daughter Jean's memoir, we see that Chester Gould employed a formula or ritual for personal success; but he also developed a very specific formula for the success of the story lines and drawing in *Dick Tracy*. As is the case with most successful (culturally representative and hence popular) story formulas, the formula in Gould's *Tracy* is a carefully crafted balance of conventions and inventions. Conventions in Gould's newspaper comic strip include very recognizable period history, newspaper headlines, and established police procedures and sciences. Inventions include the latest and upcoming scientific technologies and innovations in police procedure relative to the times in which *Dick Tracy* appeared. Gould's most famous inventions in *Tracy*, however, were the outrageous villains of his rogues gallery. Because Chester Gould felt that crime and its perpetrators were some of the ugliest elements of the human experience, he depicted them through the exaggerated physiognomy of the villains that populated Dick Tracy's world.

Like his contemporaries, world famous artist Pablo Picasso and legendary science fiction author Robert A. Heinlein, Chester Gould had an extensive career of success which can be generally, but appropriately, discussed in terms of distinct periods, subject matters, and trends. Gould debuted his famous comic strip in the early 1930s as a response to the violent urban world in which he and millions of other Americans were then living. He also drew on his frontier heritage, and in the process brought frontier law — Old Testament, quick, eye-for-eye justice — to the big city. Subsequently, *Dick Tracy* in the 1930s featured stories of the frontier — Dick Tracy actually goes "Out West" in quest of his youthful ward's (Dick Tracy, Junior's) biological father, Hank Steele. These years also showcased tales of Prohibition and Gangland, the Great Depression, a fictionalized story about Al Capone (as "Big Boy") and the

Lindbergh baby ("Buddy Waldorf") kidnapping, a story of John Dillinger (as "Boris Arson") and Gould's Pawnee friend, Moses Yellowhorse (as "Yellow Pony"). A number of the *Dick Tracy* rogues of this time period were personifications of the silver screen characters of James Cagney, Claudette Colbert, Clark Gable, Greta Garbo, Edward G. Robinson, and others. (While I thoroughly enjoy all forty-six years of Chester Gould's *Dick Tracy*, 1930s *Tracy* stories may be my favorite.)

The 1940s brought about *Dick Tracy*'s most remembered villains and stories, though these were not the villains and stories of *Dick Tracy*'s years of highest circulations—that was the 1950s. Racketeers and war criminals populated the world of Dick Tracy in the 1940s. War criminals and saboteurs such as Mr. and Mrs. Pruneface and the Brow were highlights. Flattop became Chester Gould's most famous *Dick Tracy* grotesque rogue ever. And Gould introduced a character that remains in *Dick Tracy* today. With the first appearance of Bob Oscar (B.O.) Plenty—a disheveled, unkempt, scruffy, humorous, non-villainous frontier character who, short of the title character, would become Gould's personal favorite of all his creations for *Tracy*—the artist and writer paid tribute to both his Oklahoma heritage (and some of the colorful characters of that heritage) and the old newspaper strip tradition of comic characters and story lines.

In the 1950s, *Dick Tracy* continued to feature outrageous rogues; some were wartime holdovers, and others began to emerge. Juvenile delinquents and treacherous anti-society punks were hallmarks of the famous detective strip at this time. Two of the most famous villains of this era were Joe Period and Flattop's son—two individuals who seemed to be positively cold, heartless and soulless. By the end of the 1950s, Chester Gould started to produce story lines reflective of the arriving and accelerating "space race." Themes of space travel, and high-tech crime and detection of such crime, debuted and continued throughout the 1960s and 1970s. Perhaps Gould's most popular character from these years was not a villain. She was Moon Maid, and she ultimately married Dick Tracy, Junior.

Many good—even excellent—and effective *Dick Tracy* sagas appeared after Chester Gould's retirement. But these, too, were part of a distinct era. And, as one of his successors told me years later, "We [those who followed Gould on *Dick Tracy*] were in Chet's house; he built the thing and we were visitors in that house."

Chester Gould's Family

In her writing here, Jean O'Connell relates stories of her grandparents, Gilbert and Alice Miller Gould and George and Emily Nelson Gauger. Tales of her father and mother are, of course, central. Chester had a younger brother, Ray (who later assisted him on *Dick Tracy*), and a younger sister, Helen Gould Upshaw. Gould's extended family not only contributed mightily to his success, it defined him.

Though it has been said in a variety of different ways through the generations, it is still true that the best marriages and families are the product of two strong and unique individuals who are part of an eternal partnership. Chester Gould was someone very special. His wife of almost sixty years, Edna Gauger Gould, was someone very special, too, as we begin to see here in their daughter's writing. Together as a team Chet and Edna were more than two individuals; they were one plus one plus more. As was the case with Mr. Gould, I never met Mrs. Gould in person, though I did correspond with her for a few years before her passing. (I corresponded with Mr. Gould from my childhood through my years as a university student to his passing in 1985.) She wrote me wonderful notes and letters in response to my inquiries. I still have all her letters to me.

Mrs. Jean Gould O'Connell, my dear friend whom I and my wife, Virginia, consider family, met first via the postal service. We met in person for the first time at the Chester Gould– Dick Tracy Museum during the summer week of Dick Tracy Days in Woodstock, Illinois, in 1993, when my book, *Dick Tracy and American Culture*, was about to appear in print. Jean and her wonderful family were tremendously gracious, and her family and mine quickly became the closest of friends.

While Chester and Edna Gould contributed so very much to the world including and beyond *Dick Tracy*, none of their contributions is as important as their daughter. Jean has continued her parents' legacy since the days of their retirement and, through her dedication to the highest of morality, community and family as evidenced in her work with the Chester Gould–Dick Tracy Museum, her writing (only some of which is found here), and her service, charity, and philanthropy, is a natural and wonderful extension of her parents. The vision and humanity of Jean Gould O'Connell begin to become apparent in the pages found here.

The Importance of Jean Gould O'Connell's Book to American Letters

In a speech to the Newspaper Comics Council on November 2, 1972, Chester Gould commented, "It was once pointed out to me that the *New York Times* carries no comic strips and still is a great newspaper. My answer to that was, 'Think how much greater it would have been had it carried comic strips. It might have attained a circulation almost as great as the *New York Daily News*.'" Gould's statement here is not only keen insight into the newspaper world of the twentieth century, it is excellent justification of the importance of his comic strip work, and that of some others, to a diverse international community. By providing and reflecting a universal morality and mythology for entire cultures, Chester Gould's *Dick Tracy* articulated a mindset that people embraced. In Chester Gould's day, readers purchased newspapers because of Chester Gould and *Dick Tracy*— neither Gould nor *Tracy* was a sidelight to other features in the papers of their day. They hit a responsive chord in their audiences, and they sold newspapers.

Jean O'Connell's writing here preserves a part of American cultural history that would be lost otherwise. She relates some important inside stories about her father and the world in which he lived. Her true-to-life frontier stories are important to who we are. Like the writings of Thomas Jefferson, Lewis and Clark, the great American Indian writers, Frederick Douglass, Mark Twain, Jack London, and Willa Cather, these stories are works of intellectual integrity that reveal much about the American character.

Jean's writing here also demonstrates the viability of the American Dream, the truth in the vision of America as a land of opportunity, and the virtue of hard work, persistence, and vision. In this way, more than 200 years later, she adds a new dimension to the ideology of Benjamin Franklin and other founding fathers and mothers. Jean's real-life stories are more amazing than any "rags to riches" fiction and formulas for success that Horatio Alger ever produced in the nineteenth century.

Narratives, biographies, and histories are some of our most popular story forms today. The reason for their popularity is that we want to learn of the experiences—trials and triumphs— of others who are not so unlike us. Throughout recent centuries, these genres constitute a significant percentage of what academics call "the canon" or American letters. In the pages that follow here, Chester and Edna Gould's daughter makes a significant contribution to American letters on behalf of her family.

There is so much to tell of Chester Gould, his family, and their legacy. And there is no better place to begin hearing those stories than in his and his daughter's words recorded here. Reading what Jean has written, I am convinced you will agree with me when I say that these are important stories of American life from the twentieth century.

Garyn G. Roberts is the Mystery Writers of America Edgar Award Finalist Author of Dick Tracy and American Culture *(1993).*

1

Ancestors

The Oklahoma land rush was on. The year was 1893, and on this day in September, the newly opened Indian and Oklahoma Territory awaited some fifty thousand people who would make the race and stake their claim.

My great-grandfather, Riley Wilber Miller, and my great-grandmother, Martha Ann Duncan Miller, who married in 1878, left their home in New Market, Iowa, to be part of this great movement. Accompanying them were their three daughters, Edith, Florence and Alice (my grandmother), and their son, Noah. Alice was only fourteen years old.

Taking only what furniture and belongings their covered wagon would hold, the six-member Miller family said goodbye to all they had known and headed for the open country, uncertain of what lay ahead. Leaving Iowa, the family crossed through part of Missouri, then across the state of Kansas, finally reaching the Oklahoma-Kansas line. It was a long, arduous trip. The Millers had to rely on wild game for their main food source, but Alice couldn't remember them ever going hungry. Indians were another concern and the Millers always watched the horizon for them. The family cautiously made its way, always stopping when Indians were spotted. There they would stay, very still inside the wagon, until the Indians disappeared from sight. This proved to be a safe strategy.

Thinking about this one day, Dad asked his mother, "Was it kind of scary at night?"

"No," she said.

"What do you remember most?" he asked.

"The beautiful lullaby the horses made chewing their corn. Their food box was at the back of the covered wagon where we slept, and the last thing we heard when we went to sleep was the horses chewing their corn."

With all the uncertainties of such a trip, this comforting memory stood out in my grandmother's mind.

Staking the Claim

The race must have been a thrilling one. The first ones to arrive in the territory got the best land, sold in 160-acre parcels. It would have been hard to see if someone was driving a stake on your acreage. This caused numerous arguments—most settled peacefully, or so the story goes.

Thursday Morning, April 17, 1980　　　Pawnee, Oklahoma　　　Thirty-Eighth Year　Issue No.

This log cabin was built in the 1890s and is located a short distance from Pawnee. Now used for storage, the owners plan to tear it down before long. It was once used by the mother, aunt, uncle and grandparents of cartoonist Chester Gould.

Log cabin near here to be torn down soon?

Probably the only remaining log cabin in this area will soon be torn down, according to its owner.

Located 5 miles east of Pawnee on US64, the cabin was built on land which was homesteaded by R.W. and Martha Anne Miller after the run of 1889.

They lived in a tent for a year before Miller built the cabin the 890s.

He was born in Athens, Ill. in 1850 and she was born in Memory, La. in 1854 and they married in 1878. Their children were Edith (McLaughlin) mother of Orville McLaughlin of Pawnee; Alice (Gould), mother of cartoonist Chester Gould; Florence (Haga) wife of Tom Haga and mother

the land all of his life, having cared for his mother until her death in 1965. His father, Tom Haga, built the house in front of the cabin in the early 1900s.

Other children of the Tom Hagas include Wayne Haga of Ponca City; Elsie Rhodes of Brawley, Ca. and Clifford, Robert (and Carl), all of Pawnee.

The Pawnee County Historical Society may make some effort to contact Haga in order to save and preserve the cabin, even on another site, if possible, and are interested in suggestions from area citizens.

See other photos on page 3.

The log cabin Grandfather Miller built in 1894, a year after he and his family staked a claim in the newly opened Indian Territory in Oklahoma. Although in sad disrepair, the cabin was still standing in 1980.

As the race began, covered wagons fanned out in all directions, carrying strong pioneer families to the new land. It was a rough and dangerous race, some wagons colliding with others in the confusion. The Miller family rode about forty miles into this new territory before Great-Grandfather Miller staked his claim. An emotional and exhausting journey was rewarded with the assurance that this would be their land. Though tired and dirty, Great-Grandfather must have felt pride in bringing his family safely through this difficult trip to the site that would one day be their homestead. It took all the family's energy to pitch their tent and organize their meager belongings at the end of their journey.

Vegetable farming was Great-Grandfather's livelihood in Iowa, and so it would be here. Long, hot hours in the coming weeks were spent in clearing the land, tilling, preparing, and planting the soil. Almost a year elapsed before that promised log cabin could be built. Until then, the tent and wagon had to do.

(The one-room log cabin that Great-Grandfather Miller built in 1894 was still standing in 1980, eighty-six years later, but it was now in sad disrepair. Said Gladys Kitchen, a Pawnee resident, "It was probably the only log cabin remaining in the area and historically important to Pawnee, because Chester Gould may have been born in that log cabin in 1900." She said that it was later dismantled and each log was numbered and carefully stacked on the ground nearby with the hope that the log cabin would some day be reconstructed in the town square. But that was never to be. One hot summer in the 1980s, one of a series of brush fires—started, it is believed, by an arsonist—encompassed part of the land the log cabin logs were stored on. The logs went up like tinder. All that remained were several rare photographs of the log cabin and memories of those who had known it as a home.)

Among Dad's happiest memories were the times he and Ray, his younger brother, would spend nights sleeping in the loft of that log cabin. One of the sweetest aromas to come out of that cabin was their Grandmother Miller's peanut butter cookies baking in the cookstove.

On October 6, 1902, the Arkansas Valley and Western Railway notified Great-Grandfather Miller that they were locating their railroad line over and across the northwest quarter of his land, "Section 20 of Township 21 North, of Range 6 East of Indian Meridian in Pawnee County, Oklahoma Territory." Some years later, U. S. Highway 64 came through on the other side of this property. To this day, however, descendants of the Miller family still own the major part of this original claim.

Dad chuckled when he remembered how his Grandfather Miller would come into town every spring to have his son—Dad's father—cut his hair. "All winter," said Dad, "he had let his hair and beard grow, and by spring, you could hardly find Grandpa's face." Dad said that this seemed to be a typical grooming program for the farmers, and he admitted that his B.O. Plenty character in *Dick Tracy* was created from those very memories.

The Reverend Gould

The Reverend Brainard Paige Gould, Dad's paternal grandfather, was a pioneer minister sometimes known as a "circuit rider." The Goulds migrated from West Virginia, where Dad's father, one of six children, was born in 1871. By covered wagon, they traveled as far as Colorado before settling in Kansas and, finally, the Oklahoma Territory. Over the miles of travel across the open country, the Reverend Gould found that many pioneer families were hungry for the word of the Lord. Whether his listeners were in log cabin houses, tents, shacks, schoolhouses or even brush arbors, he was there.

Though Dad remembered little about his grandparents Gould, his father, Gilbert, wrote a beautiful memoir about his minister father. Gilbert described him this way:

He was one who never had a pastorate of a great church with a handsome salary, but rather, when the Oklahoma territory opened, there was a wide and needy field to be filled by the aggressive ministers of that frontier, and the Reverend Gould was one of the first to move in.

It was not uncommon in his early years to work five days a week at manual labor — farming, stone masonry, mill work and so forth — then travel seventy-five to 150 miles in one weekend by horse and buggy, preaching his sermons, and then arrive home in time to be on his job at 7:00 Monday morning.

Not only was the Reverend Gould a profound sermonizer and forceful speaker, but he was a talented singer, supplying his own solos, and leading the congregation singing with no instrumentation except for a tuning fork. His singing lent much to the attractiveness of his ministering efforts.

Many of the United churches in Kansas were a direct result of such Herculean effort and driving work of Reverend Gould and other valiant "Soldiers of the Cross" during the 1880s.

Brainard Gould was instrumental in securing the organization of a church in the city of Pawnee and was the leading spirit in its growth. He gave full measure of devotion to its success, until one June morning in 1910, when the Lord said to him, "Enough! Come up higher."

As you can see, Gilbert Gould, Dad's father, had a beautiful command of the English language and a wonderful flair for writing. In his collection of memories one feels the rich history of the rugged pioneer days of Gil's boyhood. He writes of fishing in the creek, surviving a rattlesnake bite, driving the prairies with horses "Old Shake" and "Old Blue" — and of course about courting a girl or two, specifically Miss Alice Miller. With childhood, school and cowboy days behind him, Gilbert was embarking on a new kind of life. He was ready to settle down.

Alice Miller

High school presented a problem for Alice Miller, living almost six miles from the town of Pawnee. It was just too far for a young girl to consider traveling by horse and buggy every day to school. For many students in this situation, it was common practice to board in town with some nice family during the school year.

In 1899, Gilbert Gould was just a young man living in Pawnee, where he worked for a small newspaper. Gil's sister, Cora, better known as "Code" to her family, heard about this young Miller girl wanting a room so that she could attend Pawnee High School. Aunt Code arranged for Alice to live with her, and introduced Gil to the new roomer.

As fate would have it, Alice and Gil found much in common, became good friends, and eventually fell in love.

Alice finished high school and took a teaching job. She continued to keep her room in Pawnee but spent weekends at home with her parents.

But on February 20, 1900, wedding bells rang. Alice Miller, just twenty years old, became Mrs. Gilbert Gould.

Some fifty years later, Grandmother Gould shared with me the cherished contents of a small packet of yellowed envelopes and letters lovingly tied with a satin ribbon. Postmarks read 1899 and 1900. Never will I forget the enchantment of holding this treasured packet and sharing those most loving personal words between two people, and imagining Grandmother as that young girl addressed in those letters.

In a note dated August 6, 1899, Gil wrote:

Miss Alice Miller,

Considering our brief acquaintance, you will no doubt be surprised and maybe chagrined upon receipt of this note, the purpose of which is to ask you if you will accompany "your humble servant" for a buggy ride this evening at the pleasant hour of sunset. We can drive out to the camp meeting or not, as you like. Please answer "this kid" and oblige and delight a friend.

Respectfully,
G.R. Gould

Then a rather newsy letter dated December 29, 1899, Pawnee, Oklahoma, read:

My dear Alice,

As I agreed, I will write to you, but there is no telling when you will get it, for I understand that the Cleveland hack only makes a semi-occasionally.

I got home Sunday evening at 7:30 just before that north wind began to blow. I would have enjoyed staying longer, but when that wind rose, I was glad that I broke away. It was not a very pleasant drive as it was. The weird flap-flap of the curtains and the snow grinding and squeaking under the wheels was anything but pleasant music. The pleasure of your company for even a few hours amply repaid me for the unpleasant drive. I enjoyed Sunday's visit so much more than I used to last summer... Why??

You will doubtless want to know of the story of the small-pox affair. The doctors here as well as at other places have decided that it is not small-pox, but Spanish Itch. At Eufala, Doc Roper writes that there have been over two-hundred cases without a single death. At Blackwell, there have been about three-hundred cases and no deaths. There the people pay no attention to it, but go about their business all broken out as if there was nothing the matter. The disease is said to be contagious, but not at all dangerous. The joke is on Mr. Machaffrey (the old Gentleman). He engaged to nurse the man who had small-pox, because he had had it, and since the disease had proven to be something else, he (Mr. Machaffrey) suddenly realizes he is not exempt, and is in for a case of Spanish Itch. It is hardly likely that there will be any other cases; however, the quarantine has been so strict. Morrow, the sick man, has not missed a meal yet, but enjoys as good an appetite as he ever did. The people in the country seem to have gotten over the scare, as there was a big crowd in town today. The streets were crowded with teams.

Alice, I cannot tell you how much I have missed you these past few evenings, nor how I would love to see you tonight. You hold a place nearer the center of my affections than anyone ever did. My love, my life is yours, and no sacrifice on my part is too great to add to your happiness. But I will close for tonight.

Ever Yours,
Gilbert

On January 2, 1900, he wrote:

My Dear Alice,

Oh, Alice, I look forward with glowing anticipation when you brighten my home and life and change monotony into bliss. I do not desire to flatter or overdraw the enchanting scene just before me, but to know that I enjoy the love of a heart so pure and honest inspires me with only one desire, and that is that I may be successful in making you comfortable and happy. Though I lay all my affirmations and ambitions at your feet, it is no compensation for a love so pure, so true, so deep. May heaven bless my own dear sweet one.

Gil

No wonder theirs was a true and lasting marriage.

On November 20, 1900, Alice and Gil had their first baby. The young boy, Chester Wilber

Paige Gould, would one day marry Edna Marie Gauger and later become my father. Ray, his brother, arrived three years later. Chester and Ray's baby sister, Helen, was born eight years after Ray. Alice and Gil's family was now complete. Their lives together had created a new generation to be nurtured with love, respect and discipline.

2

My Father's Boyhood

It was right on Great-Grandfather Miller's land claim that Gil built a two-room house for his family. Not until Dad was ready for school, three years before Helen was born, did Gil have their house moved to a five-acre tract of land he had previously purchased nearer the town of Pawnee. After the move, he added a third room to the house. Now the family was just two miles away from the town of Pawnee instead of five — within comfortable walking distance to school. The new site was right across from the county fairgrounds on a nice country road. On one of those big fairground barn roofs, Dad painted an eight-foot-tall advertising sign when he was just sixteen years old. It turned out to almost be a catastrophe, as you will read about later.

While Dad and his family still lived out on his Grandfather and Grandmother Miller's land claim, Dad learned all about vegetable farming. As he grew older, his grandfather gave him more responsibility and then a chance to manage the farm during one summer.

"I guess that's where I grew to love farming. Oh, and I loved cats!" Dad told me. "If ever there was a wild or homeless cat, it had a home when it saw me. I always had a favorite one, and tried to keep it in the house, but my mother would chase us both out with a broom. Well, this one cat got to know her way around the house, and she would sneak in once in awhile, and of course, she was going to have kittens. My mother kept balls of carpet rags for weaving into rugs. The rugs in our house were all of this woven stuff, pretty nice looking. Anyway, the cat found where mother kept the rag balls, climbed in on top of them and had her kittens. And boy, that cat was in trouble! Dad took her and her newborn kittens right out to the barn, and that was the last time a cat ever came into our house."

Like most boys, Dad let his curiosity get him in trouble once in awhile — like the time his mother found him smoking dried grape leaves out behind the barn. He not only got a licking, but he got real sick. Then there was the time he went swimming in the cow pasture pond one April before it had a chance to warm up. That time he only got a cold.

Other times, he could be a hero, like one routine washday. The big chore on washday began with the heating of water in a big boiler on a wood cookstove. Dad's mother then sliced thin pieces of homemade lye soap that she and her mother had made into the hot water. Next, she poured the heated soap water into a large galvanized washtub where she scrubbed the family's clothes on a washboard. His mother used another bar of lye soap for the dirtiest spots, and rinsed everything twice.

One such washday, Dad was helping to fill the boiler, which was already on the cookstove, when his mother's apron caught on fire. Still a small boy, Dad somehow was able to pick up that boiler, and he threw the water on her. This would have been a heavy task for an adult to do.

Dad had warm recollections of the little three room house just outside of town. "I can see every board and window in that house," he told me. "It was home. I loved it. That's where my dad dug our well. He started with a posthole digger. It was only about fifteen feet from the back door, and he dug down just over twenty feet. When he hit water, he cased it and we had a well. What wonderful memories those were, filling our buckets with beautiful clear water."

On Solid Footing

The son of a minister, Dad's father came naturally to his activities in the United Brethren Church. Gil was superintendent of the Sunday School department ever since Dad could remember, and his mother was an active church worker. Ray sang in the choir, and Dad did any artwork that was needed — posters and such. Once in awhile he and Ray would be asked to play a duet — Ray on his cornet and Dad on his fiddle (the one he earned selling magazine subscriptions). "I can't imagine how that sounded," Dad chuckled. Then, in a thoughtful vein, Dad said, "You know, I had wonderful parents. It was honesty that my mother and dad tried to instill in us first. They would tell us Bible stories that at the time didn't seem important, but in later years, we realized how important they really were. All the stories had moral aspects, and today there isn't much of that. I think that is one thing we could use a revival of."

Remembering how his father taught them the value of never giving up, Dad turned to the verse in the Bible his dad often read to them from the book of Psalms: "The steps of a good man are ordered by the Lord, and He delighteth in his way. Though he falls, he will not be utterly cast down, for the Lord upholdeth." Oh, how Dad lived by those words in attaining his goal in life!

In the treasure of memorabilia left behind in Dad's small trunk were two sets of bound newspapers: *The Free Press* from Ralston, Pawnee County, Oklahoma, dated 1901 and 1902. Between the brown marble-patterned cardboard covers were yellowed pages that almost crumbled in my fingers. I wondered why Dad had saved them. Then I saw why. Under the heading "Published by the Free Press Publishing Company," were the words "G.R. Gould, Manager." This was one of the early newspapers that Grandfather Gould worked for. What a surprise! This newspaper was printed before Congress authorized the admission of the Oklahoma and Indian territories to become a state. That wouldn't be until November 16, 1907, when President Theodore Roosevelt by proclamation admitted the combined territories into the Union as Oklahoma, the forty-sixth state.

The Free Press was a small weekly newspaper with assorted articles, many relating to Indians and the territories as well as Oklahoma towns. One could see how growth and progress together were invading the Indian Territory and the tribal way of life. The paper had two features that illustrated this: "Oklahoma and Indian Territory" and "Over the Territory Gathered Up Away from Home and Gleaned from Our Exchange." Here are several short statements from those features:

Nov. 29, 1901
The Postal Telegraph Company proposes to build a line from Denison, Texas, to Kansas City, passing through Indian territory.

Nov. 29, 1901
The Cherokee National Council passed a resolution and memorial to Congress against being linked with Oklahoma in forming a new state.

Chester, age 2, with his parents, Gilbert and Alice Miller Gould, Pawnee, Oklahoma, 1902.

JAN. 3, 1902
Geronimo, the Apache Chief, has been deposed by his tribe, and Macenhorses put in his place. Geronimo challenged the new chief, who, instead of fighting the old chief, arrested him and fined him ten ponies.

FEB. 21, 1902
The Osages are the richest people in the world. They have 1,500,000 acres of very fertile lands. The tribe numbers 1,791 persons, 848 full blooded and 943 mixed bloods. These Indians receive about $150,000 annually for rent of pasture and farming land, and also have a fund of $8,500,000 at Washington, upon which the government pays them five per cent annum.

FEB. 21, 1902
Crazy Smokes followers are again in revolt. They threaten to kill Creeks who lease their lands. Their annual "stomp dance" comes soon. Many houses have been burned and robbed of winter's supply and provisions.

APRIL 1, 1902
The Choctaw Indian Nation has secured an injunction against the Fort Smith and Western Railroad restraining the company from condemning Indian lands through that nation. They demand $104 per acre for right of way and the road appraisers placed the value at $50.

MAY 9, 1902
The first train between Chickasha and Oklahoma City over the Frisco extension is expected as soon as May 10th.

Various Indian tribes lived in the Oklahoma Territory: the Cherokee Nation, the Choctaw Nation, the Creek Nation, the Pawnee, the Osage, the Seminole, the Comanche, the Apache and perhaps others.

My attention was drawn to the following obituary dated Friday, October 18, 1901:

SAUCY CHIEF DEAD: Aged and Powerful Osage Chief Passed Away
Saucy Chief, the most powerful factor of the progressive Osages, passed away at 8 o'clock Thursday morning the 10th day of October, 1901, after a lingering illness of about three months, during which time he showed most remarkable durability and faith in recovery, but the fatality of disease over-masters and carries the spirit of the great and good Saucy Chief to the far beyond where happiness and health abound.

He was born over 85 years ago, where, no one knoweth. Joined the Home Guard of Kansas in 1862 and served the government from which the Osages are now reaping the benefit; twice or thrice elected to the highest office within the gift of his people, that of the governor, and always filling the duties of that office to the best of his ability; always inviting the friendship of the whites, for he realized that it would be only a question of time until they would be the most predominating figure in his own country; ardently advising his red brethren to educate their children to meet any emergency that might arise; died with a blessing for all people on earth.

Saucy Chief good old man he was, High honored, always respected, leaving an unwritten history that memory will recall with passing time. Known to most every man, woman and child on the reservation and loved by them all for his unselfish motives and kindness of heart. Such was Saucy Chief, who lived not merely for himself, but for those he loved.

The funeral services were held in the M.E. Church Thursday afternoon by Rev. Wm Murdoch. A large audience was present to pay the last sad rites to the body of the deceased. After the ceremony, a concourse of friends, who with sad hearts saw his body lowered into mother earth, not to be raised again, but with hope that they might meet his spirit in another and better world. Farewell Saucy Chief. Your memory will shine forever and during the existence of your tribes, the deeds that you have done on earth will live, never to be forgotten by inhabitants thereof. Farewell Saucy Chief.

Saucy Chief was a wise chief who saw the change coming to the Indian Territory years before he died and prepared himself and his people for Oklahoma's statehood.

All Around the Town

Pawnee was named after the Pawnee Indians settling in that area of Oklahoma Territory long before the Land Rush of 1893. When Oklahoma joined the union, Dad was just a boy. He remembered that his father sat on the city council of this bustling little county seat of Pawnee. Dad took pleasure in recalling his home town square: "We had a beautiful courthouse, very much like our high school. I think our school must have had the same architect. Up until I was ten or eleven years old, the road around the square was just plain dirt, just dirt, not gravel. It could be so dusty, you could hardly breathe, or it could be so muddy, you could hardly walk. It was a mess! Finally, the city fathers decided to pave it with brick. What an improvement that was! The one side of the square, the east side, was never built up, that is, no stores over there, because the ground tapered off to the east. But the north side had a big hotel. In those days, the hotel was a two-story wooden structure. The south side had Marx Wheeler Clothing, Katz Department Store, Jay's Drug Store (where I worked), Ben Hues' Grocery and The Arkansas and Valley National Bank. Then there was my Uncle Bob's movie house on the corner. I worked there, too. There were several other places in between, but I can't remember what they are."

I marveled at Dad's keen memory of his hometown, a memory that he had treasured through all these years. I knew one day I would go there and see it through his eyes, remembering how he described it.

Destination — Good Times

One of the special pleasures Dad had since moving in closer to town was hearing his father come home and say to his mother, "How would you like to go out to the folks' tomorrow?" This meant a nice buggy ride to the home of Grandmother and Grandfather Miller, sitting on the rear seat that his father had rigged up, which poked underneath the buggy seat. There, he and Ray could sit, dangling their legs and watching the ground pass underneath them. They loved it, and they thought about the fun they would have playing with Frank when they got there. Frank was about Dad's age and had been raised by his grandmother and grandfather Miller since he was a baby. (Frank's mother died when he was two months old, and his father, Frank Miller, a relative of the Miller family, was grateful for the help). When Dad, Ray, and Young Frank got together, there was lots of mischief. What one child didn't think of, the other did, and though Ray was little, he got in on it all. For example, there was the time they concocted the idea of tying a string around a kernel of corn and feeding it to one of the chickens, then pulling it out. In it went, out it came, in it went, out it came, until their little experiment was found out. Then there was the game where they took turns tying each other up, went into the house and "mixed up stuff and offered it to the other guy." One of Dad's concoctions was a little vanilla and water mixed together, along with baking soda to make it fizz. That was one of the better ones, he said. There was some pretty rank criticism over some of the other mixtures and the game soon ended.

At school the kids played marbles, but the big game was called "Spike." That was spinning tops. If you could throw your top down and hit another fellow's top, it would split his, and he was out of the game. It got to be "pretty heady stuff," Dad said. Luckily, he never got his top split.

Chester, age 7, with his brother, Ray, age 4, Pawnee, Oklahoma, 1907.

Though athletic and strong (he once swam across the cow pasture pond with his cousin on his back), the thing this boy Chester most wanted to do was draw. Nothing compared with what a pencil could do. It was like holding a bit of magic in your hand. As soon as he could hold a pencil, Grandmother said, he was making marks on wallpaper, tablecloths, napkins, scraps of paper — anything. He just couldn't find enough to draw on.

By the time Dad started school, he considered himself pretty good at drawing, since everyone told him how good he was. "They'd say that about all the kids," he said. "'Oh, that's really good,' and that sort of thing." But he took this praise seriously. He felt that it wasn't so much that he could draw better than anyone else, but that he may have tried harder because he loved drawing so.

In 1906, Dad's parents gave him a box of crayons for Christmas, something he had never seen before. In all his memory, that was the greatest gift he had ever received. Even into his eighty-third year of life, he could still feel the thrill that one gift brought him. "Crayons were fairly new on the market and had to have been a turning point in children's developing a love of art," said Dad. "Kids loved them. Now they could draw the United States in color." Classroom walls were filled with colorful drawings, which had to have had a great impact on art teachers, too.

It wasn't unusual to find Dad's drawings on the school blackboard, before the teacher came into the classroom — after which they were hurriedly erased. When he was older, the margins of his papers and textbooks were peppered with drawings. This was an obsession.

The exciting discovery of crayons at the age of six brought another realization at the age of seven: Money was pretty scarce. You couldn't get much without it. All the kids in those days would save bottles and gunnysacks to sell. Bottles would go to the drugstore and gunnysacks to the grain elevator man.

Well, Dad soon discovered something bigger than this. You could go from door to door selling merchandise and win prizes. Spotting a movie machine in a company's catalogue, he knew that was what he wanted to try to earn. It was a little thing that you cranked and a continuous filmstrip would keep going around. You never came to the end of it — it just kept going around and around. The idea of a movie was just showing this over and over. So, he sold copper jewelry, rings, bracelets made of twisted copper, copper stick pins with dangling hearts, cuff links and other trinkets. He sold enough to get the projector, and he and Ray loved it and finally wore it out.

When another chance came along, Dad earned a fiddle by selling *Saturday Evening Post* magazines. Decades later, he could still remember the weight of the eighteen magazines he had to deliver each week. The strap on the carrying bag was so long, it would drag on the ground when he tried to walk with it on his shoulder. Even the stapler his dad had in the newspaper office that was used to take up the slack didn't work. It turned out to be too heavy a load for a seven-year-old. So Dad recruited Ray to help. While Ray pulled their little red wagon, Chester sold the magazines and collected the money. Ray was only four years old and would get tired and want to quit, but Dad would say, "Just think, a few more sales and we'll have enough. Think what fun we'll have with that fiddle."

He earned that fiddle, taught himself how to play it and discovered that he could play by ear. He could play any song without music.

(Dad was playing that same fiddle when he and Mother were married. He would walk around our Wilmette house playing it in the evening, while mother gave me a bath, and end up in the bathroom serenading both of us. One day, years later, when he went to the closet to get the fiddle, it had finally all sprung apart.)

The ladies in Pawnee must have thought, "Not again!" when they saw this young boy, Chester, coming up their sidewalk, this time selling everything from baking powder to liniment for sore joints, from pots, pans and dishes to shoe polish, just everything you could think of. It was all in a catalog.

"I sold a whole barrel of the stuff— that's the way it came, in a barrel," he said. That was his most ambitious sales job, and the last time he went from door to door, except for delivering newspapers.

Another Discovery

With his ambition running high, Dad was finding that it paid to work hard. Still a boy of seven, he was enjoying a newfound discovery: comic strips. He had found that the paper where his father worked, the *Pawnee Courier Dispatch*, took a service of editorial cartoons. They weren't comic strips, but he read each cartoon and studied it. He also found that the newsstand had an assortment of papers that carried comic strips, if you had the money to buy a paper. There was the *Daily Oklahoman* (later named the *Oklahoma Times*), the *Tulsa Democrat* (later named the *Tulsa Tribune*), a St. Louis paper, and more. But the best one of them all was the *Chicago Tribune*. It had the best and the most comics. Comic strips were new and exciting to him. When Dad had a few pennies to buy a paper, it was a high point in his week. The newspaperman soon learned why this young boy was so interested in newspapers, and he started saving the comic sections of old issues for him.

Taking the papers home, Dad would study and read those comic strips over and over until the next week—strips like *Mama's Angel Girl*, *Slim Jim*, *Hairbreadth Harry* and the *Katzenjammer Kids*, to name a few. This was before *Andy Gump*, *Harold Teen* and *Little Orphan Annie* appeared in the *Chicago Tribune*. But his favorite comic strip of all was *Mutt and Jeff*, which first appeared in 1906. He spent hours tracing the characters on paper and putting in his own dialogue. He was just fascinated with comic strips.

Watching his son's obsession grow, Gilbert Gould decided to talk to him about his future one day. He tried to explain to Chester how business was just beginning to boom in Oklahoma now that it was being occupied as a state. Oil drilling was growing by leaps and bounds and with it, legal problems. Oil men came in and signed up farmers for the rights to drill on their property, for which they paid a royalty. Continuous arguments about the rights and the royalties led to litigation. This was the biggest litigation issue of the day in 1907. So Gil said to Dad, "Why don't you become a lawyer, son? I have read that cartoonists are not looked upon with much dignity. They are usually impoverished artists, and I don't think you want to be that."

And the only answer Dad could give was, "No, I want to make money at being a cartoonist."

Finally, after much talking, Gil realized his son had his mind made up. "Well," he said, "if that's what you want to do, then go ahead."

As Dad reflected on his father's response he realized that his father hadn't put anything in his way. And he knew he would have to go to the top in the cartoon profession, if he was telling the truth about wanting to be a cartoonist who made money. He knew he didn't want to be a lawyer.

One evening, a few weeks later, Gil came home with the *Daily Oklahoman* tucked under his arm, and said, "You want to be a cartoonist? Look what this man is doing."

The man was Bud Fisher, the creator of Dad's favorite comic strip, *Mutt and Jeff*, which ran in the *Daily Oklahoman*. "Boy! Did my mouth water, because this man would make fifty thousand dollars a year. That was like being given the mint, fifty thousand dollars in 1907!" exclaimed Dad. Young Chester was more determined than ever to be a cartoonist.

A Taste of the Newspaper Business

A day didn't pass that Dad wasn't in his father's newspaper office after school doing odd jobs—anything. He loved that atmosphere, loved watching the typesetter and printing presses; he loved the smell of the paper and the inks and all the activity. One day after school when he walked in, his father said, "Say, the Democratic County Convention is meeting in the courthouse this week, and seeing as how you like to draw, why don't you go over there and make sketches of some of the important politicians?"

Well, that sounded okay, thought Dad. He didn't stop to wonder whether his father was serious or just offering a tongue-in-cheek suggestion to an eight-year-old. It didn't matter. Gathering the best scraps of paper from the cutting machine wastebasket, Dad put them under his arm and went over to the courthouse.

At the turn of the century there was no such thing as a photograph taken in a court-room; in fact, such photography was illegal. There was too much disturbance caused by the flash powder. A sketch artist usually sat in during the hearings and sketched the people involved in the hearing. They were remarkable drawings, Dad remembered later in life, but not what he wanted to do. He wanted to be a cartoonist.

After finding out who was who on the list of noted politicians his father had given him, he made his sketches, then took them back to the newspaper office. His father looked at them and said, "I tell you what. I'll type their names and attach them to each drawing and we'll put them in the front window."

Gil put them in the northwest window where traffic from the rest of the square moved, because the sidewalks were more improved there, and because people always passed that win-dow when they went by to pick up their mail at the post office. (There was no mail delivery service as we have today.)

When Dad saw his drawings go up in the window, he knew his father had figured it out; young Chester would have a captive audience. He stayed there all the rest of that afternoon and watched the people stop and look. His sketches, he admitted, were far from professional, but now and then he would see a passer-by laugh. He could see fingers pointing and heads nodding. Staying there after school the next day, he saw the same things. Then a man came into the newspaper office and asked to buy a sketch of himself, and it turned out to be a lawyer on the state Supreme Court. He left one whole dollar on the counter. The impact of this expe-rience had a lasting effect on Dad's future.

Testing the Water

By the age of fourteen, Dad was more eager than ever for any chance to draw. One day, his Uncle Bob, who owned a movie house on the main street of Pawnee, showed him his lat-est issue of a movie trade magazine, and Dad's eyes lit up. The magazine advertised a cartoon contest, with a first prize of five dollars for the best cartoon illustrating the popularity of the movies. Excitedly, Dad hurried home with the news, and by evening had a cartoon penciled and inked, with the title "The Drawing Power of the Movies." He had drawn a giant horseshoe-shaped magnet pulling a multitude of people into Uncle Bob's movie house. As he climbed into bed that night, Dad felt the excitement of what he had done. First thing the next morn-ing, he mailed his entry and tried to settle down for a spell of patient waiting.

If ever a fourteen-year-old was excited, it was the day the letter arrived for him stating that he had won the first prize and five dollars. Not only that, he saw his own cartoon appear in the next issue of that movie trade magazine. For weeks, Dad basked in the thrill of having won his first contest. He knew he had to find other contests to enter.

That's Entertainment

Uncle Bob's movie house was always an exciting place. Between the thrilling silent movies (talkies didn't exist yet), there were stage shows of every sort. Dad remembered people flocking there as much to see the stage show as the movie. What a day it was when he became a part of these surroundings! He was fourteen going on fifteen when Uncle Bob hired him. Whether it was sweeping floors in the movie house, cleaning the stage, helping the acts backstage that came to town, or being the official corn popper, it didn't matter — Dad loved it all. Once in a while he even had a chance to run the projector.

A pianist always played during the movie, enhancing the excitement of the moment. It was a fascinating experience to listen to piano moods change with the silent movie story. When Uncle Bob asked Dad one night if he would like to join the pianist and play his fiddle, the answer was a rousing "Yes!" Uncle Bob even hired Dad's friend who played the banjo. On nights they played, they each earned twenty-five cents playing all evening. That was a lot of playing, Dad said, but those were wonderful memories.

One time, there was a cowboy actor from California who came through Pawnee, and he made a movie right on Uncle Bob's Stage. It seems he needed a baby for one of the scenes, so Dad asked his mother if his baby sister, Helen, could play the part. His mother agreed and brought Helen to the theater, and Helen played the part all wrapped in a blanket. There was talk about her being a movie actress because she was so good. She slept through the whole thing.

When performers weren't coming through town, Uncle Bob had his own dog act. He trained these dogs himself, and had worked up an act people really enjoyed coming to see. The day came when Uncle Bob asked his energetic nephew if he would like to help with his dog act, and of course, the answer was again "Yes!" Uncle Bob always wore a big bloomer clown costume when he was performing, all made by his wife, Dad's Aunt Code. Well, on his first exciting night, a long-haired blonde ballerina came on the stage with Uncle Bob, complete with tutu, white tights and ballet shoes. It was Dad! There he was, tiptoeing around the stage with his magic wand as if helping the dogs go through their routine tricks. He loved the laughter and applause.

Uncle Bob had even trained two of his dogs to walk abreast around the town square, wearing hats and signs hanging around their necks advertising their own show. He would stick a cigar in their mouths and they would hang on to those things until they got back to the movie house. It had to have been a funny thing to see.

Confidence, ambition and most certainly a sense of humor were molding the character of this fifteen-year-old. Chester was finding life was what you put into it. Right now, he knew it was important that he make as much money as he could to put away for college. With that in mind, when he heard that Cecil Jay, the owner of Jay's Drug Store, was looking for help, he was right there. He was hired to do a cool job: to work behind a twenty-five-foot-long soda fountain with a fan directly overhead. Working every day after school, he earned six dollars a week. But one summer, he earned fifteen dollars a week working from 7:00 A.M. to 7:00 P.M. — long hours, but the money helped a lot. The soda fountain was big business, especially in the summer. It was one of the most lucrative parts of the drug store.

Remembering when American Indians came in for something at the fountain, Dad said they always wanted "red," and of course in terms of an ice cream soda, the only reds were cherry and strawberry. So, when he saw them coming, he would simply prepare one or the other; it didn't seem to matter, so long as it was red.

Cecil Jay carried several models of Victrolas from the Victrola Talking Machine Company. With Christmas drawing near, Dad desperately wanted to buy one for his parents, but figured he couldn't afford it. It wasn't a large cabinet, just a small Victrola that sat on a table, but the music was beautiful. One day, Mr. Jay, who had watched this boy over the weeks admiring this machine, said to him, "Listen, you take this home. Don't worry, just take it home. Pay me a dollar or two a week, whatever you want." So that's the way it was. Mr. Jay was very kind to him.

Chester, age 16, is on the far left, behind the soda fountain at Jay's Drug Store, Pawnee, Oklahoma, 1916.

During that summer, what young Chester had been watching for caught his eye in *The American Boy Magazine*: another cartoon contest, this one with a first prize of ten dollars. That was a lot of money! He was eager to submit a cartoon and have a chance to win. This one required a lot of thought. The cartoon had to pertain to World War I (the United States had just entered the war). With diligent thought, he at last came up with an idea. Though the hour had grown late, he kept at it until the cartoon was drawn, inked, titled and ready to mail.

Weeks passed, and finally, in the mail one day, a letter arrived addressed to Chester Gould from *The American Boy Magazine*. Dad couldn't get it open fast enough. Inside was a short letter of notification with the words "Chester Gould—first prize winner." He had done it again! As with the movie trade magazine, his drawing was printed in the following issue of the magazine. Describing it, Dad said, "I drew some soldiers marching down a country road. This was the beginning of our country entering World War I. They walked past this farm boy who was hoeing in the cornfield. Hoeing was necessary between corn rows, because a team of horses would break off the cornstalks. It was a hot, tedious job, hotter than hell. No air. Anyway, this kid was hoeing, and he looked up and one of the soldiers was looking at him. They were looking at each other, each coveting the other's job. I titled the cartoon, 'Golly, What a Snap he's Got!'" (A "Snap" was an easy job.)

Dad's life was busy from morn till dusk with school, jobs, studying, and chores. Now with summer coming, and the end of his sophomore year of high school, Dad wanted to really make some money. His bank account, though small, was growing little by little for college. Having had practice in lettering, he decided that was where he would begin: doing

Dad's winning cartoon in *The American Boy Magazine*, 1915.

professional lettering. When school was out, Dad called on the mayor of Pawnee. Maybe he would like his name lettered on his door.

"I got seventy-five cents on a big contract deal to put 'J.V. Orton, Mayor' on his door at the top of the stairs," Dad said proudly. "I did nice black letters outlined in gold leaf and thought it looked very professional." When he finished, he asked the mayor to come out and take a look.

"Well," said the mayor, "the lettering is all right, but I don't think it's worth seventy-five cents."

"That's what we agreed on," replied Dad.

"I'll tell you what," answered the mayor, "I'll give you fifty cents for it."

Dad had a single-edged razor blade in a little box in his pocket. He calmly took it out and, without a word, he went over to the door and scraped off the whole sign, just like that. Then he turned and went downstairs.

"I was always proud of my work," he said. "I don't know what the mayor did. Probably wished he had kept his mouth shut."

Other small lettering jobs came along; then came an ambitious undertaking for Mr. Bruington. Mr. Bruington was the owner of a very successful hardware, paint and furniture store and he said he would be interested in a sign. In those days, in rural areas, merchant's signs were often painted on barns or other buildings; in that era before radio and television, such signs were an important form of advertising.

Dad knew that Doc Waters had a big barn that could be seen almost a mile away, and he got Doc's permission to paint this advertisement on the side of Doc's barn.

"Can you do it?" Bruington asked.

"I can start tomorrow."

"Fine. I'll give you twenty-five dollars and pay for the paint," Bruington said.

"That was big money for a boy who hadn't quite reached seventeen years of age," Dad recollected years later. "I went out there and painted the sign, a big sign. 'Bruington's for hardware, paint and furniture. Quality and price,' and that sort of thing. It took a lot of paint on that old barn siding. Bruington always had a format for his ads: down in the right-hand corner, a picture of his head and under it 'Our Founder.' He was a kind of 'heady' fellow, very good looking and very influential in town. After finishing the sign, I asked him to come out and see it. He liked it and paid me the twenty-five dollars, which really helped my savings account."

Only a few days had gone by when Mr. Bruington stopped Dad as he passed his store on the way to school. "Say, listen," he said, "the paint job you did on my sign is fine, but have you been out there lately?"

Dutch doors were at each end of the barn. On one of the doors, Dad had painted "Our Founder" on the lower half and Mr. Bruington's picture on the upper half. In the hot weather, the farmer had opened the upper half of the door. There, as Dad put it, "you could see the ass and the tail of a big Prussian horse, and under it, 'Our Founder.' That's the way it happened," he said, "and everyone had a laugh, including Mr. Bruington."

The reputation of this new sign painter was rising, and before long he had his next job, a big one. Another local Pawnee store hired him to paint a sign on a fairground barn roof.

The roof was almost an eighth of a mile long. The back side faced the busiest side of the road, and that's where the sign would be painted. It couldn't be missed by anyone coming into the fairgrounds. Everything was laid out and set to go. "Marx Wheeler Clothing," it would say in eight-foot letters.

Since Dad lived just across the road from the entrance gate, he could wheel his paint over everyday in a wheelbarrow. One morning, he was in too much of a hurry and tipped over the whole thing. Red and white paint ran all over. But that didn't discourage him. He bought more paint and started again.

He finished the job in about ten days. The big white letters against a red background were beautifully readable to about a half mile away. Dad remembered: "I wanted to get the full impact of my finished job. I walked back as far as where the other road turned into this road to read it and saw that it said 'Marx Wheeler *Clothng*.' I had left out the 'i' in clothing. So I squeezed it in there. It didn't look too bad, but it didn't look too good, either. Mr. Bruington paid me a whopping seventy-five dollars for that job, more money than I had seen in my whole life."

Summers were filled with weeks of sign painting. No sooner would Dad finish one job than he had another. Mr. Swalley, who owned the well-respected meat market in town, hired Dad to paint a sign for him, knowing just what he wanted it to say. "Make it simple," said Swalley. "Swalley's Meat Market—fresh meats cut to order—we deliver."

Not far from the center of town, an abandoned railroad boxcar had been on a spur of the railroad track ever since Dad could remember. It was agreed that Mr. Swalley's sign would be painted right on the side of the boxcar. Large bold letters would catch anyone's eye. It was a striking sign, and Mr. Swalley liked it. In less than a year, however, the strangest thing happened. The boxcar suddenly disappeared from the railroad spur, after having been there for so many years. No one knew where it went, but probably Mr. Swalley's ad had greater exposure than he ever anticipated.

By this time, anyone who wanted an advertising sign or any kind of a sign painted knew where to go. That boy Chester Gould could do it! He knew his business. He worked hard and gave one hundred percent in terms of effort and was rewarded handsomely. His savings for college were growing. Wise beyond his years at seventeen, he insisted that his parents share in his good fortune.

Dad had learned well the effort it took to earn money. He was frugal with his savings. However, one day while looking at the paper, he noticed an ad that read, "The W. L. Evans School of Cartooning and Caricaturing"— twenty lessons, twenty dollars, with purple-ink criticism and remarks made right on your drawings by Mr. Evans. If ever there was an ad meant for Dad, this was it. He knew he would part with twenty of his hard-earned dollars to enroll in this correspondence school. Within two weeks, he received his first lesson and was absorbing every word, every instruction to its fullest, then returning each completed lesson to Mr. Evans for his purple-ink criticism.

This course was the only formal training Dad ever had in cartooning and caricaturing. The first two lessons concentrated solely on mastering the use of the dip pen. Controlling thick, thin and curved lines without the ink spattering when one of the two pen points wasn't in proper alignment was a challenge. With the techniques he learned, Dad could attain great shadow and texture effects, called hatching, cross-hatching and curved hatching. Dad mastered the techniques and used them for most of his forty-six years of drawing the *Dick Tracy* strip.

The following letter attests to the expenditure of twenty dollars for this course.

CHESTER GOULD
CARTOONIST TULSA DEMOCRAT
TULSA, OKLA.

July 8 '19

W. L. Evans School of Cartooning,
8th Floor Leader Bldg.,
Cleveland
Ohio

Dear Mr. Evans:

In regard to your course in cartooning, I'm going to say right at the first that it is the most complete and thorough course I have ever seen.

Your personal purple-ink criticisms and remarks right on the drawing itself links the student and the instructor together in a spirit of good fellowship and understanding. I feel as if I had been personally associated with you for years.

My situation here on the Democrat is most pleasant and I enjoy the work immensely, all of which is due to your instruction, ABSOLUTELY!

As a final word , I will say that I shall always recommend your course to the fellow desirous of aquiring an education in newspaper cartooning. To the student of limited means it is the only course. IT IS ECONOMICAL.

With the very best wishes and personal regards for you and the school,

I am sincerely,
A satisfied student,

Chester Gould

Dad's letter to W.L. Evans School of Cartooning, July 8, 1919.

School Days

By bringing home excellent grades and deportment in grade school and high school, Dad showed that he applied himself. In seventh grade, however, his teacher noted on his report card, "Inclined to too much mischief, and he whispers too much." I think the trouble was that Dad was filled with humor and silly antics. Even during assembly, he freely offered to play his harmonica that he had rigged with dangling bells. His classmates didn't lack for entertainment when "Chet" was around.

Otis Porter was Dad's classmate and good friend, and lifelong resident of Pawnees. He was 93 years old when I visited with him in 1993. Otis remembered Dad getting into trouble when he drew cartoons of teachers, including one who threw ink bottles at misbehaving students. As Otis and I sat on a park bench in Pawnee, in 1993, in front of the old *Pawnee Courier Dispatch* newspaper building where Dad's father worked, Otis described the following incidents as if they happened yesterday.

"Ches was sittin' there jus' drawin,' an he'd look up at the teacher, then look down an' draw, an' draw, an' draw some more. Then someone in the room hollered, 'CHET! an' he ducked. He jus' had a suspicion of what was goin' on. An' here comes that ink bottle sizzling right out an' over his head an' through the winda' an' busted out on the wall that went around the gym."

Chuckling, Otis continued. "An' right above the *Pawnee Courier Dispatch* newspaper where your dad's father worked was the *A. N. P.* That was *All Night Prowlers*, our club, an' our reason for bein' wasn't too clear. Anyway, for initiation, they laid y' down on yer back an' covered yer eyes, then tell y'to open yer mouth, an' some ole boy'd make the sound of spittin,' and they'd drop an oyster in yer mouth. I saw some a' them boys go plum to the ceilin'!

"Chet got a hold of an ol' portable phonograph, took the spring outa' the thing so yu'd have to turn the handle t'make it go fast or slow, an' the horn on that thing'd be stickin' out the winda and we'd turn it up all the way an' blast that thing. That meant we were havin' a meetin.'"

Otis confessed that they gave the Pawnee sheriff plenty of headaches. "We played cops and robbers. Different ones of the A.N.P. would hide on top of buildings around town. We'd shoot off a shotgun then watch for the sheriff; when he'd get close to the one who fired the shot, a shot went off in the other direction. We kept 'em goin' all night."

American Indians

Dad and Moses Yellowhorse, a Pawnee Indian, went to school together every day — Moses on his pony and Dad walking alongside. As Moses grew older, he developed a serious love for baseball, and when old enough, he joined the Pawnee County Baseball League as a pitcher. It was there he was spotted by a Pittsburgh Pirates talent scout and was signed up by the Pirates. During his first game, he pitched a no-hit, no run game. This was in 1922, the year after Dad came to Chicago. During one of Moses' games in Chicago, the two of them met for the first time since their school days in Pawnee. That was the last time Dad ever saw Moses.

Moses Yellowhorse was the first full-blooded American Indian to ever play major league baseball. In 1994, he was inducted into the American Indian Athletic Hall of Fame.

In 1935, an incidental character appeared in the *Dick Tracy* strip by the name of Moses Yellowpony. Dad thought he might hear from Moses, but he never did.

Joe Shannontong, another friend and a full-blooded American Indian, gave Dad a pocket knife when he left Stillwater for Chicago in 1921, one of those big knives that had everything on it — a screwdriver, a punch, a corkscrew, a nail file, scissors and two knife blades. When I was a young girl I remember seeing that same knife in Dad's taboret next to his drawing board where he kept his pencils, erasers, inks and pens, and he told me what fine people the American Indian people were and deserving of much respect.

High School

Just about everyone in high school had a nickname. Dad's nickname was "Ches," shortened from "Chestnuts," which sometimes just ended up being "Nuts." Dad's best friend, Waite Clark, was known as "Chunk."

These two friends were elected all four years of high school as president and vice-president of their classes. One day Ches said to Chunk, "Why don't you be president?"

Chunk said to Ches, "I'm a better manager. I'll be the power behind the throne."

So that's the way it was, all four years.

During their senior year, the two collaborated on an idea for a small, bound, twenty-six-page softcover book called *Class History of 1919*, a ten-year history of the class. The book's credits ran as follows:

```
Editors  . . . . . . . . . . . . . . . . . .  Ches and Chunk
Business manager  . . . . . . . . . .  Ches
Advertising Manager  . . . . . . .  Chunk
Illustrators  . . . . . . . . . . . . . . .  Ches and Chunk
Society Editors  . . . . . . . . . . . .  Ches and Chunk
Sporting Editors  . . . . . . . . . . .  Ches and Chunk
Historian  . . . . . . . . . . . . . . . .  Chunk
Prophecy  . . . . . . . . . . . . . . . .  Ches
```

Chunk, the historian, began:

And when morn did come, lo our city did behold the first day in September in all its glory. Yes, upon that eventful day, in September, in the year of our Lord, Nineteen Hundred and Six, there was given unto the world a great hope, for, started upon the long rough journey of knowledge was that class to be remembered onto generations to come, the class of Nineteen Nineteen. Truly a multitudinous selection was this new class in Pawnee.

It was a gallant opening that led to recalling twelve eventful years, their sentimental and memorable moments.

This book, measuring only five inches by eight inches, was filled with memories, recognitions, and quotations from professors, teachers and students. All the student body and faculty alike found themselves nicknamed with their pet expressions added. This seemed to be a popular trend of the day.

The "Class Prophecy" was Dad's:

Class Prophecy
By Chester Gould

It is with the advance of twelve long years that I arouse myself and look about me to see just where I am and what is taking place.

Oh, now I remember — oh yes — I had been asleep, but now I was awake. You see, I had fallen asleep during the sermon. Yes, it was an interesting sermon, too. But now, the minister was closing and it was almost noon. Soon everyone would be going home — Yes, here comes the minister now, shaking hands with everybody.

"Good morning, Mr. Johnson," said I, shaking hands.

"Well, Theodore, old boy, how are you?"

"Just fine," said he.

"Better come have dinner with me today, Ches."

"Can't do it today — sorry — but my train leaves for Albany — leaves at 12:20, you know — that's where Major Grimsley lives and he wrote me to come over and inspect a new fangled invention of his for opening baled hay."

"Well, well, give Major my regards and tell him he has Rev. Johnson's hearty support for his new project."

"That I'll do, Harlow," and with that I left the church.

The station was only a five minute walk, so I took my time, for it was a very warm day. On the way down I stopped at the Red Star café for a sandwich. You know Frank Johnson is proprietor. He serves short orders and everything. Louise Krauss and Frank furnish music there during the meal hours. Even as I entered, they were rendering Paddlewhiskey's 'Pair-of-Dice-Lost,' Louise at the piano and Frank beating the drum. The rendition was perfect and as I came in I saw a young lady scratching her ham sandwich and spreading mustard on her ear, so absorbed was she in the music.

I seated myself and was waited on by Lloyd Tennyson. He is head waiter and in a confidential talk told me he was receiving as much as ten dollars a week and was due for a raise now any time.

I devoured my sandwich to the strains of "Ave Maria," and proceeded to the train. I was startled by the whistle and to my surprise saw my train pulling into the yards. By quickening my pace, the train and I pulled into the station at the same time.

"Hello Nuts," said a voice from the express car as the train passed by. "Where are you going?"

It was Fuzzy Webber, you know he's third assistant on the Santa Fe between Skedee and Tallahassee. However, I was in such a hurry, I never answered him, but proceeded to purchase my ticket and scramble on board.

The train was crowded and I had to stand up, but I didn't care because there were several young ladies standing up also, and to my surprise found them to be a troupe of vaudeville actors, headed by Helen Tansey.

I knew only two of the girls, Helen and Florence Bevins. They were on their way to Memphis. We all began to talk of old times, of course, and I was surprised to learn that George Toler was in Kalamazoo in the movie business and also that Marcia Dawson was married and living in a Minnesota town. This surprised me very much, for when I last heard of Marcia, she was in Kansas City at a hospital nursing.

Florence asked about several of the old P.H.S. class and when I had seen George Moore last. I told her how he was running a combination furniture store-manicure parlor in Chicago, having given up scenery painting at the request of his mother-in-law who disliked the smell of turpentine very much.

Helen asked especially about Ikey Marx and Chunk Clark, both of whom were in Milwaukee manufacturing near-beer.

She felt very disappointed in Ikey whom she felt would have made a lovely villain in light farce. But as for Chunk, she said he always was peculiar.

I told her about Buck Beshears who was interested in a corkscrew concern in Indiana where now he was residing with his family.

At this stage, we were interrupted by the news butch whom we discovered to be Harry Caughey. He had his mouth full of Hershey Chocolate covered almonds at the time however, and at his confusion on meeting us, became choked and was forced to retire to the smoker to recover. He soon returned however, and we all joined in a merry chat.

Harry had received a letter only the day before from Bessie Feaster but refused to exhibit it. He told us she was giving dancing lessons in St. Louis, where she had been since 1920. He also told us that Mrs. Lincoln, who had been residing on a California orange ranch, was in Baltimore where she was running for county attorney on the Anti-Face-Paint party ticket.

Harry suddenly became very sad when he related how Marion Nimerick, who was with the side show company as juggler, had let a keg of nails which he was juggling on his nose fall, hitting him squarely between his eyes and breaking the nose bone.

Of course I wanted to know where he was now and Harry informed me that he was in the Davies hospital at Nigra, operated by Al Judy and Drudie Davies. I decided I would stop over and see Marion as my train went through Nigra. So bidding Harry and the girls good bye, I made arrangements for disembarking.

We soon reached Nigra and I had no sooner landed than I was surprised to be greeted by no other than Leslie Lehew. He is running a jitney line there and of course he took me out to the hospital. He told me that Helen Sterling was running a correspondence school of manicuring in the city, assisted by Mae Compton and Marie Cavitt.

I was certainly surprised. I asked him if he knew where Vernon Livesay and Anne Moore were. He said yes, that Vernon was married and living in Washington. D.C. where she was at the head of an Anti-Powder-Puff party and through Ruby Caldwell, Congresswoman from Oklahoma, was using her influence to boycott Colgate's tooth paste until it should return to 26 cents a tube.

And as for Ann, she was in Chicago singing the latest hits for the Columbia Talking Machine Company, drawing an enormous salary and two Coca Colas a day. However, because of an ingrown eyelash, she was forced to retire to her father-in-law's country home in Hampton Rhodes.

Asking why a large bunting was draped around a shop window, I was told it was in honor of Reva Manning having been newly elected county treasurer. This was a shock to me because when I last heard of Reva, she was in Paris taking voice lessons from De Blowhard.

Presently we arrived at the hospital and met Al Judy. After chatting for several minutes, I asked for Marion. For our disgust, we learned that he had just left, having fully recovered. Three operations were performed on his nose and six-eight penny nails and a piece of wooden keg had been extracted.

So bidding all adieu, I proceeded back to the station, where I was to take the next train to Albany.

"Any word you want to send to Major?" said I to Leslie, upon reaching the station.

"Nothing, I guess," said he, "only tell him you saw me. But say Ches," he continued, "you remember Juanita Coonrod and Nellie Morphis? Well, I saw in today's paper that they have been awarded the honor of cleanest of any other two county officers in the state of New York. For this they will receive a pension of fifty bucks and two powder puffs the rest of their lives. I claim that is a record to be proud of, eh?"

"Why most certainly," said I, "give my congratulations the next time you see them," and with a hand shake and a good-bye, I entrained.

The ride to Albany was uneventful and I was met by Major at the train. He took me out to his home and it was here I was introduced to the Missus. She was an ideal woman — tall and graceful. She was sweeping the northwest bedroom when we arrived, and became very much embarrassed at the unexpected arrival of her guest. Major did not seem to be affected in the least, however, by the peculiar circumstance and after cracking some joke, which I did not catch, about the wife looking like a stage hand for a side show, we retired to the parlor to await supper.

It was a splendid meal and I enjoyed it immensely.

After supper, we all went down to the theater to hear Helen Peter and her troupe of singers give a recital. It was certainly fine. It was composed of old war songs of the war of 1914; such noted composers as Cohen, Fiest, Harry Von Tilzer had prominent numbers on the program. One of the best numbers of the evening was "Ja-Da," sung by Miss Helen, who was dressed in purple organdie trimmed in a broad bodice and wearing a cowslip of bright red across her bosom. She rendered an encore of "The Old Gray Mare."

After the show, we visited Leona Wheeler and Myrtle Bell's beauty parlor, after which we left for home.

We were all chatting while waiting on the corner for a street car when I was suddenly hit by a terrible blow from behind on the head. I tried to speak, but I could not make a sound. I thought at first that I had been attacked by a thug, but decided that this could not be, for there was no one near to do the deed. Even Major and the Missus had disappeared.

Suddenly a voice called, "Well, if you want to stay on the floor all night, take these covers and stay there." With that a bunch of covers hit me in the face and all was quiet.

Then I realized that I had been addressed by my brother, that I had been dreaming and had thoughtlessly strolled off the bed and was lying on the floor, face upward, somewhat chilled and uncomfortable.

There was only one course to pursue, and that was to climb back between the blankets and resume my night's rest. This I did.

Ches and Chunk's classmates and faculty must have been proud of this one-of-a-kind Class History of 1919 created by two fellow seniors. The senior class picture, titled, "Charter Members," of which there were twenty-three, was the only photograph in this small book with the exception of one other, which appeared on the last page. Looking out at the reader upside down was a picture of Ches and Chunk.

Said Dad, "Chunk and I were constant buddies. Chunk's father, a wealthy lawyer in Pawnee, bought him a used Ford car, when he turned seventeen. Chunk proceeded to do what all kids did to their cars in those days. He stripped it down until nothing was left but four wheels and a place to sit. The seats were still fastened down, but when you looked down, you could see the road go by." Somehow, Chunk had managed to fasten the spare tire on to the back of what was left of the car and on it painted "Ches and Chunk." They drove all the way to Oklahoma City in this car, some ninety miles away, leaving after school on a Friday and arriving at Chunk's aunt's house in Oklahoma City around 10:00 that night.

"Just when most people were going to bed, here's ol' Chunk knocking on his aunt's door," chuckled Dad, "and she welcomed us with opened arms."

They stayed there that night and had breakfast the next morning before starting back.

"Waite Clark was a great friend," Dad said with a deep respect, "a very sharp guy and highly intelligent. Soon after graduating from college, he became a prosecuting attorney in Pawnee County and we kept in contact all our lives."

3

Off to College

If fate ever played a part in Dad's life, it was the day after Thanksgiving in 1917 right in his hometown of Pawnee. A student from Oklahoma A&M College was visiting a fraternity brother in Pawnee. They were standing on a corner talking to some high school kids about how A & M had beat Oklahoma University 9–0 in football. One of the boys, a sophomore in high school, asked to borrow the game program one of the college students was holding. When he returned the program, along its margins were five of the A & M College players sketched so anyone would know them, along with a witty comment written about each.

The A & M College student, a senior, was Frank Martin, vice president of the Educational Society on campus, an editor of the *Redskin Yearbook* and a talent scout for the college. The high school boy was Ches Gould. So impressed by Dad's sketches was Frank Martin that when he arrived back on campus, he pinned them up on the main campus bulletin board, the college's quickest way of communication in those days. Frank later ran these same drawings in the college newspaper. That was Oklahoma A & M College's introduction to Ches Gould.

After seeing Ches's work, Miss Maude Cass, the managing editor of the *Redskin Yearbook*, asked Frank to try to get Ches to come to Stillwater (a thirty-mile trip from Pawnee), and spend weekends on campus and work with the art department staff. Amazed and exhilarated over the thought, and after getting his parents' consent, Dad enthusiastically accepted — and so he entered into a new world. It turned out to be more work than he anticipated. He was asked not only to select a few prominent people around campus to caricature, and to draw what they called the frontispiece for each campus department and activity, but also to draw a few cartoons to scatter throughout the yearbook. That kept him plenty busy during his junior year in high school — all that drawing while he tried to maintain passing grades. But when Miss Cass asked him if he would continue with the artwork for the college yearbook the next year, he accepted most willingly.

Several weeks before high school graduation in 1919, another opportunity came Dad's way. A telegram arrived for him from Charles Page, the editor and owner of the *Tulsa Democrat*. Mr. Page had learned about Dad's talent and wanted to hire him for a temporary job drawing a series of editorial cartoons for his paper. The hot issue of the day involved a five-million-dollar bond issue to create the Spavinaw reservoir for the City of Tulsa. Page was against it and wanted eighteen editorial cartoons to that effect. He offered Dad thirty-five dollars to do the job, which Dad eagerly accepted. "Page was a pretty impressive guy. Not only did he own the *Tulsa Democrat*, but he was an oil magnate and philanthropist," said Dad. "He carried a lot of weight."

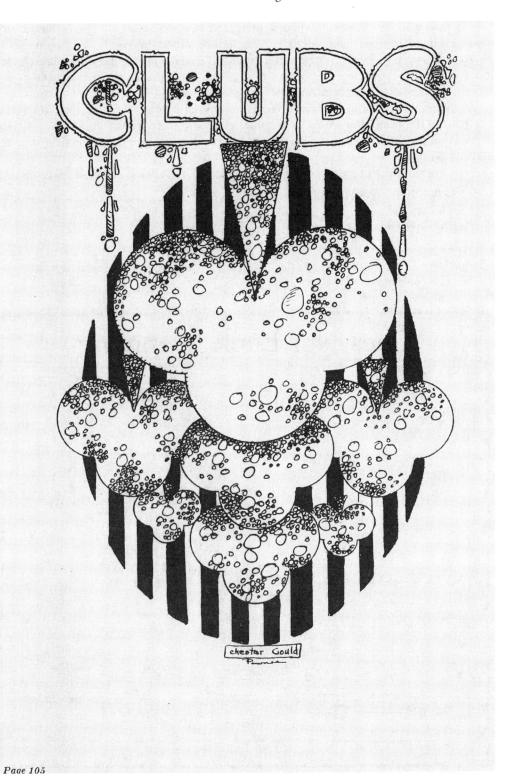

A frontispiece, drawn by Dad while he was still in high school, designating college clubs for the Oklahoma A & M (later Oklahoma State University) *Redskin Yearbook*, 1918.

So, leaving for Tulsa right after high school graduation, this young aspiring cartoonist welcomed his first "big time" newspaper job. After finding a room to rent, he went right over to the *Tulsa Democrat* to meet Mr. Page and to listen to his views against the referendum. It took about a month to complete the eighteen drawings. Mr. Page seemed pleased and paid Dad—even though the bond issue passed anyway. For a nineteen-year-old whose dream was to become part of the newspaper world, this short career as an editorial cartoonist only whetted his appetite.

Just twelve years after Dad's high school graduation and his drawing those editorial cartoons for the *Tulsa Democrat*, *Dick Tracy* made its debut in that paper (by then renamed the *Tulsa Tribune*).

Looking through our library of fascinating books one day, I found a book whose cover read:

The First Works of Chester Gould
June–July 1919
Assembled by the Tulsa Tribune

These were the very editorial cartoons that Dad had drawn for Mr. Page. Here they were, reprinted and presented to him years later in an attractive book from the newspaper that gave him his first professional newspaper job.

Above and following page: Three of the eighteen editorial cartoons drawn for the *Tulsa Democrat* (later named the *Tulsa Tribune*), summer of 1919, before Dad entered college.

Realizing the Consequences

Leaving Pawnee

The summer of 1919 saw a change in residence for the Gould family, who moved to Still-water. Living in the same town as Oklahoma A & M College, where Dad would attend as a freshman, would save him room and board fees.

Up until this move, the Gould family had never had electricity or indoor plumbing. What a luxury this three-bedroom bungalow would be! You could walk straight through the living room and the dining room into the kitchen, and there stood a wonderful sink with hot and cold running water and a gas stove. Adjacent to the kitchen was a bedroom. Between the other two bedrooms, on the south side of the house, was a bathroom with a big bathtub on claw feet. Next to it stood the water heater waiting to supply a warm bath at a moment's notice, and the pedestal sink — what a beautiful sight! Best of all, no more trips to the outhouse! Electric ceiling lights were in every room, and in the living room, a handsome potbelly stove was just waiting to take the chill out of those cool days. The low-sloping roof shaded a porch that ran across the whole front of the house, and an inviting swing hung at one end of the porch, a place where many a relaxing hour would be spent. A large backyard promised exciting rewards with plenty of room for a vegetable garden and flowers, too. This was definitely a welcoming new chapter in their lives.

Gil, with his knowledge of the newspaper business and all the mechanics of printing, had obtained a job in the college's printing department — a place where Ches would find time to visit.

CHESTER & SISTER. HELEN

19-year-old Chester and his 11-year-old sister, Helen, the summer of 1919. He would be entering Oklahoma A & M College in Stillwater, Oklahoma, in the fall.

College 1920–1921

Although Dad was a freshman, his artwork for the yearbook and publications had made Ches Gould's presence known all over campus. It didn't take him long to find that one of the most popular spots for students and faculty alike was the campus bulletin board, which was where all the important information and notices were posted. Now it also included the ever-changing cartoons by Ches Gould. Dad never missed a chance to expand on his cartooning experience. No sooner had he become a pledge of the Lambda Chi Alpha Fraternity than he was drawing caricatures of all the members. But this wasn't why he entered college.

A more serious side of college soon surfaced. Dad had promised his father he would go to college and work hard. Time and money were valuable commodities. So this fun-loving, light-hearted individual who dreamed of cartooning and entertaining people found himself majoring in commerce and marketing. But he was preparing for the future. He knew that someday he would be a cartoonist, but he also knew he needed a good business head on his shoulders. He wanted to make a lot of money like the cartoonist Bud Fisher, his childhood idol. He wanted to prove to his dad that he could.

So the next two years at Oklahoma A & M College were devoted to commerce and marketing. Still, his passion for cartooning crept into the classrooms. He was known to have passed an examination by making cartoons of his answers. An example took place during his first year of chemistry. One question read: "Describe the difference between diluted and concentrated hydrochloric acid."

Dad's answer showed a student bent over with his hands on the floor and his bottom up in the air. Behind him was the professor with a bottle tipped so that drops would hit the student's bottom. The student was smiling. That must have been diluted hydrochloric acid. Then he showed the same student in the same position, and again, the professor was tipping the bottle so that drops hit the student's bottom. But this time, steam and smoke arose and the student was yelling and screaming. That had to be concentrated hydrochloric acid.

Above and on following pages: Cartoon artwork for the *Redskin Yearbook* at Oklahoma A & M College, 1920.

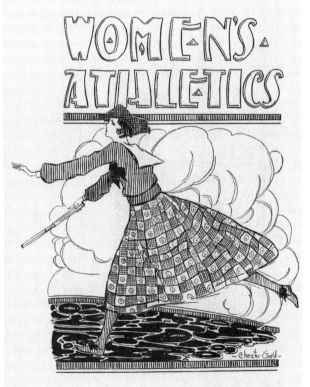

When Bernice Baldwin was asked her opinion of H. B. Meeker, she replied something like this: "Oh, Meeker, may be alright in his way, but he don't weigh enough."

Lois Castle says, "A girl should start early and land a man, and then she will have the rest of her time to devote to more profitable work."

BUT

Florence Kraemer says, "First pick don't always stick."

Futoransky thinks our National Air should be—"All the World Will Be Jealous of Me."

Prof. Andrew (in Geom. 22.)—"Miss Rouse, what is a secant?"
Miss Rouse: "A secant is a thing that goes around with both ends out."

Dola Tyler (in English Exam.): "Squire Cass was a *bachelor* of Raveloe, who had three sons."

At Last

Fellow Students:

In closing the joke section the editor ast me would i like to say a word about the cartoons and jokes. I supose he ment did i want to poligize for any bad brakes which i have puled herein if any. Or maybe he wants me to take al the blame for certain picktures of indivijuals.

It gives me exquisite pleasure to anounce that each and avey pickture re-prospected in this book is based on facks and trooth compiled by the campus-ology ed., bus, manger and ed. in chef, to sy nothing of my self. No ficticious pickture was printed on less as a joke.

Ef a purson sees himselves or herselves in a spasm do not get sore and run, or rase h—l with the managment, whitch would show no good colege spirut, but jus bite your upper lip and forgit it.

Hoping you will take this in a joking manner and not feel hurt ef some-thing makes you sore,

I am yours completely

—Ches —

Post Mortem.

The managment is leaving town on the same train this blueskin comes in on.

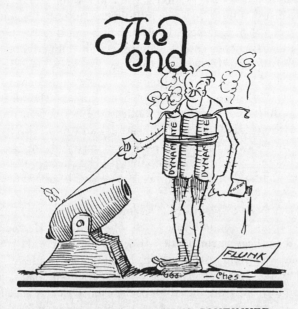

CAMPUSOLOGY PICTURES CONTINUED

Dad was a good student, but chemistry was another story, and it became more and more difficult for him. As Ora Blanch, a student assistant to chemistry professor Dr. Hilton Ira Jones, explained, "At the time Ches attended Oklahoma A & M College, grading papers of freshmen chemistry students was part of my duties. Despite the best that Professor Jones and I could do, Ches continued to fail."

One day, while waiting for Dr. Jones in his office for a conference about those failures, Dad sketched a picture of U.S. president Woodrow Wilson that was hanging on the wall. Then, from memory, he sketched Professor Jones. When the professor arrived for the conference, he saw the sketches, looked at Dad and said, "Why are you taking chemistry?"

Answering with the only reason he could give, Dad said, "Because all freshmen have to take it."

It seemed that right then, a bond of truthfulness and admiration formed between the two of them. Thereafter, Professor Jones wholeheartedly encouraged Dad to become a cartoonist, and gave him a final passing grade.

In fact, during the rest of the year, the unique pairing of professor and student combined chemistry and cartooning on several occasions and entertained the college student body during several programs in the big auditorium. On one occasion, under the direction of Professor Jones, Ches drew a cartoon on a large poster board, which was then chemically treated, causing his drawing to disappear. With great fanfare, during the performance, Dad sprayed a chemical solution on this same board, causing his drawing to magically appear. The students roared with approval, whistling and calling out, "How did you do that?" So popular was this stunt that during the next assembly program, they tried something more daring — the use of a blowtorch. The heat from the blowtorch would bring out the cartoon. Well, that one went up in smoke, calling for some quick fire extinguishing, making it the hit of the show anyway.

Dad never forgot Professor Jones. In 1932, just twelve years after that near failure in freshman chemistry class, he sent the professor a drawing of Dick Tracy and Junior. Tracy was saying to Junior, "If it hadn't been for 'Doc' Jones, you and I would still be taking chemistry!"

Later, when Dad and Mom were living in Wilmette, Illinois, Dr. Jones left his professorship at Oklahoma A & M College to take a job with a chemical research company in Chicago. When Dad learned that Dr. Jones and his wife resided in Wilmette, he contacted him. They rekindled their friendship and college memories, and their wives heard some stories that they might never have heard. Dad called on Doc Jones' advice a number of times to keep Detective Tracy's police lab work absolutely correct when it came to chemical analysis.

After Dad's freshman year at A & M College, he decided to relinquish his artwork for the college yearbook and college publications and apply himself diligently in his studies. Thanks to Professor Jones, he had passed chemistry his first year. For that, Dad was grateful, and he had done well in his other subjects. The strong pull of cartooning was still complicating his thoughts, though, when he should have been focusing on marketing and commerce.

September ... October ... November ... December. Dad was really buckling down, and the months passed quickly as he found himself well into his major. He had some social life, and he still stopped at the college's printing department almost every day to say hello to his dad and lend a hand once in awhile just because he loved that atmosphere.

In late March of 1921, Frank Martin, now a close friend of Dad's, contacted him. Frank wanted Dad to meet Mr. Harrison, the editor of the *Daily Oklahoman*, a newspaper published in Oklahoma City. In fact, Mr. Harrison, already acquainted with Dad's work, had requested some samples of his drawings. Dad sent him several. Mr. Harrison bought a multi-paneled cartoon for $3.00 and really liked Dad's work. In fact, he offered Dad a job with the paper, despite the fact that Dad was still in college and was some eighty miles from Oklahoma City. Distance didn't bother Mr. Harrison a bit.

"We can work something out," he said. "I'll put you in touch with the sports editor."

And that's what he did. The plan was that every other week, Dad would send the paper a six-column sport cartoon featuring pen and ink drawings of newsworthy Oklahoma athletes, along with some interesting facts about each one. This feature, called *In the Sport Spotlight*, turned out to be very popular with the readers, and soon Dad was making $15.00 a week.

(In 1957, thirty-six years later, Dad was a guest on Ralph Edwards's popular *This Is Your Life* television show. Mr. Harrison, one of the surprise guests, when introduced, took from his suit coat pocket a fragile, well-worn piece of paper and carefully unfolded it. There was the drawing Dad had sold him for $3.00 in 1921. This was a complete surprise, seeing Mr. Harrison and the drawing he had kept all these years, and it touched Dad deeply.)

The *In the Sport Spotlight* feature was such a pleasurable assignment that Dad found he could juggle both classes and job and still get respectable grades. But as his sophomore year was coming to a close and his sports cartoon feature was growing in popularity, a feeling of unrest beckoned him. He knew he wanted to follow that feeling. Even Mr. Harrison knew of his dream, could see that he was ready, and encouraged him to go, as much as he wanted him to stay.

Above and on following pages: In the Sport Spotlight, a strip created and drawn while Dad was at Oklahoma A & M College in the winter and spring of 1921.

Y'S ERROR IN NINTH COSTS INDIANS SECOND AT

IN THE SPORT SPOTLIGHT - + - By Chester Gould

TE TENNIS TOURNAMENT OPENS HERE SEPT

IN THE SPORT SPOTLIGHT - By Chester Gould

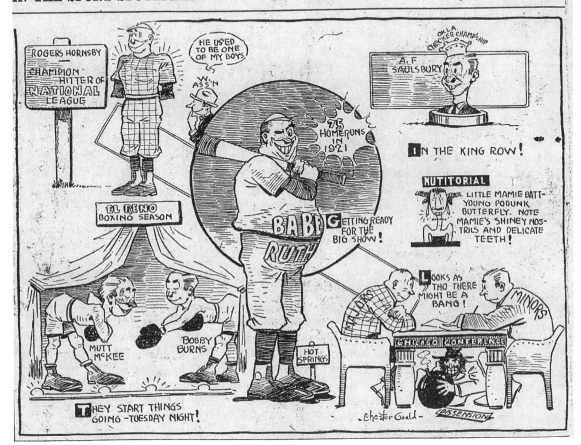

The main concern Dad had was for his parents. They didn't approve of his going to Chicago, "the gangster-ridden city," so they had read. He needed to talk to someone — someone who knew about his dream. His good friend Frank Martin — Frank knew. Frank had told him everything. It seemed so important to ask Frank what he should do.

One afternoon, excitement and uncertainty churning within him, Dad called on Frank. In later years Dad remembered so vividly how nervous he was as Frank listened to him patiently. Then, with complete sincerity, Frank leaned forward and said, "Ches, if I had your ability, your personality and your drive, I would go to Chicago if I had to ride the rods on a freight train."

That's all Dad needed to hear. His pent-up desires had suddenly been released. He knew it was time to pursue the plans that he had dreamed about since his childhood. He was ready!

4

Chicago

On the evening of August 30, 1921, a train pulled into the Dearborn Street Station in Chicago and a young man from Oklahoma, just shy of twenty-one years of age, stepped off the train and into the beginning of his dream. He had his savings of fifty dollars in his pocket, his suitcase, and his portfolio of editorial and sports cartoons. He even wondered why he had brought so much money with him when he would soon be working as a cartoonist for the *Chicago Tribune*. It was a hot, sticky night, but after walking a couple of blocks up Clark Street, he was so exhilarated and overcome by being in this big city with all his plans that he hadn't a care in the world.

A neon sign hanging over the sidewalk flashed, "Hotel." He went in, registered and stayed there for the night. Recalling that night, Dad said, "It seems to me that my room was on the second floor; there was no air conditioning then, so windows were left open. My room faced the alley, and as soon as I got into bed, I heard a band playing, a typical jazz band, and it thrilled the dickens out of me. I thought, 'I'm in Chicago, and that's the welcome I'm getting.'" Dad went to sleep listening to that jazz band. He loved that room with the music.

The next morning he headed for Northwestern University in Evanston. There he registered for fall night classes, continuing his major in the School of Commerce and Marketing. Getting into subjects like American commercial law, statistical methods, political economy, supply and demand, theory of economics, typing, and English writing would demand a good span of time for study. Northwestern's night school classes weren't held on the Evanston campus but in the old Oliver Typewriter Building, which was near State and Dearborn streets in downtown Chicago.

The plan was to get a room near Northwestern's campus so as to attend university functions—namely Lambda Chi Fraternity functions—but for the time being he took a room at 1100 North LaSalle Street. The room cost him $3.00 a week.

Within days of writing his parents with his new address, he received a letter back from his mother, saying, among other things:

Dear Son,
   I just read about the gangsters in Chicago. They are killing people, shooting them down in the streets for no reason, and you with fifty dollars in your pocket. Come home at once!
   Your Loving Mother

Dad assured his parents that he was safe, and that this was where he wanted to be. His only goal after arriving in Chicago was to get a job as a cartoonist with the *Chicago Tribune*.

He didn't know how, but he wanted to be a part of that paper, drawing cartoons. Dad thought if he just had one of his cartoons on the back of their delivery truck, that would be a great start.

"I didn't have any particular worries," said Dad. "I was entirely alone, which meant I had fewer responsibilities than some of my fellow college student friends."

"My mother and dad were comfortably well. I had no excuses of any kind. My track was clear. I had nothing to do but go ahead, and I said, 'I'll set this place on fire!'"

His first three days after registering at Northwestern night school and getting a room were spent making heavy rounds of all five Chicago papers, starting with the *Chicago Tribune*, but nothing came of it. In fact, they all said the same thing: "We can't use your work. You don't have the kind of artwork we want."

Toward the end of the third day, Dad made a return visit to the *Chicago Journal*, a well-respected evening paper. Just that very day, the head of their art department had been suddenly taken to the hospital with an appendicitis attack and would be out a month.

"Your qualifications look fair. We can take you on for just a month," said the interviewer.

"That's fine," Dad replied. "What is the salary?"

"Thirty dollars a week," was the response.

Dad was just amazed. So, he had a beautiful job for thirty dollars a week for one month. That really boosted his morale and helped him in every way.

He did a little of everything: retouching photographs, drawing little cartoons, doing some lettering (including special lettering for headings), and just doing all-around art department work.

He was able to live on six dollars a week, three dollars for a room and three dollars for food. He used the cheapest mode of transportation, his legs, and never paid for streetcar fare if he could walk. He bought his shoes at the cheapest store, his clothes at the cheapest places, all on Clark Street. Regimenting his eating habits to one good meal a week, in 1921, for sixty-five cents, he could have a number one dinner: meat, potatoes, gravy, salad and dessert. A donut or sometimes a sweet roll was a nickel and so was a cup of coffee. Breakfast was a dime. He could live pretty cheaply.

But one day, Dad became a little reckless with his money. He bought a radio for twelve dollars. Radios were just becoming popular and the most common set of the day was known as a crystal set. "It had no internal maintenance at all, but there was a little 'cat's whisker' you had to fool around with," said Dad. "That's what it was called. It had to touch this little hunk of stone with a handle and hit a certain spot. Then, you got reception — no tubes or batteries were needed."

When he got back to his room with the radio, he couldn't bring in anything but a crackily voice now and then. Pondering what to do, Dad noticed across from his window, on the other side of LaSalle Street, a maple tree growing, and thought, "If I had two insulators and wire, I'd have an aerial."

He bought the wire and insulators, attached one insulator to his window sill with one end of the wire secured to it, and went across LaSalle Street, dodging the traffic and holding the wire high over his head. He shimmied up the tree with the wire wrapped around his waist, the other insulator to the tree, attached the wire and pulled it tight.

"Boy! Was I nimble in those days. I only weighed 130 pounds."

When Dad returned to his room, he couldn't wait to turn on his radio. Did that aerial ever work! He had the greatest reception.

The old German and his wife who owned the house didn't see the aerial for a number of weeks. Then, one day, there was a knock on Dad's door, and the old German demanded, "Did you string that wire across LaSalle Street?"

Dad said, "Yes, I did. That's the aerial for my radio." He thought the man would be impressed, but he wasn't.

"Take that thing down. If the police see that, I'll have to pay a big fine, and so will you, too."

Dad was still impressed with his aerial and never took it down. When he later moved to Evanston, he thought the man probably thanked him for that aerial, because nobody else had an aerial across LaSalle Street.

After one month with the *Chicago Journal*, Dad collected his last paycheck, shook hands around and said goodbye. He had already started his night school classes at Northwestern, three nights a week, and the other two nights were devoted to classes in figure drawing at the Chicago Art Institute. It was imperative to know how to draw the human figure in any position — how to foreshorten an arm or leg or the head in an angled position, and to do it automatically.

Even with this rigorous schedule, working during the day, attending classes at night and studying, Dad continued to find time to create cartoon ideas late into the night, to submit first to the *Chicago Tribune*, then the *Chicago Daily News*, then the *Herald Examiner* and finally the *Evening American*. As soon as one paper would return his work, he would send it out to another. This system worked pretty well, but it didn't get him another job. What it did do was to create a collection of rejected ideas that he placed in a box labeled "Dead Letter Box."

(In the 1936 *Tulsa Tribune*, Dad's sister, Helen, in an interview about her brother, said, "Chet had a pretty tough time when he first went to Chicago. He often spoke of those first hard months of living in a small dingy room, attending night school, studying hard, being homesick, not eating enough, not having money for shows or recreation and denying himself many things. But he doesn't like to think of those times.")

Luckily, Dad had a little backlog of money in the bank to carry him over, but he couldn't seem to get anywhere. Picking up the paper one day and turning to the want ads, he saw that out on Vaughn Avenue, the A & P store had an opening for a stock boy. He took a streetcar out there to apply for that job.

"See that fellow over there?" said the manager. "I just hired him."

Coming back, Dad thought, *Well, now what do I do?*

When he stopped at his favorite cigar store the next day, there was the same customer whom he had often seen and who knew of his plight through casual conversation. ("Haggerty is the name.") He told Dad about Zuckerman's Ad Service, a place on South Dearborn Street. They had lost a fellow. The position called for a commercial fashion artist, not Dad's specialty — but it was worth a try. Dad was hired and found that his duties were that of an office boy, erasing drawings, pasting drawings down and carrying work to the engraving department. It was a disappointing job, but it was a job.

During the year he spent at Zuckerman's, Dad continued making the rounds to all the papers on a weekly basis, always aiming at the *Chicago Tribune* first. This he did on Saturday mornings, before the art departments closed at one o'clock. Persistence was of the utmost importance to him, but each week brought him no closer to his goal.

"I didn't care how they treated me. They couldn't insult me. They couldn't depress me. I knew I was going to make it."

One day again at the cigar store, Dad ran into Haggerty, who had given him the tip about Zuckerman's. After a short exchange of conversation, Haggerty told Dad that he was working at the *Chicago Tribune*. There was an opening in the Art Services Department, where he was assistant manager. It was available if he wanted it.

"That was the last place I wanted go," said Dad emphatically. "I wanted to go to the *Chicago Tribune* as a cartoonist with an exclusive office with my name on the door."

But when he was told the job paid fifty dollars a week, he took it. "That was big bucks in 1922." And he suddenly felt that maybe he was beginning to get somewhere.

1923: Breaking into the Chicago Scene

The job at the Art Services Department would do just until he could get into cartooning. In the meantime, his efforts were directed at the Hearst papers, namely the *Evening American*, an afternoon paper. He learned that the top man in the editing department was a hot-tempered Irishman by the name of "Curly." That was the man he wanted to see. Curly was one of Hearst's top men.

On the day of his appointment, Dad loaded himself with editorial cartoons, gag strips and cartoons of every sort, and soon found that Mr. Curly wasn't one to beat around the bush. He couldn't use any of it. He didn't like any of it. But, one thing he would do was listen and talk.

"I can't promise you anything," he told Dad. "It has to come from New York. If I think you have something, I'll tell you to send it to New York to King Features."

After that visit, Dad deluged Mr. Curly with ideas on a weekly basis. These included comic strips about office boys and one about the Stock Market. (Dad knew nothing about the latter, but would read the business section and write gags about it.) Another was a strip called "Midget Encyclopedia." He also wrote gag strips, lots of gag strips, just everything he could think of, but nothing was what Mr. Curly wanted.

One night after leaving the *Chicago Tribune* (the Tribune Tower hadn't been built yet) Dad walked to the *Evening American* with a plan in mind. He first checked on the time the cleaning women were in Mr. Curly's office, which was about 5:25 P.M. Then he just looked around the building. He bought an *Evening American* and a candy bar, and headed back to his room in Evanston.

Seated at his drawing board, he opened the paper to the editorial cartoon by T.E. Powers. Powers was the *American*'s top editorial cartoonist, in Dad's estimation. His cartoons were strategically placed in the newspaper, covering a four-column width on the back page of the second section of the paper.

Dad carefully measured the dimensions of Powers' cartoon. This done, he sat at his drawing board late into the night, creating his own cartoon of the same dimensions.

The next evening after work, Dad went over to the *American*. With his shirtsleeves rolled up and his cartoon under his arm, he walked right into the engraving room.

"I'd like to have a cut made of this," he stated with authority, handing the man his drawing. (A "cut," in newspaper terms, was a picture engraving plate used in printing newspapers. In this case it would print Dad's editorial cartoon onto newspaper newsprint.) This cost him a whole six dollars, one week's living expenses.

When Dad's cartoon was printed, he carefully cut around the edges of his drawing, making sure that they matched exactly the edges of T.E. Powers' drawing. With rubber cement, he glued his freshly made proof right over Powers' editorial cartoon.

Walking into Mr. Curly's office, looking like an employee, Dad placed his mock-up on the editor's desk. "Chester Gould's" editorial cartoon was open and faced Mr. Curly's desk chair.

"So, instead of Powers, it was Gould," Dad said, describing the incident years later. "It was a shocking thing to look at. I almost knew that with Curly's temper, he was going to order me to stay out of his office after hours. I just knew it. But I was willing to face the music. I wanted him to know just how much I wanted the job."

About ten o'clock the next morning, Dad received a phone call at work. It was Mr. Curly's secretary.

She asked, "Can you get over here to see Mr. Curly today?"

Well, thought Dad, if you asked me if I could jump out of a ten-story window of that building, I'd have said yes.

"I certainly can," he replied. "I'll be over at 11:30."

Fearing that this could be his downfall, he went over with a feeling of trepidation. When Dad arrived, there was Mr. Curly with Dad's handiwork in his hand.

"Did you draw this?" demanded Mr. Curly.

"Yes, I did," came the response. "I wanted to see how my work would look in your paper."

"Well, you damn near fooled me," Mr. Curly retorted, shaking his head as he sat down. "I think the best way to get rid of you is to hire you."

Dad's blood pressure must have jumped twenty points. Not only was he hired, but his salary went up another ten dollars a week from what the *Tribune* was paying him. (As Dad was telling me this, his eyes filled with tears as the emotion of that memory came back to him. Through his tears he continued.) "That's the type of thing you had to do in the cartoon business, when you weren't known. It was about the most imaginative thing I could think of anyone ever doing. I did that trick just once. It was a once-in-a-lifetime gamble, and it worked. It takes courage to get something unattainable. I never expected to sell him with that idea, but nevertheless, that was my intent." This was 1923.

After working for the *American* for a year, Dad signed a five-year contract. He started out as an artist in the *American's* Advertising Art Department doing layouts and promotional ads. Dad chuckled as he clearly remembered a weekly bakery ad he was assigned to draw. The ad was supposed to show a coffee cake. The cake didn't come in until 3:00 in the afternoon. Still warm from the oven, its aroma filled the art room. Well, the art department fellows were the problem. Dad had to the have drawing in the engravers' hands by 4:00 in order to make the morning paper. By the time Dad was putting the finishing touches on the drawing, the coffee cake was the size of the palm of your hand. "Do you know what that did for me?" Dad said, smiling and shaking his head. "I learned to be accurate and quick, but it was kind of tragic at times, because drawing a coffee cake is not as sweet a job as eating it."

His boss, Bill Jennings, liked Dad's work and one day invited him to be his luncheon guest at a new club that had just been dedicated. This had to be about 1928. Bill was a charter member of this exclusive Tavern Club in the 333 Building on Michigan Avenue in Chicago. For Dad, determined to reach the top, this was a real eye opener.

"I never knew why Bill took me up there, but I was grateful. The glamour was, without question, something I would never forget."

During this impressive luncheon, Bill offered Dad an invitation to join the Tavern Club through his sponsorship. Dad's heart skipped a beat. He thought if he ever got to be a success in the comic strip business, he might take him up on it, but now, it seemed way over his head. Instead, he extended his appreciation to Bill and declined. (Thirty-four years later, Dad became a member of the Tavern Club.)

As months passed, Dad's talents expanded in numerous directions. He had already created a comic strip called *The Radio Catts*. The name for the strip was taken from the "cat's

The Radio Catts. The Catt family begins their adventures with the latest invention: the radio (1924).

whisker" of the radio—the same kind he had tried to tune in his LaSalle street room. The characters were cats, and the comic strip stories of the Catt family involved humorous situations encountered with the new invention of radio. (In today's high-tech world, it is fascinating and often funny to read the strips and look back on that time.) For some reason, less than a year into the strip, Dad had the Catt family climb into the inkbottle in one panel of the strip and come out as the Lane family, real people, in another panel. The story continued without an explanation, but it was a clever stunt that could only happen in the funnies. From then on, the strip was called *The Radio Lanes*. Dad's trunk of work from the 1920s contained several 1924 radio magazines that he undoubtedly referred to while learning about the radio.

One day in 1928, at the request of his boss, Dad was asked to create another strip, in addition to *The Radio Lanes*. This was to be an adventure strip, fashioned after Ed Wheelan's *Minute Movies*, a very popular strip at that time. The word was that Hearst had tried to get Ed Wheelan to join the *American*, but without success. Dad's reply to his boss was, "Nobody can imitate Ed Wheelan properly." But, his boss told him, "Do it. Do what you can."

So Dad created *Fillum Fables*, starring Jack Storm and Dolly Darling, the adventurous

The Radio Lanes, 1924: the metamorphosis of the Catt family.

couple forever escaping George O. Silverrough's evil traps. It was a popular strip, but one Dad was never happy with, since it was a take-off on another man's work.

Now he was doing two comic strips along with a feature called *Lotsa Things Happening.* Here, in a light, airy feature that ran across the top of a page, he caricatured people and places around the Chicago loop with bits of news about each. Yet another feature he did reviewed the top billings at the Palace, the Rialto, the Majestic and the State Lake theaters with capsule interviews and caricatures of the stars as they made the vaudeville circuit. That's how he met

Fillum Fables, 1928.

Dad rewiewing his *Fillum Fables* strip in 1928.

Al Jolson, Eddie Cantor, Sophie Tucker and numerous other stars of the day. He also drew editorial cartoons on a routine basis. One of those he sent to his parents in a scrapbook, and penciling underneath it, "Hearst went crazy over this." The drawing referred to the approaching summer in the form of a beautiful lady holding behind her a bag of wind, a bag of slush, a bag of sunshine and a sprinkling can. A little man holding baseball bats, fishing poles, golf clubs and bag and other sundry sports items looked up at her and asked, "Now tell me, are you going to be a good girl this year or aintcha?" The title of the editorial cartoon was "He'd Like to Know." This is what caught Hearst's eye.

In 1923, Dad created a new feature called *Why It's a Windy City*. This took him all over the city interviewing business men and what Dad called "big shots." "I would go and see a well-known judge in the news courtroom and maybe the manager of the Congress Hotel and maybe a president of a bank. I'd ask them to give me an anecdote or a funny story and some-

One example of Dad's reviews from the Palace Theater, 1924.

times that wouldn't be funny. Then, I'd make a caricature of each, which wasn't always perhaps an attraction in itself, but they got cartooned and quoted in this column. I think it went over big. Curly liked it, too." This feature ran down the entire first column of the page, from top to bottom, making it a definite eye-catcher.

Dad illustrated a sports column daily. He added cartoon sketches to society page photographs. Anywhere in the newspaper where a snippet of a cartoon was needed, he did it. It seemed he was doing the work of three people.

At one time, Dad counted eleven pieces of his work that appeared in the paper in one day. His comment to all this was, "The Lord gave me a good body. I couldn't help myself. I had finally hit a goldmine. I didn't sleep. I would be sitting at my drawing board at the *American* when the art department fellows were going home. That department was right in the editorial department, what they called the newsroom. There were four fellows, and their day was over when the last edition of the *American* was out, just about the time commuters were going home. They would put their coats on, put the latest edition under their arm and say, 'Goodnight.' When they'd come back the next morning, most often I would still be there just finishing something. And one would say, 'Hey guys, come here. He's still here!' And the other would say, 'He's nuts! What do you do? When do you sleep?' I would just keep working. They got my goat once in awhile, but I'd just laugh it off. They'd have to go home to their families, but I didn't. I had no family, nobody that I was responsible to, no reason to go home at five o'clock. I could just sit there and work and reach my goal in half the time that these monkeys would, even if they worked hard."

Above and following pages: A sampling of advertising art, editorial cartoons and features drawn for various Chicago newspapers between 1921 and 1925.

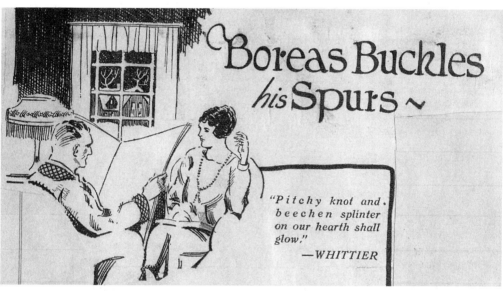

"Boreas Buckles *his* Spurs ~

"Pitchy knot and beechen splinter on our hearth shall glow."
—WHITTIER

To be Sure of Used Car Satisfaction Buy from a Reliable Dealer

Most of Chicago's Reliable dealers advertise their Used Car values every day in the Herald and Examiner!

You want to know that the Used Car you buy will be replete with satisfaction in every way. The appearance you can judge for yourself—and many used cars look like new but the service and performance must be assured by the dealer from whom you buy. Therefore you can see the importance of buying from a reliable dealer and you can find these dealers advertising their best used car values daily in the Herald and Examiner.

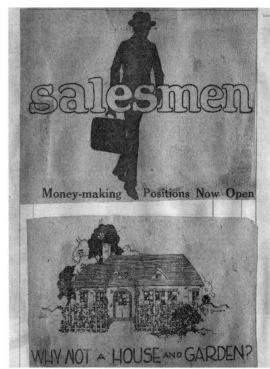

Working through the night at least twice a week was now a general routine. Dad's life seemed to be nothing but work. Mealtime was replaced by a candy bar all too often. But somehow, he was keeping himself in shape, swimming at the YMCA after work as often as he could. It was there he met the Olympic swimmer Norman Ross.

Since 1922, Dad had been living in Evanston, rooming with a wonderful family named Thrumston who greatly admired him. He had graduated from Northwestern University night school in 1923 with his degree in commerce and marketing and had attended any number of Lambda Chi Alpha Fraternity functions. At the young age of twenty-four, he was purchasing a piece of property in Kenilworth, an exclusive suburb of Chicago. He had bought a 1924 Maxwell Coupe from a good friend he had met since arriving in Chicago, George Florey. The car, only a month old, had blue leather upholstery and was pretty natty looking, with shiny natural wood wheels, and it sported a spare tire sunken into a wheel well on the left fender. (The Maxwell Motor Car Company was soon to be bought by a fellow named Chrysler.) George, like Dad, was working his way up the ladder of success, and went on to become a top advertising executive. (In 1958, Mr. Florey was instrumental in getting Dad to California under the pretense of seeing a *Dick Tracy* promotional idea. The real reason for the trip was that Dad was the honored guest on Ralph Edwards' *This is Your Life* TV show.)

Though success was making its mark in Dad's life, his determination to become a cartoonist for the *Chicago Tribune* never wavered. On a routine basis, Dad continued submitting new comic strip ideas to Captain J.M. Patterson (the cousin of Robert McCormick and co-owner of the *Chicago Tribune*), who hired the cartoonists for the *Tribune* as well as for his *New York Daily News*, but there wasn't a glimmer of success.

Above and on following pages: Eight of the sixty comic strip ideas rejected by Captain Patterson over a ten-year period. The sixty-first idea was *Plain Clothes Tracy*, which became *Dick Tracy*.

MIDGET ENCYCLOPEDIA -

BRIGHT LIGHTS BRADY -

GIRLIE -

One night as he sat working at his drawing board in his room in Evanston, there was a knock at the door. June, the Thrumston's daughter who was soon to be married, had been waiting to find a chance to talk with Dad. He hardly knew her. After some small talk, the subject turned to June's best friend, and how nice it would be if June and her fiancé, Bill, could take Dad over to meet this friend. She lived in Wilmette, not far from Evanston.

Dad's immediate reaction was *no*. He wanted to tell June: *Don't feel sorry for me! I'm working my way to the top*! But instead he said, "All right."

June approached her friend, Edna, about meeting this handsome roomer who had dark wavy hair and horn-rimmed glasses. Just that afternoon, Edna had her studio portrait taken by a most unattractive photographer with dark wavy hair and horn-rimmed glasses, and she said, "No!"

But on October 3, 1925, they met. June and Bill introduced Chester to June's best friend, Edna Gauger, and to her parents, Emily and George Gauger, and her brothers, Bill and Dick.

"I liked her," confessed Dad. "She was a lively, attractive girl, so natural, no frothy little attempt to make believe or be sophisticated. I say that because some parents have sons and daughters who they want to meet important people. I never looked for anyone that was important. I just wanted someone I could believe in, and I found her parents were the kind of people that were all family, down to earth. There was no phoniness about them."

The two couples left for a casual dinner at the Chicken Shack, a popular restaurant in "No-Man's Land," a place between Wilmette and Kenilworth where young people went. Dad found that you could treat a date to a nice chicken dinner for thirty cents in 1925. His first date with Edna — my mother — cost him sixty cents.

Mother was pleasantly surprised at what a handsome, interesting and entertaining person Dad was — nothing like the photographer.

The next morning at 8:00, the phone rang at Mother's house. My grandmother called upstairs, "*Edna*, telephone!" Yawning, mother wondered who could be calling her so early in the morning. Dad's voice was on the other end of the line. He had just called to find out how she was. He asked her to join him that Saturday night at the Edgewater Beach Hotel's Marine Dining Room. It was just the hottest place on the North Shore, with big bands and dancing. He had only heard about it — he had never been there.

The night of their date, Dad really "put on the dog" and pulled his shiny blue Maxwell right up to the hotel entrance to have it parked. To his surprise it cost him a whole quarter.

He never forgot how the waiter seated them, placing a napkin in Mother's lap with a low bow, then handing each of them a giant menu. "I'd been used to hamburgers and sodas," said Dad. "I looked down the right side of the menu. I didn't bother to look down the left side. I had five dollars and fifty cents in my pocket when I left home. I knew that was more than enough. It was dangerous to carry that kind of money. Well, your mother, my dear wife-to-be, ordered a whole live lobster."

(Mother often enjoyed seafood and fish of all kinds at home that her father bought at a fish market on the way home from his Chicago office. So she thought nothing about ordering lobster.)

Said Dad, "Believe it or not, a whole live lobster in the Marine Dining Room was two and a half dollars. I remembered I had spent a whole twenty-five cents to have the car parked."

Pondering for a moment what to do, he heard himself order *two* whole live lobsters! He would just make it, but there wouldn't be enough for a tip. That night Dad couldn't wait to get out of that hotel, because he didn't have enough money for a tip. But he knew one thing. This was the kind of girl he wanted.

Mother's father, George, who had never been impressed with any of Mother's dates and said as much each time she brought a new beau to the house, was quite taken with this small-town Oklahoma boy. He knew the stock market, had a good business head and had ambition running through his veins. In fact, the whole family liked him.

Edna and Chet went to plays, took rides in his Maxwell, listened to the radio together, had tea and muffins (Dad never liked tea), went dancing (he didn't dance either), played cards (which he didn't usually do either), and walked Buster, the dog (he liked that). Mother often went with him when he reviewed the billings at the theaters, and she found they were generally seated in the first row. If Dad had work to do at night, which he often did, he brought it to Mother's house to finish. His life had suddenly taken on an added direction, one that seemed to grow with love and caring, and with someone whom he could share his dreams.

Dad's thoughtfulness, his sense of humor, and his enthusiasm for his work seemed to create an aura around him and was everything Mother loved. She knew that was the world she wanted.

(A charming disclosure to all this was a diary that had undoubtedly lain undisturbed for some sixty-eight years among Mother's special keepsakes in her cedar chest. When I discovered it after her death in 1994, I picked it up and hold it close to my heart, recalling the happiness and wonderful life they had shared together. Carefully opening it, I saw nothing until October 3, 1925. That was the day she met Dad. Day-to-day records of phone calls from Dad, dates and activities that they enjoyed together, filled its pages. And as suddenly as this diary began, it ended with just six words, on June 29, 1926: "Chet asked me to marry him.")

When wedding bells appeared to be on the horizon, Mother's father took Dad aside and said, "About that piece of property you have in Kenilworth: I think you should live in a more modest area for awhile." Dad wasn't too sure about that, but thought maybe he should consider this.

Then Grandfather Gauger told him that he had access to some property on 17th Street in Wilmette, so they drove over there. It was beautifully located on a nice street with trees. "I'll build you and Edna a house here," Grandfather said. "Take that money from the sale of the Kenilworth property and buy furniture for the house."

"I've never had a deal any better than that in my life," Dad told his future father-in-law, and he was so proud of what Grandfather had offered to do.

Mother and Dad in their courting days, 1925.

Life Taking on an Added Direction

Grandfather Gauger believed that home is where life begins and life ends; it is the heart of one's existence. And home is where Edna Gauger became Mrs. Chester Gould, right in the sunroom at home on November 6, 1926. She was twenty-five years old. Festoons of bridal garlands and flowers filled the house. From the grand piano came the stately wedding march as the beautiful bride descended the staircase. Relatives and close friends looked on while this small but wonderful wedding took place, the beginning of a marriage that would span fifty-nine years, until Dad's death in 1985.

After their honeymoon trip to Mammoth Cave in Kentucky, the newlyweds returned eager to begin their new lives in the house that Mother's father had built for them.

A shiny blue Maxwell could be seen parked in the driveway. The lawn around the house was manicured with precision by Dad, who was filled with love and appreciation for what Grandfather had done for them.

With the adjustment of married life and Dad's rigorous routine, patience and understanding were a necessity on Mother's part. She knew how hard he worked. Her father, ever since she could remember, had worked long hours, many times bringing work home in the evening. Chester's life would be very much the same. She had already accepted that.

Dad had been with the *Evening American* now for four years and was three years into his five-year contract with them when he and Mother were married. At home in the evening, he worked at his drawing board, constantly creating new ideas to send to J.M. Patterson at the *Chicago Tribune.*

Their two-bedroom bungalow was completed with Mother's special touches. Their baby grand piano certainly lent a feeling of elegance to the living room, and Mother, having studied piano at the Chicago College of Music, brought beautiful music into their home. She was also becoming quite domesticated in the kitchen.

This is the pink Spanish bungalow on 17th Street in Wilmette, Illinois, where Mother and Dad began their married life together.

One night, Dad arrived home with a dinner guest, Ferd Johnson, creator of the comic strip *Texas Slim*. They found Mother standing on a stepladder in the kitchen, crying and wiping the condensed milk off the ceiling. It seems the hole she had poked in the can of condensed milk before heating it in a pan of water was too small. Then she forgot to check it while she was busily fixing the rest of the dinner. Suddenly it boiled and spurted straight up out of that hole onto the ceiling. Mother's tears of frustration were soon eased when Dad and his cartoonist friend pitched in and eased a tragic moment into laughter.

Move Over! Here I Come!

Just nine months after they were married, on August 18, 1927, there were three of us. Said Dad, speaking of my arrival, "You were born in the Evanston Hospital, and I had to fight with the doctor and nurses to see that you arrived all right. I said, 'That's my wife! She's going to have our baby, and I have to be there.' I pushed my way into the delivery room, I didn't care, and they had to put a gown on me. I stood right there and saw them spank you and everything."

Mother and Dad hadn't decided on a name for me, so there I was in the nursery with Betty Louise Brown, William Brian Jones, Sally Jane Smith, and "Baby Gould." Luckily, when they brought me home, I was "Jean Ellen Gould."

I was born into a home filled with love and happiness, which I recognized years later to be the greatest of all blessings. We loved our little pink Spanish bungalow on 17th Street and lived there until 1936 when we moved to the country. That is where the comic strip, *Dick Tracy,* was born — in that wonderful little house.

The fireplace wall divided the living room from the dining room with wide arched openings on either side of it — the fireplace was open to the living room only. Dad and I would play tag running around and around the fireplace until he would catch me and swing me up in the air. Then we'd start again.

Just Dad and me, 1927.

A favorite early family photo.

The sunroom was actually an extension on the north side of the dining room. Here is where Dad's drawing board, chair and taboret stood. This is also where two comfortably padded wicker chairs (one a rocker) and a small table and lamp were situated. On the floor near one of the chairs stood a basket of yarn and knitting needles; this was where mother sat in the evening with the radio playing softly to keep Dad company while he worked at his drawing board.

Never did an evening pass that Dad didn't play with me before he worked at his drawing board. One of the games, my favorite, I later found was a game Dad and Ray played with their little sister, Helen. I must have been about four or five years old and such a lightweight to carry, he said. First, my head was covered with a towel, then I was twirled around. Then, picking me up, Dad would say something like, "Well, I think we'll go downstairs," meaning the basement. Imitating going down stairs, he would get lower and lower and say, "Well, here we are downstairs in the basement and the lights went out. There is something wrong with the lightbulb and I'm getting scared." But that didn't scare me one bit with my Dad holding me. At last, he pulled the towel off my head, and I found that we were still in the living room. We had never gone downstairs.

Sometimes starting in the living room on one of these imaginary trips, we would go across water on stepping-stones or we would walk right through it, and Dad would get his feet wet. We would duck under low hanging branches, even fit through narrow passages, bumping against things. Finally, he would say, "We're going into a cave now, and it's very low." He would put his hand on my head to protect it, then duck down. Carefully putting me down on the cave floor, he would pull the towel off my head, and there I would be under the kitchen table. Oh, how I loved that game!

We even developed a wrestling team, so Dad called it. He would sit on the floor, and I would toddle over and push him, and he would fall over. As I grew bigger and stronger, one day, I gave him a push that landed right under his chin. He coughed and laughingly said, "This has to stop—the fun is over." I had grown too big for that game.

Eating watermelon while lying on our stomachs in the front of the living room fireplace, we competed to see who could spit the seeds the farthest into the fireplace. This was a game Mother must not have appreciated.

Even going to bed was a production in our house—one Mother and Dad played along with. After I was ready for bed, the train formed in the living room. Dad was always the caboose, Mother the passenger car, and I was the engine. Well, of course, the engine always took the long way around to the bedroom, weaving through every room in the house, with the caboose making us laugh with the silly antics that only Dad could think up. The fun didn't stop after we reached the bedroom. While mother went to the kitchen to get a small glass of warm milk for me to drink before climbing into bed, Dad and I would hide in the closet.

"Now, where did they go?" Mother would say upon returning. And of course, we would jump out of the closet and say, "Boo!" I would jump into bed so pleased with our game. No matter how many times we hid in that closet, Mother never let on that she knew where we were. After a bedtime prayer and goodnight kisses, I had been thoroughly put to bed, while the soft music of Wayne King played in the background, lulling me to sleep.

The closeness and time my parents so lovingly shared with me have had a lasting influence in my life, one that I have tried to pass on to my children. I feel that the bond of love, trust and respect taught to me by their example is the greatest gift any child can receive during the early formative years. That sets the pattern for life.

ORIGINAL AND CARBON COPY

Dad took this picture of Mother and me in the back yard in Wilmette, 1929. His caption is what caught my eye. He wrote under the photo "original and carbon copy."

The Pursuit Continues

In 1928, seven years after arriving in Chicago, now married and with a baby daughter, Dad had made a name for himself at Hearst's *Evening American*. He was going strong. His work was recognized and well read, and he was making good money and taking it to the bank. But ever since Hearst had asked Dad in 1925 to create a cartoon strip like Ed Wheelan's *Minute Movies*, it had gnawed away at him. Dad had heard that Hearst had tried to get Wheelan to join the *American* without success. So he accepted the job knowing it would be a take-off on Wheelan's work, something he never wanted to do. But he swallowed his pride and developed *Fillum Fables*, which turned out to be a big hit for the *American*.

Now there was a rumor that Hearst was looking for someone in the art department to do *Little Annie Rooney*. Dad knew that if he were approached to do that strip, it definitely wouldn't be for him. He was at a crossroads in his career. Should he sign another five-year contract with the *American*, or leave the paper? It was a decision to be made right when he was riding the waves of success. If he followed his gut feeling, he knew he would be out of a job. Recalling this time in his life in 1928, Dad said, "Here I was only twenty-eight years old and had an ego so big that I felt I would never be out of a job — but there I was, out of a job."

Strangely enough, a few days after leaving the *American*, and right in front of the newly built Tribune Tower building on Michigan Avenue (dedicated in 1925), Dad once again ran into Haggerty — the man who had given him a job in the Advertising Art Department of the *Tribune* back in 1922.

"Well, you're doing very well on the *American*, I see," said Haggerty, as he cheerfully greeted Dad. "I've been following your work."

"Well, you won't be following it anymore, because I left the *American* the day before yesterday."

Haggerty looked surprised. "Are you out of a job?"

"Yes."

"I'm with the *Chicago Daily News* now, and we're enlarging our art department," said Haggerty. "What were you making at the *American*?"

"A hundred dollars a week."

"I can only pay you fifty a week, but you can start tomorrow," was the answer.

"You've got your man!" Dad responded enthusiastically, and he went home with a grateful heart.

So, it was back to the old commercial artwork: lettering and drawing ads for foods, furniture, rugs, and housewares — ads you see every day and think nothing of.

Some time after settling into his job at the *Chicago Daily News,* Dad was notified that the boss in the editors' office wanted to see him. For some reason, Dad felt nervous about this.

"I understand you had some experience with the *American*," the editor began.

"Yes," responded Dad.

"Well, we need a girl strip in the *Daily News*. Can you draw a girl strip?"

"I sure can," Dad responded without hesitation.

"Let me see what you can do and we might start using it right away."

And that's how *The Girl Friends* began in the *Chicago Daily News* in 1929. It was a light-hearted, humorous strip about two girls and their frivolous lives. Dad wrote and drew this strip until he left the *News* in late 1931.

The Girl Friends comic strip, *Chicago Daily News*, 1929.

Nine Years and Counting

With 1930 approaching, Dad was thinking over his last nine years in Chicago. He had worked on all the other papers in the city and gotten nowhere with the *Tribune*. He had submitted comic strip ideas of every conceivable subject to J.M. Patterson but collected only a series of rejections in return. Finally, he decided he had to meet Patterson face to face. "I was prepared mentally to go to my grave, if necessary," he said, "but I was determined to get something for my effort. I said, 'I can't miss. The practice and effort I'm putting into this is bound to bring some kind of reward.'"

In looking back years later, Dad reflected that these are the most important years in a man's life: the years before he reaches his goal.

He made an appointment with Captain Patterson, who had moved to New York City to oversee his newspaper, the *New York Daily News*. (During World War I Patterson served as a captain of Artillery, then as a war correspondent in France and Belgium. Upon re-entering civilian life, he retained the title "Captain.") After the war, Captain Patterson's sharp newspaper sense was utilized in hiring the top cartoonists in the country. They were a major factor in the faithful following of his newspapers' readership.

So Dad loaded a satchel with an example of every kind of work he had done over the past nine years and boarded the train for New York City. He figured it just might impress Patterson to see this man who wouldn't take no for an answer.

Patterson greeted him cordially and looked at every piece of his work. He didn't slight anything. Shaking his head, he said, "You've done a lot of work here. I just can't use any of what you have. Right now, I'm looking for an editorial cartoonist. But whenever you get anything you think could be worthwhile, be sure to send it to me."

Dad picked up on that last sentence and felt his effort to come to New York had not been in vain. Thanking Patterson for taking the time to look at his work, Dad said goodbye. As he waited for the elevator, Patterson's words rang in his ears. Then the adrenaline began coursing through his veins as he thought, "An editorial cartoonist is what he wants."

Dad got off the elevator at the second floor and went in and subscribed to the *New York Daily News* for one month, including Saturdays and Sundays. The paper would be sent to his Wilmette home. He wanted to study what this paper was promoting, politically and every other way.

As soon as the first *New York Daily News* arrived, he read the editorial writers' columns. He continued reading them every evening after he settled down at his drawing board. He even cut them out and taped them up on the wall in front of his drawing board so he could absorb their content.

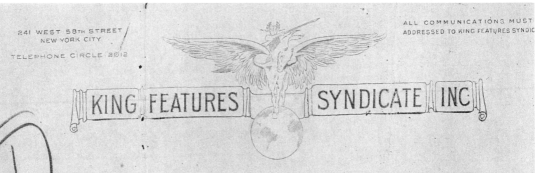

241 WEST 58TH STREET
NEW YORK CITY

TELEPHONE CIRCLE 2012

ALL COMMUNICATIONS MUST
ADDRESSED TO KING FEATURES SYNDIC

KING FEATURES SYNDICATE INC

December 21, 1922

Chester Gould, Esq.,
Room 217, Hearst Building,
Chicago, Ill.

Dear Mr. Gould:

     This is in acknowledgment of your letter of
December 15th.

     I shall write you frankly about your feature.
Your drawings and your ideas give every indication of
your ability to develop a successful comic feature.

     I don't care for the idea "Our Nuto-Grovure
Section". Won't you please try your hand on a new idea
or on several new ideas? Can't you do something along
the line of "Little Willie's Slate", with which I as-
sume you are familiar?

     Won't you get down to this without delay and
send me some samples for presentation to our comic editor?

     Please interpret my letter as meaning simply
this: that we like your stuff but we do not think it
will achieve satisfactory results if devoted to the "Nuto-
Grovure Section" series.

     With best wishes,

               Very truly yours,

MK*K

On this page and the next are a few of the rejection letters Dad received over the course of ten years,
between 1921 and 1931.

Liberty

247 PARK AVENUE

NEW YORK

J. M. PATTERSON
PRESIDENT

August 5, 1929.

Mr. Chester Gould,

 230 -17th Street,

  Wilmette, Ill.

Dear Mr. Gould:

   Thank you very much for giving us the opportunity of seeing your cartoons. I am sorry to say that we haven't the space to take on your feature at the present time.

   Sincerely yours,

   J. M. Patterson.

Liberty

220 EAST 42ND STREET

TELEPHONE VANDERBILT 6900

NEW YORK, N.Y.

J. M. PATTERSON
PRESIDENT

April 24, 1930

Mr. Chester Gould,
230 - 17th Street,
Wilmette, Ill.

Dear Mr. Gould:

   Yesterday, Mr. Patterson asked me to write you that he thinks your cartoons are very good, but he is not looking for a cartoonist at the present time. He has been seeing them as they were received.

   I have them all together and shall be glad to send them to you, if you wish me to do so.

   Sincerely yours,

   Secretary to Mr. Patterson

Liberty

220 EAST 42ND STREET

TELEPHONE VANDERBILT 6900

NEW YORK, N.Y.

J. M. PATTERSON
PRESIDENT

August 21, 1930

Mr. Chester Gould,
230 - 17th Street,
Wilmette, Ill.

Dear Mr. Gould:

   I thank you very much for letting me see the originals of the cartoons which recently appeared in the Chicago Daily News. I am returning them thinking you might wish to preserve them.

   I think you do good work.

   Very sincerely yours,

   J. M. Patterson

Liberty

220 EAST 42ND STREET

TELEPHONE VANDERBILT 6900

NEW YORK, N.Y.

J. M. PATTERSON
PRESIDENT

January 2, 1931

Mr. Chester Gould,
230 - 17th Street,
Wilmette, Illinois

Dear Mr. Gould:

   I suppose I am pretty discouraging, but I do not believe we have room for this feature.

   I hope you will keep on trying, because some day you may be able to make a connection.

   Sincerely yours,

   J. M. Patterson

After several weeks, he decided on a campaign to make it appear as if he were working for the *New York Daily News*. This strategy turned out to be similar to the one he had used with Mr. Curly of the *Evening American*.

Dad laid in a stock of envelopes and cardboard fillers, the size of the cartoon to be drawn (11" by 14"). He pre-addressed each envelope to the attention of:

> Captain J.M. Patterson
> New York Daily News
> 42nd Street
> New York City, N.Y.

Every night, he created an editorial cartoon to mail to J.M. Patterson the next day, including Saturdays and Sundays. He did that for thirty days. During his lunch hour, he would walk over to the Dearborn Street Station and put his drawings on the Twentieth Century Limited that left for New York daily. This train had a mail car, just like the post office. You could mail letters or packages right there.

"I'd hand my work to the fellow," Dad explained, "stamped and ready to go first class, and after a week or so, they thought I was a big shot sending important stuff to New York, and then, it was 'Hello,' or 'Hi, how are you?' I did that for one month, never missing a day. I call that the greatest piece of salesmanship I ever did. So every morning, Patterson came down to his office and there was an editorial cartoon by Gould. I heard nothing, no answer, nothing."

When Dad did hear something, it was the package of his thirty cartoons being returned by Miss Higgins, Patterson's secretary, who wrote, "Captain Patterson likes these very much but doesn't seem to believe your work is what he is looking for."

A few days later, a note from Patterson himself arrived, saying, "Thank you so much for letting me see your cartoons, which came every day. They are not quite what I am looking for, but please, see that I get any other work that you think I would be interested in."

Looking back Dad said, "A lot of people that would like to be successful, in my estimation, simply don't have the desperation back of it. They'll say, 'Well, if he can do it, I can do it.' The heck you can! You've got to have more than that! People will say, 'Well, I did the best I could.' That to me is an insulting answer. You're not supposed to do the best you can. You're supposed to do the best. So, I was working under a complex of desperation, in that I would never be any younger, nor would the opportunity ever be any closer to me than now, right now. I couldn't sleep. I was on a racetrack. My belief is that we don't have much of that anymore. You have to maintain a high degree of pressure within yourself. You can only do that in your younger years, and I was in my thirties then, but I kept it up until I was seventy-seven."

Above and top right: When Dad's efforts failed as a cartoonist, he tried his hand at editorial cartooning. Here are three examples of the thirty editorial cartoons sent to Captain Patterson in New York.

A day at the Wilmette beach. Dad and I haven't started playing yet. Dad, not quite 30 years old, was working at the *Chicago Daily News.* This was just about one year before he created *Dick Tracy.*

As Dad continued with his work at the *Chicago Daily News* well into 1931, he still had the taste of the editorial cartoons in his mouth. What could he do that was different? What could he do that Patterson would like? He recalled something that Patterson once said: "Keep things natural, go for the man on the street, tell it to Sweeney." Sweeney was the man on the street, the average American citizen that Patterson aimed for in his *New York Daily News*. The paper's circulation had climbed to 3,000,000 on Sundays and better than 2,000,000 on the dailies. Dad had to get something that was real and right now, something that was happening now that would be newsy. Something he could tell to Sweeney.

5

The Birth of *Dick Tracy*

One May evening after dinner, after I was tucked in bed, Mother sat down in her usual chair to knit; Dad sat at his drawing board reading the evening paper while the radio played softly. It was quiet, a comfortable setting, but this would be a night that would change our lives forever.

Dad carefully scanned the pages of the newspaper, stopping to read articles that caught his interest. Then, folding the paper, he gently dropped it to the floor. Just as it hit the floor, however, his eyes for that split second caught the headline: "*Another Gangland Killing.*" The headline might as well have been in neon lights the way it caught his eye. Dad thought, "*Gangsters!*"

Gangsters were thriving on the effects of the Depression of 1929. Everyone was fed up with crime, graft, dishonesty and disrespect for the law. Even the law was questionable at times. Gangsters were escaping their punishment. There were fixed juries and fixed judges, and all kinds of crooked business was going on. Convictions didn't seem to matter. Hoodlums and gangsters involved in murder would come to court and the lawyers got them out scot free. They'd bring them in around 8:30 in the morning, and the lawyers would have them out walking the streets by 11:30. All this ran through Dad's head in what seemed like a flash.

Dad pondered those headlines, and he remembered how he loved to read Arthur Conan Doyle's Sherlock Holmes detective stories when a boy. He realized what a shrewd-thinking detective Holmes was, always tracing clues and getting his man. He thought, "That's what we need today: someone who can either shoot down these public enemies or put them behind bars where they belong." Then he remembered: "*Tell it to Sweeney.*"

Sitting back in his chair, he slowly rolled his pencil between his fingers, looking nowhere in particular in complete concentration. What would a modern-day Sherlock Holmes look like? He reached for some paper, his hand racing to keep up with his mind. Not a two-peaked English deerslayer cap, but a snap-brim fedora — and under the hat a sharp nose for tracing clues and a sharp chin to denote strength. He stopped for a moment, aware that his heart was racing with this exciting realization. Then his pencil continued in a long downward motion, putting a long coat over this clean-cut man's suit and tie, to finish the look. And there was his detective!

Jumping to his feet with all the assurance that Patterson would go for this idea, he exclaimed, "Edna, I've got it!" Handing her the rough sketch, he continued, "A detective strip, an honest, sharp-thinking detective who always gets his man. I'll call him 'Plain Clothes Tracy.'"

Mother, in complete surprise, dropped her knitting and took the drawing Dad had handed her. She listened to him develop the concept as she studied his drawing.

"Plain Clothes Tracy. It sounds like a wonderful idea, Chet," she answered. And they both relished the moment of great expectations. Dad always respected and counted on Mother's comments, and it was no different tonight. After talking for what seemed to be hours, Dad finally kissed Mother goodnight.

Still, feeling the exhilaration that this night had brought, he couldn't sleep. He didn't want to sleep. All that night, and into the early hours of morning, Dad sat at his drawing board, unaware that there was another world beyond the circle of light that flooded his work. His body was exhilarated as his mind carried his pencil from panel to panel.

At Mother's breakfast place at the table the next morning lay Dad's six strips, all inked in and complete. With enthusiasm, she carefully read and studied every strip. Looking up at Dad, Mother said, "Chet, you have a winner here."

Dad had added a title strip with "PLAIN CLOTHES TRACY" in five-inch letters across the whole page. "I used every bit of psychology and salesmanship I could think of, except to trip Patterson with a rope," he said.

Mailing those strips first thing before he went to work that morning, Dad started counting. One week, two weeks, three weeks, four weeks—nothing.

He continued diligently with his job on the *Chicago Daily News*. Now he was writing and drawing *The Girl Friends*, drawing editorial cartoons and still working in the advertising department. In fact, he was drawing a complicated Persian rug with all its intricate floral work when someone in the art department said, "Chet, telephone." Glad to take a few minutes away from that rug, Dad answered the phone to hear Mother talking excitedly.

"Chet, a telegram just arrived from New York. Shall I open it?"

"Yes! Yes! Yes!" was the reply. "Read it!" He heard her tear it open.

"August 13, 1931—— Your Plain Clothes Tracy has possibilities. Would like to see you when I go to Chicago next. Please call *Tribune* office Monday about noon for an appointment. J.M. Patterson."

Here is how Dad described what happened next: "All of a sudden I began to break out in a cold sweat and I got the shakes and a little dizzy. I said, 'Finally! It's here!' I sat down to finish the rug and I couldn't do it. The pen was shaking. I asked Hatton, another artist, if he would finish the rug. He said, 'Sure.' I went downstairs and ordered a malted milk. I bought a cigar. I bought a package of gum. I had all this at the soda fountain, and I could hardly drink the malted milk. Finally, I did get it down. Then, I began to calm down. I went back upstairs. This was all spontaneous. It hit me almost in a frightening sense. I said to myself, 'Surely this is not the thing I've been looking for,' but it had to be."

(Dad considered that telegram his most cherished possession until the day he died. It represented the most emotional moment of his ten-year struggle to reach his goal. He was proud to show off this telegram, which always hung on the wall next to his very first *Dick Tracy* Sunday page, dated October 4, 1931, but no one could ever have known how deeply his emotions were tied to this simple little piece of paper. Mother and I saw his eyes well up with tears on many an occasion, remembering.)

Dad immediately made an appointment with Captain Patterson, then went out and bought a new suit, shirt, tie, shoes and hat. And on August 15, 1931, Patterson—wearing old Army boots and no tie—greeted Dad. He was holding Dad's strips in his hand.

"This is a very thrilling day for me," said Dad. "I'm so happy to be here."

"Good. Good," responded Patterson. "I think the name is too long."

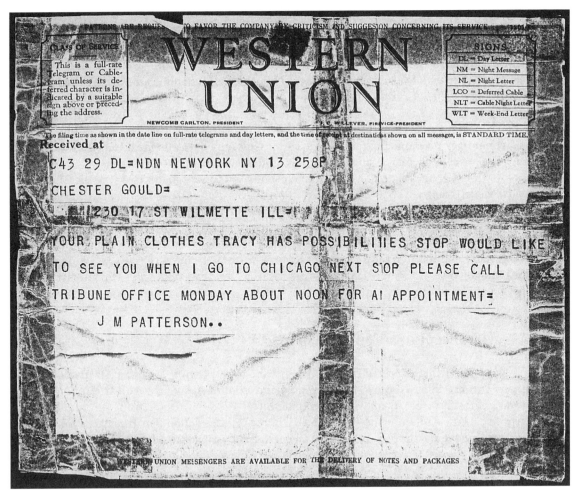

The telegram that Dad received that ended the ten-year struggle, August 13, 1931.

Dad had to listen attentively. The captain was not one to waste any words.

"We've got to get a shorter name for this strip. John Tracy, Fred Tracy, Dick Tracy. Let's call this fellow 'Dick Tracy.' They call detectives 'Dicks.'"

Dad heartily agreed, wishing he had thought of that idea.

"Now for starters," continued Captain Patterson, "why don't you have Tracy going with this girl whose father owns a delicatessen, and they live upstairs over the store. The old man customarily takes his days' receipts upstairs at night and puts them in a small safe under his bed. That night thieves break into their apartment and kill the old man and take the money. You take it from there. Can you have two weeks' work in to the *Chicago Tribune–New York News* syndicate in New York by September first?"

"You bet I can," exclaimed Dad. "What a whale of a start. It's a beauty!"

Patterson could see the determination in this amazing young man who wouldn't give up. Dad, extending his hand in an enthusiastic handshake, thanked the captain and left his office realizing that at last his childhood dream was at hand. After ten years and sixty different comic strip ideas sent to this man, he had finally hit the mark.

"Fierce determination and a belief in yourself is what it takes," said Dad. "You can't give up. *Dick Tracy* was my sixty-first idea."

For the next two weeks, Dad averaged two hours' sleep a night, getting those strips written, drawn, inked and in the hands of Molly Slott in New York, as Patterson had directed.

During those days, having never been a policeman, Dad had to learn the routine. He immediately contacted the *Tribune*'s top police reporter, an Irish fellow by the name of Jim
Dougherty. Jim took Dad over and introduced him to the 1121 South State Street Police Headquarters and the policemen and their department, where he received a carte blanche to come
anytime.

Then, at Patterson's suggestion, Dad enrolled in Northwestern University's special School
of Criminology, a unique program that even the Chicago Police attended. Here Dad learned
about ballistics, microscopes and all the tools used in police laboratories in the study of criminology from Calvin Goddard. Northwestern eventually transferred this course to the Chicago
Police Department.

Criminology books, magazines and every kind of law enforcement magazine that Dad
could get his hands on were now a part of his library. Through his class he subscribed to the
Journal of Criminal Law Criminology. There would be no doubt that Tracy was going to be as
comfortable and sharp in the police laboratory as he would be out on a case. He would know
the latest in police techniques and police procedure. Sure, he would use his gun and fists, but
they would be a last resort.

A New Concept in a Comic Strip

Dick Tracy first appeared on October 4, 1931, in the *Detroit Mirror*, a *Tribune* owned
paper. This had to have been a highly exciting and emotional day for Dad. Patterson figured
it was going to be a big hit and wanted to pull out all the stops in advertising this new comic
strip (all the promotion coming from New York). The circulation departments of both the
Chicago Tribune and the *New York Daily News* wrote and sent ads to *Editor and Publisher Magazine*. They wanted to put the strip and the advertising on the market simultaneously.

Above and following pages: The first ten days of *Dick Tracy*.

Dad sitting in his Tribune Tower office, shortly after he had begun writing and drawing **Dick Tracy.** **Chicago Tribune** photo, 1931.

They wrote:

Dick Tracy: *Chicago Tribune* detective thriller comic, although only a few months old has won the widespread approval of readers and publishers.

Packed with adventure, suspense and surprise, *Dick Tracy* is an up-to-the-minute comic about a sleuth who is determined to squelch gangland ... It's refreshing ... It's new ... It's surefire ... It's bound to be popular. Write or wire regarding exclusive rights in your territory, prices and proofs. Chicago Tribune Newspapers Syndicate, Tribune Square, Chicago.

"Those were the most thrilling days a man ever had," Dad recalled, "creating something that had never been done before, a serious comic strip. It was somewhat frightening. Even the guys at the news syndicate, when they saw some of the first strips showing some mean crooks, they said, 'Nobody will print these.' I think the first year, we put on close to one hundred papers, and it kept going up from there."

Instant Popularity!

A sampling of letters sent from publishers:

Where are our *Dick Tracy* strips? We have had 500 telephone calls from readers who want to know why *Dick Tracy* did not appear in the *World* today.
    —*Newport (Kentucky) World*

Dick Tracy is getting over big in New York. In fact, I have heard more favorable comment on this strip than on anything we have used. When we announced that we were going to use it also as a Sunday feature in colors, we got a great response in the way of increased Sunday business.
    —J. S. Sullivan, Manager of Circulation, *New York News*

I consider *Dick Tracy* an outstanding feature. It appeals at once to young and old and is proving one of the most popular comic strips the *Chicago Tribune* has ever printed. Readers and dealers are enthusiastic about it. Recently, we gave away 300,000 *Dick Tracy* buttons to Chicago children and our office was swamped with thousands of letters requesting these buttons.

— Louis Rose, Director of Circulation, *Chicago Tribune*

Knowing His Stuff

On one of his trips to the State Street Police Department, after the strip had been running in the paper for a few weeks, Dad met Al Valanis, a young officer who did the "foot work," they called it, which was the toughest part of police work. Al must have seen *Dick Tracy* in the *New York Daily News*. It was so new it hadn't appeared in the *Chicago Tribune* yet, but he had already become an ardent Tracy fan. Al had tried his hand at a police strip, but without success.

Some years later, Al played an important part in the strip, when Dad contacted him and asked him for information in a panel requiring a fingerprint scene.

"Would you tell me where an officer stands and how he holds a suspect's fingers when he is fingerprinting him?" Dad asked.

"I'll do better than that," responded Al. "I'll draw it for you."

With great detail, Al sketched the table, the positioning of the inkpad, the roller, the position of the suspect and the policeman, everything that entailed the correct procedure. Dad was overwhelmed. Dad knew that this was a man he one day wanted on his staff.

Remembering Al, Dad said, "He went on to become one of Chicago's top plainclothes detectives and undercover men. He was a brilliant man, having a mind that took details just like two cogwheels. There couldn't be any misunderstanding about the facts, because it could mean a life, or a terrible gun battle or somebody getting needlessly hurt." Teaming up with Stanley Sarbarneck, another tough and brilliant man on the Chicago force, Al worked on many of Chicago's most horrible crimes.

In 1953, after his retirement, Al joined Dad's staff as his technical advisor, meeting with Dad and his assistants in his Tribune Tower office early on Monday mornings. For two hours, they would banter ideas about, and Al would check over Dad's penciled Sunday page for correct police procedure when it was used in the story. Al kept Dad abreast of new police techniques and lab work, often illustrating a point rather than describing it and, if possible, bringing a piece of equipment to Dad's office from the police lab.

In 1949, Dad created the *Crimestoppers Textbook Tips*, which appeared in the top right hand corner of every Sunday page. Each week it had an interesting bit of factual police information for the reader. When Al joined Dad's staff, he supplied the *Crimestoppers Textbook Tips* with factual safety tips for adults, teens, children and police rookies and expanded this feature into a most informative and popular addition to the *Dick Tracy* strip. Most of those tips are as applicable today as they were then.

During his police career, Al drew keen sketches from descriptions given by witnesses to crimes. Sometimes the likeness was almost photographic as an amazed Brinks hold-up man discovered when he saw the sketch of himself.

When Al died in 1974, Dad lost a greatly admired friend and assistant. Al's knowledge in police work had brought vast credibility to the strip.

At its height in popularity, *Dick Tracy* ran on the front page of the Sunday comic section of the two biggest newspapers in the United States, the *Chicago Tribune* and the *New York*

Daily News; for forty-five consecutive years it ran on the front page of the *New York Daily News*. That has to be some kind of record.

Said Dad, "The only reason for a cartoonist existing is to sell newspapers or to mold opinion as the editorial cartoonists do; I considered myself a glamorized newspaper boy. It's all based on circulation. Captain J.M. Patterson in my opinion was one of the greatest visual editors in the world."

In his early years of doing the strip, Dad had no schedule. "I just kept working until I had the work done for that week, and — I could work all night and all the next day — and I did. You know, when you're fired up and you are at that age — I was thirty-one — you've got all the vigor in the world. You don't need anything but just to have somebody fire the gun — GO! And that's it.

6

The Farm

New York seemed so far away, but that's where Dad considered moving in 1935. Leaving our relatives and friends was something Mother and I didn't even want to think about. Dad and other *Tribune* cartoonists were encouraged to make this move to New York so as to be closer to the Chicago Tribune–New York News Syndicate, where cartoonists sent their work each week. (Captain Patterson, who lived in New York, was editor and publisher of the *New York Daily News*, but he also had an office in the Tribune Tower. He hired the cartoonists. Molly Slott headed the Chicago Tribune–New York News Syndicate in New York.)

Around this same time, Mother had just visited a friend who seemed to have amazing perception and would often read tea leaves and cards. During a social visit one day, this friend read Mother's tea leaves. With a surprise in her voice, she said, "Why, Edna! I see a farm. You and Chester are going to buy a farm."

"What?" exclaimed Mother. "This just couldn't be true. We're not moving, and you know, Marge, I've always been a city girl." Something was about to change that.

One day, as the spring of 1935 approached, Dad was talking to Al Loewenthal, his agent, who handled all the *Dick Tracy* dolls, games, books, rings, badges, detective sets, toys, and so on. Al said to Dad, "Chet, have you ever thought about living out in the country, maybe buying a farm? I pass through some beautiful farm country when I leave Chicago for the weekend at my home in Marengo. There are some farms for sale near the little town of Woodstock. It's about sixty miles northwest of Chicago."

Al and Dad had talked about the effects of the Depression of 1929. The economists, the financial advisors and all the noted writers were saying the same thing: "If you want protection during the next depression, buy a farm." Al was a very sharp individual and proved many times that his greatest concern was Dad's best interest. Dad and Al had tremendous respect for each other, not only from a business standpoint, but also as trusted friends. *Dick Tracy* products zoomed in sales with Al's masterful business sense. After their talk, Dad thought about a farm and even mentioned it to Mother. But nothing more was said.

That August, as we passed through this little town of Woodstock, the town that Al had mentioned, on our way back to Wilmette from a vacation at Big Sand Lake Club in Phelps, Wisconsin, Dad suddenly decided to stop at a real estate office. Just like that! We didn't know anyone, so we stopped at the first one we found.

"Sure, I've got some of the best in the land to show you. When do you want to come back?" asked the realtor, knowing that we were on our way home from vacation.

Dad and Mother looked at each other with a nod of agreement. "Let's take a look right now," said Dad.

So, into his car we climbed, driving about five and a half miles east of town on bumpy, dusty, hilly, washboarded gravel roads, churning up a trail of dust as we went. Turning onto a path with two dirt tracks straddling grass, we approached a hill that appeared to have a forty-five degree drop. As we crept downward, the realtor pointed to a house set back from the road on the left. "See over there, that shack almost hidden by the trees? No electricity, no running water. That's where Old Man Miller has lived for years."

Old Man Miller, as the realtor referred to him, was the caretaker of the sixty acre abandoned farm we were about to see at the foot of the hill. We crossed a beautiful babbling brook, and soon turned into what had once been a driveway but which was now waist high in weeds.

Set back about a hundred and fifty feet from the road were a house, a barn and several shacks, all tumbled down. The barn was leaning to one side. It had broken windows, and discarded old junk stood in the weeds around it. It was a mess. These were old, abandoned farms out here, and we were later to find out why.

We got out of the car. Grasshoppers were jumping everywhere in the weeds. (We later found ourselves covered with cockleburs from the waist down — or in my case, since I was shorter than everyone else, practically from the neck down.) We climbed over a missing stair into the house — and there we were, in a living room among bushels of rotting cucumbers that Old Man Miller must have put there and forgotten. Over in the corner stood an old Franklin stove with part of the stovepipe dangling. Bees had found a nesting place in the wall opening. Stepping over debris, we walked into another small room that opened to the back of the house. To the right of this room was the kitchen, a large room with a door leading to the outside on the south side of the house, and next to it an old chipped enamel sink and hand pump showing signs of rust from years of neglect. (This same hand pump was later restored and installed at the bar sink in their rotunda, when Mother and Dad remodeled in 1967.)

The wood-burning cook stove stood near the west wall. It had to have seen years of use and must have filled the kitchen with warmth and wonderful aromas of food cooking. On the northeast wall, a rather narrow low door opened to a flight of steep, narrow stairs descending to a dark, musty basement below. A flashlight beam directed us down to a dirt floor surrounded by a foundation of fieldstone. Undoubtedly the stone had been gathered from the property some seventy years ago, when the house was built. That would have been in the 1860s, during the Civil War era. Scattered among the debris on the floor of the basement were abandoned canning jars, empty cans, collapsed shelving that once must have held a storehouse of food. It was too dark to see much else. I was relieved to leave the dark and primitive basement and climb back up those stairs to the kitchen again. Another door on this same kitchen wall led to a bedroom. When I opened a door in the bedroom expecting to find a closet, I instead found a stairway and another door. This door, I found, opened into the living room, where we had first come in. These two rooms could close off the stairway that led to the second floor. As we carefully climbed this narrow, steep set of stairs, the combination of stale air and freshly disturbed dust told us that it had been years since anyone had gone up there.

Generous walk-in closets accompanied each of the four bedrooms. There was no bathroom. Looking through the wavy glass windowpanes, I realized that none of the windows had been broken. Outside of an east window stood a pump and windmill with an old tin cup rhythmically clinking against the windmill's hanger. Somehow, the clinking of that tin cup on the windmill brought back childhood memories for Dad. He loved it.

Then Mother called, "Chet, you won't believe what I found outside this window!" There it was — the old outhouse. It looked as if a strong wind would blow it over, yet there it stood after all these years.

Again outside, our eyes scanned the vast wooded hills around us, with a deep valley nestled in between the hills.

"It's just beautiful," said Dad, and Mother agreed.

"Those are mostly red oaks and shagbark hickories up there," the realtor said, pointing to the hill in front of the house. "But wait until you see what's at the south end of this property."

Here were the grasshoppers and cockleburs again, as we trudged through the weeds heading south of the house. Passing a small cluster of apple trees, we helped ourselves to an apple as we followed the realtor. Before we saw it, we heard it: a brook winding its way across the south end of this property, the same one we crossed on the road. The crystal clear water magnified everything on the brook's bottom. A beautiful sight and a great place to play, I thought.

Then Mother exclaimed with excitement, "Chet, come here! Look at this beautiful watercress!"

By the time we made our way back to the barn, Mother and Dad knew that this place had great natural beauty and potential. And it was there on the side of the barn, that very afternoon, that Dad wrote a $200 check as a deposit. It was that sudden. We were on our way to owning a farm at $50 dollars an acre. I couldn't have been more excited thinking about cows, pigs, horses, chickens, cats, dogs and who knew what else.

Soon after purchasing the farm, Dad found out why so many farms were abandoned in this area. It was all gravel! If you dug down about five or six inches, past a kind of topsoil, there was gravel. As Dad put it, "We had bought sixty acres here and seventy acres across the road (three years later). We had bought two piles of gravel!" The good farmland was all north and west of Woodstock. But Mother and Dad didn't care. The beauty of this acreage was what they loved.

Mother joined the Woodstock Memorial Hospital Auxiliary after moving to the farm and began to make new friends. Among them was Mrs. Green, the wife of the president of the First National Bank of Woodstock where Dad planned to open an account. Mr. Green had his office near the entrance of the bank so he could see everyone who came in and went out. Recalling this certain day, Dad said, "I went in to make a deposit and was just leaving the bank when Mr. Green came out of his office with his hand thrust out and said, 'You're Gould, aren't you? Well, I'm glad to know you.' And in the next breath he said, 'Why in the devil did you buy your acreage in Bull Valley?'"

Shocked, Dad replied, "We just thought it was beautiful out there. It's got water, hills, trees, a brook and a little farmland."

"Well," said Mr. Green, "I'm going to tell you something. You'll never grow anything on that farmland. It's all gravel!"

"Is that right?" said Dad. He was getting a little angry by this time and didn't want to say something for which he would be sorry.

They shook hands, and Dad thought to himself, I just went in there to put a little dab of money in his bank, so I'd feel like I belonged.

Several years later after the house and farm were complete and we had moved in, we were eating out. As we were leaving the restaurant, who should come in the door but Frank Green and his wife. Dad had not forgotten what Mr. Green had said to him.

Mr. Green took Dad's arm and pulled him aside. "I want to have a word with you," he said. Dad wasn't too sure he wanted to hear what he had to say.

"You know what I told you before about that property you bought?"

"I'll never forget it, but we still love the place just the same."

"Well," said Mr. Green, "You have the damndest most expensive land in the county."

Mother and Dad had been trailblazers in this farm country, as were several other families in 1935 and 1936. Dad was soon going to find out however, how unwelcome he was.

Getting the Wheels in Motion

As soon as the closing on the purchase of the farm took place, Dad immediately lined up a Woodstock contractor to rebuild the barn and build a silo, corncrib, chicken house, milk house (for cooling the milk), pig pen and bull pen. The concrete man set the stanchions (for the cows) in the cement floor of the barn as well as for the feed troughs, following the recommended blueprint for dairy barns. In the meantime, construction of the new house was begun while the farmhouse was being remodeled.

We were so anxious to see the progress that we spent every weekend at the farm. We even ate lunch in the old farmhouse kitchen on a temporary table that Mother had covered with oilcloth. It was exciting to see the progress. The new part of the house was built right up against the restored farmhouse. All the fieldstones used in building the two fireplaces in the new house were found on our property, and each stone was chiseled to fit into a pattern that was just beautiful. With Dad's studio right above the living room, the fireplaces could share the same chimney, but each had different flues. Dad's drawing board would have a perfect location along the north wall of windows. When he was working at his board, he could look up and see the cattle grazing. The walls and cathedral ceiling were all finished in a rich satin-finished knotty pine paneling, as were the two supporting beams. A wagon wheel light fixture was a must for Dad's studio. The little town of Ridgefield that we passed through on our way to the farm had just what he wanted. Stopping at the blacksmith's shop on the corner in that little town one day, Dad asked the blacksmith where he could find a wheel.

"I got wagon wheels right over there," stated the bewhiskered blacksmith, "but why in Sam Hill do you just want one? They only come in pairs."

NEW ADDITION LOOKING EAST   1935-1936

Construction of the new house in 1936. It was exciting to drive out to the farm every weekend and see the progress being made. It would be almost a year before it was completed and we would move from Wilmette to Woodstock.

So Dad bought a large pair of wagon wheels that had signs of wear, just the look he wanted. The unused wheel just stood leaning against the back of the barn, attracting vines. The other was electrified with ten candle fixtures and hung by a series of large chains that converged at the center of the ridge in the ceiling. It had a wonderful masculine and country look that was outdone only by a big elk's head mounted on the wall opposite the fireplace. This was a gift from a friend.

The old outhouse had probably never been used as much as it was that year, throughout all the construction. But now that the house had indoor plumbing, it was no longer needed.

We often brought Grandmother and Grandfather Gauger out to the farm with us. They both loved the country as we did, and they, too, lived in Wilmette. Grandfather was a partner in a very successful Chicago commercial contracting company, so he enjoyed watching the building progress.

Well, one hot summer day, things were going along as they should until Grandfather took a match to the outhouse. That August was exceedingly hot and dry, and though the outhouse had been moved to a wide-open area away from the front of the house, it was cause for alarm when that old shack went up like tinder. Sparks ignited the dry grass in every direction. By the time we learned what had happened, Grandfather had recruited all the workmen, some dozen of them, to haul pail after pail of water from the windmill pump and the newly turned on water spigots on the outside of the house. Other men were digging trenches. Sparks would cause little fires to pop up in one place while men were working on another. It was an insidious thing. The main concern was the house.

It took most of the morning and all afternoon to put the fire out. It had burned all the way up the hill and under the fence into Old Man McDonald's property. He lived to the north of us, and already he didn't like Dad. Now, he was mad as a hornet.

"You'll pay for this, Gould!" he yelled. "You doggone city slicker. You don't belong out here!"

For weeks that followed, the old dried cow and horse dung from years before smoldered and had to be watched. The workmen were all rewarded for their efforts. Try as he might, however, to atone for what happened, Dad found that "crabby" Old McDonald never let him forget that he didn't belong out there.

With the farm buildings and the farmhouse about finished, Dad started interviewing farmers from the area and soon found that none of them wanted to use tractor-drawn machinery. Everything had to be horse-drawn. So, after hiring Jo, a farmer from Elgin, to help him, Dad went out and bought a team of horses. It just happened that the horse barn that auctioned and sold top quality horses was owned by Frank Green, the president of the First National Bank. But Dad bought a team of horses anyway. He named them "Tom" and "Jerry." He also bought "Cookie" and "Danny," two riding horses. Stopping at a harness shop on the way home, he and Jo bought all the equipment the workhorses needed, and two saddles and bridles for the riding horses. (Years later, after our riding days were over, the saddles hung over a beam in Dad's studio—until 1967, when they became clever seats in Dad and Mother's rotunda bar.)

The first piece of farm equipment purchased was a small plow the farmer wanted in order to create a large vegetable garden for Mother. There just happened to be a Sears and Roebuck catalog in the back seat of our car, so Dad and Jo climbed in, sat down in the back seat, and opened the catalog to farm machinery.

"That's the one right there," Jo exclaimed, pointing to a one-horse plow, the kind you hold and walk behind, guiding it while the horse pulls it. The price was $15.00. (That same plow sprayed gold, thirty years later, became a centerpiece in an indoor garden in the foyer of Mother and Dad's newly built house.)

The rest of the farm machinery was likewise purchased — a rake and disc for working the ground and four or five other pieces of equipment, all built to be pulled by a team of horses.

Jo and his wife moved into the farmhouse. Meanwhile, the painters were finishing our house. In our kitchen, Hotpoint had installed an oversized electric range (gas hadn't been brought out to the country yet). This range had two ovens, five calrod surface units, and a deep well for making soups and stews. Mother was planning on doing a lot of entertaining. Four years later, in 1939, we had a Hotpoint dishwasher, a remarkable appliance.

For one year the farm and house construction had occupied Dad's time. When he wasn't sitting at his drawing board in Chicago, writing and drawing *Dick Tracy*, he was out at the farm checking on the progress.

Next came the farm animals. Grandfather Gauger had found a place near Chicago where a small herd of cows could be bought.

"Put in Brown Swiss," recommended the man. "Their butterfat is much higher than ordinary white face, and their production is better."

Dad found the man was right when he bought a herd of fourteen Brown Swiss cows, and he started selling milk to Borden Weiland Dairy in Woodstock. Two milk cans of Grade-A milk a day brought the ridiculous price of fifteen to twenty dollars a month, but at least it was a monthly check coming in. Dad remembered it went up to thirty dollars a few times. The Depression was still on. Carpenters on the job were making fifty cents an hour.

Next on the scene were a

DADDY & GRAMPA GAUGER 1936

Dad and Grandpa Gauger in 1936, visiting the windmill pump at a calmer time for a drink of ice-cold well water. Dad loved drinking from the tin cup he is holding, which always hung on the hook at the pump.

hundred laying hens. They arrived in the back of our new yellow pick-up truck. One day on his way through McHenry to buy pigs, Dad saw some ducks and bought them. Our farm was growing.

The fields now looked beautiful. To the east of the house, Jo had planted alfalfa that went clear down to the brook. Across the gully was our cornfield, looking bigger than the all out-doors. There were soybeans to the south of the ridge and oats on the southwest side of the house and north of the driveway — all to supply our small dairy farm.

Something was missing: a farm dog. So Dad bought Blackie, a mixed breed, part black Lab and part something else. He had a long, shiny black coat of fur and the kindest brown eyes. Blackie proved to be the most loyal, gentlest dog we ever had. He had been raised an outdoor dog, never wanting to be in the house. I was always amazed to see him during the winter make a nest in the snow and curl up with his nose tucked in his fur. Feeling sorry for him, I tried to bring him in the house, but it was too warm for him, and Dad assured me Blackie could go into the barn and sleep in the hay if he wanted to.

During one hot summer, Blackie had his hair shaved off. Dad felt sorry for him and took the electric clippers to his beautiful coat of long hair, except the hair around his neck. The poor dog looked like two dogs put together. Blackie was never embarrassed like that again. That wonderful dog spent thirteen happy years on the farm with us.

The Big Move

On September 6, 1936, bidding a sad farewell to our neighbors, our friends and our lit-tle pink Spanish bungalow, we left Wilmette, heading for a new life that would span nearly fifty years. Mother's brother, Bill, and his family would now enjoy that wonderful little house in Wilmette that we had so loved.

A few months before we moved, Dad bought a beautiful 1936 Lincoln Zephyr car. Never mind the bumpy, dusty, washboarded country roads, we were going to the country in style. As it turned out, however, that car gave us nothing but trouble after moving to the country. So Dad traded it in and came home from Chicago one day with a long, sleek-looking black Fleetwood Cadillac. It was a beauty, sporting a spare tire encased on the front left fender and a luxurious interior trimmed in genuine walnut. We drove that car for almost ten years.

Mother had a new life to adjust to, not having the convenience of the city and stores close by, or her Wilmette friends and family.

I remember how at least once a month Mother and I would dress up — which included hats and gloves in those days— and take the Chicago Northwestern train into Chicago to spend a day shopping at Marshall Field and Company. It was a large, beautiful department store that prided itself on personal customer service. Their toy department was a child's dream come true. There seemed no end to it. A few of the foreign dolls in my collection came from their marvelous foreign doll department. Mother and I would leisurely shop until noon; then, after a lovely lunch in the Walnut Room on the seventh floor, we headed for the model house on the furniture floor. The exterior looked like a one-story ranch house, and the interior had all the rooms such a house would include. It seemed remarkable to me, here in a department store. You could live right there.

By the end of the day, Mother and I were bushed. We took a cab over to Dad's office in the Tribune Tower and found him finishing his work for the day. His assistant, Jack Ryan, was also winding down. Marshall Fields had delivered our purchases to Dad's office, some-thing they did free of charge. As he packed up his work to take home, we all left together, say-ing goodbye to Jack as we exited the building. Walking down a flight of stairs to the lower level, which led to the parking lot up against the Tribune building, we got into our car and drove home with Dad his jovial self.

Now that we were living in the country, Mother had to think twice about running out and picking up one or two items. It was a five and a half mile trip to the nearest store. But an amazing thing happened. She seemed to take to the country like a fish to water, and she couldn't wait to have their first party and invite her city relatives (Dad's relatives were in Oklahoma). This would be Dad and Mother's first big party.

Were those city relatives in for a surprise when they saw a whole roasted and glazed pig, complete with a glazed apple in its mouth, at the end of our buffet table! This was Dad's idea, of course. He had met a man in town who had a big commercial oven, and he offered to roast the pig if Dad had it butchered and dressed. The day of the party, Mother had decorated a huge platter with parsley and glazed apples, which made a flattering setting for the pig. Still, it was a startling sight. Already we had eliminated one pig from our farm, but everyone loved it and country life seemed very satisfying — and the party was destined to become an annual event.

Early fall brought harvest time. Farmers in the area usually hired several temporary farmhands to help bring in the crops, but still it took several days to get the work done. When Dad caught sight of the team pulling the flatbed wagon into his fragrant mown alfalfa field, the temptation got the best of him. He put down his pen and his cigar, corked his ink bottle and pushed away from his drawing board, as if a childhood memory beckoned him. He went out into the field, asked for a pitchfork and began tossing the alfalfa up on the flatbed wagon, just like the rest of them. The horses slowly moved along, hesitating at the farmer's command, while the grasshoppers and other bugs sprang up all around. They went up one direction, down another, until the field was clear and the wagon was piled high with alfalfa.

Dad lasted less than twenty minutes before he handed over the pitchfork to one of the hands, who smiled, realizing that this man was a little out of his element. But Dad had satisfied a feeling of nostalgia, remembering his boyhood days helping his Grandfather Miller on his farm in Pawnee, Oklahoma.

ZEAK STANDING 1936 DADDY ON WAGON TOM & L JERRY

Dad takes time out from his drawing board to get a taste of farming, 1936.

Among her many talents, Mother was gifted with a green thumb. She loved flowers and plants, and they thrived under her care. Along with the hard work of it all, she had found a secret ingredient. First thing in the spring, after the frost was well out of the ground, she conducted a collection drive that led us up on the hill in front of the house. Each of us carried a paper bag. It took some getting used to, picking up dried cow dung. She even recruited her mother and father, if they happened to be visiting. When Mother's friends saw her zinnias, eight inches across, they couldn't believe their eyes, and had to have the seeds from those flowers. They never knew that Mother's secret ingredient did the trick.

Adjustments for a New Kind of Life

Going from Wilmette telephone service in 1936 to Woodstock's country service was a big change. Now our phone was a wooden box attached to the wall. I was just eight years old and had to stand on a step stool to talk into it. If you didn't hear someone on the line (we were on an eight-party line), you turned the crank on the side of the box to get the operator. Woodstock people in town had phone numbers like 647 or 516; ours in the country was 1645M1. Years later, we chuckled as we remembered our frustration when we wanted to make a call and someone was on the line. Dad was especially frustrated. He called the Chicago Tribune-New York News Syndicate office in New York City often. Said Dad, "I'd invariably pick up the

The summer of 1936, the year we moved to Woodstock. Already we had adapted to country living. What a complete change it was from suburban life! I was soon to be eight years old, but all of my friends were back in Wilmette.

phone to crank the thing and hear something like, 'Mabel tell'm t'git the vet over here quick. I think the mare is sick!'" It took a little over a year until we could get a private line.

Our telephone book in 1939 measured 6" × 9" and contained eighteen pages, which contained all residential and commercial phone numbers of Woodstock, Crystal Lake, McHenry and Harvard. By 1942, the year after we entered World War II, the phone book had grown to thirty pages, but stayed the same 6" × 9" size. On the cover of this book was a notice from the Illinois Bell Telephone Company that read: "ATTENTION: Please do not make Telephone Calls During or Immediately After an Air Raid Alarm or Other Unusual Occurrences as It Is Essential That the Lines Be Kept Free for Use by the Defense Authorities. If Your Telephone Rings, However, Answer It Promptly."

Another big change in our lives—especially Dad's—was commuting from the farm to the Tribune Tower in downtown Chicago. It was still a six-day-a-week commuting schedule, as it had been in Wilmette, with work until noon on Saturdays. Train travel was limited from Woodstock. The Chicago North Western Railroad had one steam engine that made it into Chicago from Crystal Lake, a nearby town, in one hour, but it didn't fit Dad's schedule. So for the first four years, Dad drove the sixty-mile trip from the farm into the Tribune Tower in his little Ford coupe, "the puddle jumper," leaving the house at 5:00 A.M. He drove this way and that way, finding the shortest route and the least traveled roads he could find. There were no tollways, just two-lane highways, and luckily for him, not much traffic that time of day. He made it into the city and was parked on the lower level next to the Tribune Tower building in one hour.

I had entered third grade in 1936, when we moved to the farm, and that was the last year the little one room schoolhouse we passed every day operated as a school. Mother and Dad wanted me to attend school in the town of Woodstock, so I never saw the inside of that schoolhouse until a neighbor family purchased it some years later. They turned it into a charming country home, enlarging it for their needs, but keeping the original schoolhouse look, including the school bell atop the roof.

Mother was a real trooper, taking me to school and picking me up each day, a five-and-a-half mile trip each way in rain, snow, fog or ice—on all gravel roads. On particularly bad mornings, Dad worked his schedule around taking me to school, then taking the train into the city.

Whether it was working with the Woodstock Hospital Auxiliary, playing bridge with her newfound Woodstock friends or her Wilmette bridge foursome, knitting, planning parties or working in her beautiful gardens, Mother kept busy. During the summer, our kitchen hummed with activity. Mother canned vegetables from our garden (beans, corn, tomatoes, and beets) and made applesauce, jellies and pickles. She was just remarkable doing all this work herself, having known nothing but city life up to this time. Dad never failed to recognize this.

Home freezers were not yet on the market in the early 1940s, and when Dad had the chance to buy a used ice cream freezer, the kind with six cylindrical deep wells that drug stores used, it suddenly became the most exciting addition to our home. Mother could freeze our garden vegetables now, and we could keep all kinds of ice cream and ice cream bars in it. The excitement of opening the lid and finding all this was just like being in a drug store, only better. But first you had to get past the rayon stockings. Freezing was thought to extend the life of the fiber. (Nylon, during the war, was used for parachutes and wasn't available for stockings.) Then Dad had his Robert Burns Panatela Cigars in another well (freezing was good for them, too). That freezer served any number of purposes, and we loved it.

We found those first years in the country a real wilderness, however. The only people who had snowplows were the railroads, mostly in the northwest. We had seen some snow drifts go over the tops of the fences. After a big snow, the only way to get out was to shovel. And we

did. On some snowy mornings, Mother, Dad and I went out with shovels at 5:00 and shov-
eled the driveway all the way out to the entrance gate and then back to the garage, a good 150
feet. It took hours to do, with a lot of effort and a lot of laughing to get through it. Our dogs
loved it. Dad later found that the milk truck, which was able get through at about 6:00 A.M.,
had wide dual tires that made wide ruts in the snow. Having learned from Jo, the farmer, how
to put chains on the back wheels of the car to get traction, Dad could drive with one side of
the car wheels in the truck ruts and get out.

A few years later, we had a secondhand International Harvester tractor with steel cleats
on the wheels. The country roads were still all gravel. This tractor helped fight the snow problem. The cleats were in triple rows, triple sets, all around the wheels and were meant to dig
into the ground to get traction. One just didn't believe that the tractor would get stuck under
any condition. But what happened, Dad found, was that the cleats were so severe, so deep,
that during the cold winter months, the tractor threw snow out the back just like a dog kicks
up dirt. "You'd be sitting still," said Dad, "while the cleats bounced on the ice underneath."
He even got stuck on the big hill south of our house (better known as Miller's hill) with that
tractor and almost tipped it over trying to get a car out of the ditch. Days later, that tractor
disappeared from the barn and was replaced by a tractor with big rubber wheels.

What a Father!

One thing I loved about Dad was that he was so animated. He had a way of making the
most menial job a fascinating and often funny experience to watch. Stoking the furnace was
one example. Our new home had a big rectangular furnace in the basement that needed stoking with coal every night. But first, it was necessary to remove strange-looking things called
clinkers, a volcanic-like coal residue left from the burned coal. One by one, these clinkers
were plucked out and dropped into a galvanized bucket. This just fascinated me, seeing Dad
with these long handled tongs reach into this fiery opening in the furnace and remove the
clinkers one by one. Like everything he did, he performed this task with great finesse.

When the ominous coal bin door was opened, a complete black abyss was exposed. One
time, a barn cat jumped out when the door opened, and we about hit the ceiling. It must have
gone in from the outside when a coal delivery was made, and it had spent the entire day there,
coming out all black except for around its mouth. It couldn't wait to get outside.

It took four or five coal shuttles filled with coal to satisfy the furnace, and each one was
tossed through the small door opening, making a "whooosh" sound as it hit the remaining live
coals. If I was watching, Dad couldn't resist getting a little silly, but he never missed the door.

He left that part of the basement immaculate before moving over to the laundry tub to
wash his hands. Opening a cabinet, he took out a cup and a box of salt and mixed a little salt
into warm water, which he poured into his cupped hand. With a horrible sound, he sniffed
this stuff up into his nostrils, and then blew it out. He did this several times, claiming that it
cleaned any coal dust out of his nasal passages. Undoubtedly this was something learned in
Oklahoma.

On some Sunday mornings before breakfast, especially in the spring, Dad and I would
go out to the barn, saddle up Danny and Cookie, our two riding horses, and slowly ride
around the country section, which encompassed about five beautiful miles of farmland. The
crisp morning air would smell so good as our horses clip-clopped along the gravel roads, taking us past farms that were stirring with early morning noises and activity. As we rode along,
Dad would sometimes make up stories about a pheasant or a horse we saw, or even a crow
sitting on the fence. I loved those special mornings.

Welcome to Woodstock

The town of Woodstock was, and still is, built on a town square with a beautiful park in the center and stores around the perimeter. Not a single store was outside that perimeter. (In many ways, Woodstock's town square still resembles the town square of Pawnee, Oklahoma.) Back in the mid–1930s, traffic went around the square both ways. With parking in front of the stores, as well as on the park side of the square, driving could become pretty congested, especially if a farmer brought his horse and wagon into town to pick up feed, coal or fertilizers, then stopped on the square for something. Not too many years ago, indications of high curbs where horses were once secured still gave the square historic charm.

Each store was typical of small towns of that time. There were clothing stores that carried fabrics, sewing needs, and table, bed and bath linens. There were hardware stores and grocery stores, a drug store, saloons, a millinery shop, several other shops and more saloons.

"There were also some characters in this town," said Dad, recalling his first encounter with one of the Woodstock merchants. "One of the hardware stores, which later became Dacy Appliance, was run by a really sharp-tongued little guy. The first time I walked into his store, I saw he had stuff clear up to the ceiling in little drawers and things stacked high up on the floor and on display. He had a book that he would get the number out of which showed what drawer your item was in. Then he'd climb up a ladder, like they used in department stores, and would push it along a track until he found the drawer with that number that contained what you wanted. He was a cranky little guy, but a darn good man and had a lot invested there. But the first day I went into the store, he came out from behind the place where the bookkeeper sat,

Dad kept close track of the farm operation and enjoyed pitching in once in awhile.

on a sort of platform that had a little brass rail around it, and said, 'Well, I suppose you've been to every store in Woodstock, and you finally came here. What d'ya want?' That's just the way he said it. I tried to smile, and he didn't. I thought, Geez, I ought to turn around and walk out, but this guy may have what I want. I wanted a bolt cutter, which is a high leverage mechanical thing that will cut bolts, steel or anything. I said, 'I want a bolt cutter, not one of these big ones, but one I can handle.'

"'I know just what you want,' he said, 'but I don't have one. I'll have one brought out tomorrow with my order.'"

Dad thought the owner was giving him a line and was about to tell him to forget the whole thing. But on second thought, he didn't want to make a fuss in this town. This was his first time purchasing anything in Woodstock. The next morning he had a bolt cutter.

"I finally got to understand this little guy," Dad chuckled. "He was always crabby. So I'd go in there and say something insulting to him, and we were on good terms."

Back on the farm, Jo was bringing us fresh milk from the barn (we had grown used to drinking unpasteurized milk since we had been on the farm) and fresh eggs from the chicken house. Our garden was abundant with vegetables of all kinds. We could even get a chicken for a Sunday dinner, which we did once in awhile. After Dad butchered the chicken, all three of us plucked the feathers. Dunking it first in boiling water was necessary to help the feathers come out more easily. If you have ever smelled wet chicken feathers, you know how horrible they smell, and how those smelly feathers stick to your hands. By the time we got to the inside of the fowl, Dad sounded like an old pro. "See the oyster shell and other food in its crop. It's heading for the gizzard, to get ground up to help make a harder egg shell. And look here, it's the beginning of an egg," and so on. It was like a biology class and the job didn't seem half so bad. Then Mother took the dressed chicken in the house, washed it inside and out and prepared it for our Sunday dinner. One year, Dad butchered twenty-one chickens for a party. Boy! Did our chicken population go down, and were we busy plucking and cleaning those birds. By then we had Julia, a live-in maid, who was a wonderful cook and a lot of fun. She pitched right in with the chicken cleaning.

7

Dad at Work and at Home

By 1940, Dad changed his commuting schedule. Instead of going into the Tribune Tower six days a week, he went in only on Mondays and Tuesdays. These were the crucial days of the week, when Dad completed the writing and penciling of the *Dick Tracy* Sunday page and six daily comic strips. This involved concentrated thought and, sometimes, long hours. Early Wednesday mornings, Russell Stamm, Dad's assistant at that time, drove out to the farm. By late Thursday afternoon they had finished their work. Russ, having learned Dad's technique in lettering, took on that job, as well as the job of inking in some of the backgrounds. One by one, as those strips were finished, they were laid out on the hickory table in the studio. By the time Russ left, all six strips and the Sunday page were on the table waiting for Mother and me to read. This was a weekly ritual Mother and I loved — one that Dad depended on for our comments regarding the clarity of the story. However, we rarely, if ever, found any of his stories unclear. At a most crucial time in a story, after reading the week's set of daily strips and Sunday page, I couldn't wait to find out what was going to happen next. Invariably, to my disappointment, Dad's answer was, "I don't know." How could he not know? How could Dad get Tracy backed into a corner and not know how he would get him out? Dad not only thrived on this way of writing, he knew his readers wouldn't know what was going to happen if he didn't know. He became a master storyteller using this technique, incorporating unpredictable twists and turns throughout his stories.

Dad explained, "A comic strip has to follow contemporary thinking to be popular. Then the cartoonist has to be darned alert to see that he doesn't get in a rut. There is no such thing as having it made in this business. The only morning you have it made is this morning, you hope. Tomorrow morning, you have to make it again.

"The facets are so numerous that you have to please the young and the old. You have to please the biased. You have to try to get the people that don't read the comics. You have to prevent the person who has followed you for years from saying, 'Well, I'm tired of that, and I don't read it anymore.' There is no end for what you set for yourself. It's like being on a train track and a train is chasing you and you can't get off the track. The pressure is always there."

By bedtime on Thursday, there were Dad's strips and Sunday page rolled securely, wrapped, sealed addressed, and ready to mail to New York the next morning. Until then, they spent the night next to his bed on his night table.

101

Thursday wasn't by any means the end of this work week. Aside from business mail, paying bills and tending to personal business, Dad had fan mail—and lots of it—to be read. He responded to as much as time permitted. Over the weekend, he read law enforcement magazines, *Criminology Monthly*, and FBI magazines that informed him about police procedure and police lab technology that he could use in *Dick Tracy*.

On Saturday and Sunday, ideas were taking shape for the next week's Sunday page. During the summer, much of Dad's thinking took place on his mowing machine. Mowing acres of grass around the perimeter of the house and barn provided Dad with a relaxing job away from the drawing board, and a time to think about the mess he had gotten Tracy into.

My dad trimmed bushes, fixed fences, hauled broken tree limbs to an area behind the barn for future firewood and kept up with outdoor maintenance, even though there was help to do that. It was important for him to know that everything around the farm was done the way he wanted it. I can remember that on some hot summer days after trimming the long hedge near the garage, Dad would come in for lunch and his arms and hands would be quivering from the continuous physical exertion in using the long hand clippers. (This was before electric trimmers.) It took about ten to fifteen minutes for his arms and hands to stop quivering.

Dad seems to be contemplating: "Well, I've done it again. Dick's in a heck of a mess!" 1945. (Photograph courtesy Saturday Evening Post Society, ©1949 www.saturdayeveningpost.com.)

On Sunday afternoon, seated at his

drawing board with the blank Sunday page laid out in front of him, Dad would pick up his pencil and begin. Again, with no story plan written on paper, no notes, nothing before him, he began writing in longhand, word-for-word dialogue, just as it would appear in the finished lettered balloons. This dialogue might include, "What's the idea?" And in the same panel, "Crime Stoppers. We're going to do a little talking." Panel after panel the story would unfold in this manner, going right from Dad's head to the blank panels on his Bristol board. He would think about the next week's story over the weekend, and he always put an immense amount of thought and research into each story, but nothing would be written down until he sat at his drawing board to draw that week's six daily strips and Sunday page.

Techniques

Dad's two-dimensional drawing style was by no means accidental. He drew his strips in a simplistic manner so that the reader could easily pick up the paper, turn to *Dick Tracy* and, at a glance, easily see what was taking place in each panel of the story before reading the dialogue. (Dad never forgot J.M. Patterson's words, "Keep it natural. Go for the man on the street.") His unique technique in using solid blacks brought dramatic visual contrasts and strength to the strip. He knew how to use black to direct the reader's eye to the interest at hand, a formula he had down to perfection — never overdone, never underdone.

Anyone lucky enough to own an original *Dick Tracy* strip might notice what looks like a scorched area on the back of the strip. This resulted from Dad hurrying up the drying process by holding a lighted wooden kitchen match under the freshly inked-in black area, which was still wet. Sometimes a blacked-in area took longer to dry, depending on its size. Dad's drying technique always left a black, sooty area on the back. When this was wiped away, the Bristol board was scorched. Once in awhile, if the flame lingered too long, it would leave a slight bubble, but luckily, Dad never had the burn go through to the front of the drawing.

I remember how Mother discouraged Dad from using his handkerchiefs to wipe the soot off the back of his strips. The handkerchief was the first thing he grabbled, not a rag, because the finer fabric did a better job of removing the soot, but the soot left permanent stains that Clorox couldn't remove. So his handkerchiefs were tattletale-gray. Only when he went out or we had had company did he have a new handkerchief — and before long, that one, too, became tattletale-gray.

Thanks to his training in the W.L. Evans Cartooning correspondence course way back in high school, Dad was in supreme command of the "Gillott" dip pen, the only pen point he ever used. Going from the boldest to the finest hairline stroke was something Dad had easily mastered. I loved watching him ink in his strips. His hatching and cross-hatching, also learned from his correspondence course, were also techniques he used masterfully every day. His use of contrast and line was outstanding. I didn't know a cartoonist who could draw more beautiful snowflakes than Dad.

It was exciting to watch Dad put the finishing touches to one his miserable, windy, rainy, stormy night panels. This he accomplished by taking the corner of a single-edged razor blade and making long scratch lines right across his drawing. I would hold my breath when he did this, but the roughed-up lines on the Bristol board gave a perfect effect of rain or sleet blowing at an angle every time. Those memories are so vivid to me today.

Panels showing techniques in black and white.

A Giant Heap of Trouble

Only once do I ever remember Dad not knowing how to get Tracy out of a life-and-death situation. It was in 1942. Jacques, one the minor crooks in the strip, captured Tracy and took him to the city limits where several twenty-foot-deep caissons were set for digging a new extension bridge.

"Push him in," said Jacques to his cronies, and they did. With the help of the car, they pushed a giant granite bolder into the hole, on top of Tracy. The huge jagged rock dropped until it struck an irregular projection of clay. Then it stopped, but its weight forced it slowly through the damp clay and it dropped again — tons of life-crushing weight. It moved another foot ... and another.... What could Tracy do now? What could Dad do?

His solution, which never appeared in print, showed Tracy looking out from the paper and saying, "Gould, you've gone too far." In the next panel, Dad drew his hand, holding a piece of art gum and erasing the giant bolder. As he drew, he was thinking, "Gee, this will be a first."

When Captain Patterson saw that Sunday page, he called Dad immediately. "You can't do this," he said. "It will kill all your readers' faith in you. You won't have anything to hang on to."

Dad knew Patterson was right. By the time the Sunday page was returned to him, Dad had it figured out. As Tracy stomped around sweating bullets, his heels made a hollow sound. He found that he was on dirt-covered boards which were part of the ceiling form for concrete. By yelling, he managed to get the attention of the workmen below. They cut a hole and he jumped down and rolled out of the way just seconds before the giant boulder dropped down. Dad got him out of that one. The caisson turned out to be a ventilator shaft for a new tunnel — a lucky break for Tracy.

A Different Sort of Fan Letter

I must have been about ten years old when I started writing fan letters to some of my favorite comic strip cartoonists. There was Carl Ed, who drew *Harold Teen*, Milton Caniff, who drew *Terry and the Pirates*, and Walter Berndt, who drew *Smitty*, to name a few. Dale Messick, the creator of *Brenda Starr*, surely would have been at the top of my list, but Dale hadn't yet created *Brenda Starr*; that strip began in 1941, and this was 1938. My hope was that I might receive autographed drawings of these favorite comic strip characters that I could frame and hang on my bedroom wall. Of course, I knew that Dad's drawing would be an easy one to get. Dad liked my idea and said that he would make me a nice drawing, but later, when he had more time. So I started my campaign of letter writing. I think I wrote half a dozen different cartoonists.

Within a month, one by one, each of their autographed drawings arrived in the mail. To open each envelope and find a delightful comic strip character looking out at me with a special greeting just for "Jean" was such a thrill!

Mother and I were going to drive into Woodstock to get these treasured drawings framed and ready to hang, but I still didn't have a *Dick Tracy* drawing from Dad to add to my collection. No matter how often I reminded him of this, he would lovingly put his arm around me, give me a kiss on the cheek and say, "Honey, I haven't forgotten." Then one day he added, "I have a piece of Bristol board in my *Tribune* office, just the right size." Well, that gave me hope. I waited a few days, but nothing happened. That's when I decided to write Dad a fan letter.

We didn't have a typewriter, so I wrote the letter in my most careful long-hand writing, what we call cursive today. I tried to be professional by following the form of a discarded business letter I found in Dad's wastebasket. I really wanted to impress him. I sat down at my little desk in my bedroom and took my dictionary off the shelf so as not to make any careless mistakes in spelling. Mother had given me Dad's address. The letter went something like this:

Mr. Chester Gould
Chicago Tribune
435 N. Michigan Avenue
Chicago, Illinois

Dear Mr. Gould,

If you searched the world over, you could never find a more faithful *Dick Tracy* fan *anywhere*. Ever since I could read, and I am 10 years old now, I have read *Dick Tracy every* single day.

I would do almost anything for an autographed drawing of Dick Tracy for my bedroom wall collection. It would always be my favorite drawing.

Thanking you, if you think you have time to do this. Please! Please!

Yours truly,

Jean Gould
P.O. Box 191
Woodstock, Illinois

I mailed the letter and waited. After three or four days, I began watching Dad's reaction when he came home from work. No reaction. Did he get my letter? A week passed — still no reaction. Maybe he didn't get my letter. Should I ask him? No. I'll wait a little longer.

It was a day or two after that when Mother picked me up after school. There on the car seat lay a manila envelope. I saw that familiar *Chicago Tribune* name in the upper left-hand corner and above it, "Chester Gould." It was addressed to "Miss Jean Gould, P.O. Box 191, Woodstock, Illinois." I can still hear myself saying, "He did it! He did it!" as I tried to open the securely sealed heavy manila envelope. "Jean! Jean!" I heard that definite assertive voice of a mother who really means what she says. "Wait until we get home and use a scissors so you won't tear or bend the drawing." *How can you tear or bend Bristol board*? I thought to myself. *It's tougher than I am.* Well, I impatiently waited, shaking the envelope, pinching it, and scrutinizing it until Mother was probably ready to sit on me.

As soon as we arrived home, Mother and I opened the envelope together, and there was a most wonderful autographed drawing not only of Dick Tracy but also of Junior, and they were talking to me. Dad had drawn me right there in the picture, too. The drawing that I waited so long to receive is one of my most precious possessions. That dear Dad of mine put so much love into that one drawing that it was almost embarrassing at my young age to show it to my peers. It was such a treasure of love.

The treasured autograph from Dad that I waited so long to receive.

A Bold Step

In 1941, the United States entered World War II, and it wasn't long before rationing began. There were ration books allotting so many stamps per month for gas, for sugar and for meat, and it wasn't unusual to find store shelves low on certain grocery items. We were very happy for our farm as it permitted us to have a "B" gas ration book that contained more gas stamps than the "A" book. This was because gas-operated tractors were a necessity in planting and harvesting crops.

Due to the war, a new butter replacement was put on the market. Mother bought white, pasty one-pound blocks of stuff called oleo. It came with a yellow capsule of color, which had to be mixed into this block of white stuff to make it look like butter. That was my job. But the color didn't help the taste. It was miserable.

Dad sold the dairy farm that year and bought a small herd of young beef cattle, with plans to graze them during that spring and the summer then sell in the fall. Hired farmers were either going into the armed service or into defense factories, where they could make more money.

One day, Dad said to Mother, "Honey, what would you think of our butchering one of our beef cattle? We'd get the full taste of country living and that would be our emergency beef until we can buy meat again." Mother hesitatingly agreed.

Bill Fleming, who worked for us as a gardener, was a wonderful old man who had been born in a log cabin not far from us and who had been a farmer most of his life. On the day Dad spoke to him, he was doing his usual trimming around the house.

"Bill," Dad asked, "will you help me butcher one of our beef cattle?"

Bill was down on his hands and knees trimming around a rock pile near our rock garden pond. He looked up and without hesitation said, "Sure, Gould. Y'know where we could hoist that carcass? Right over one a' them big beams in the corncrib." Bill was a sharp "old timer" and knew everything about farm life.

Mother's two brothers, Bill and Dick, converted our springhouse, which was built partially underground to keep foods cool in the summer, into a walk-in-refrigerator. Dad put hooks in there on scaffolding to hang the sides of beef to age, and they were ready to go.

The next thing was to visit the butcher in town. Mr. Asmus owned a fine meat market and Dad wanted to see if he had a diagram showing the cuts of meat on a side of beef.

"Sure, I've got one right here. Take it along," he said.

"We're going to butcher our own beef," said Dad.

"Well, good luck," replied Mr. Asmus, no doubt wondering if they knew what they were getting into.

Dad purchased two meat saws and two butcher knives before heading for home. Mother had rented another drawer at the freezer plant in town and had bought freezer paper and marking pencils while there.

The day arrived. Dad loaded his .38 pistol, picked out a steer with Bill's help and got it in place.

"Gould, get up there on that saw horse and shoot this animal at close range, right between the eyes," Bill instructed. "When he drops, I'll cut his throat."

"And that's the way it happened," said Dad. "Then we arranged a pulley, and we put these hooks right through the tendons of the hind legs, and hoisted this animal up to drain. It was very important that the blood drained out. Then we cut the animal down the middle and gutted it, skinned it and cleaned it. When we finished the job, we were a mess, but we washed off at the pump and carried the halves of beef down to the springhouse and hung them on those hooks to age for about a week. On the given day, after we took you [meaning me] to school, I brought one side of beef into the house. Mom had our white enameled kitchen table all ready with leaves extended and covered with oilcloth. It was a little after 8:00 in the morning and we didn't get through until 8:00 that night. One hundred and four pieces of meat, cut, wrapped, labeled and delivered to the locker. I don't think any two people were ever so tired. We had bone dust all over the kitchen floor. We were sliding in it. We had it down our necks, in our hair, inside our clothes, inside our shoes, everywhere. Chips of meat and fat had been stepped on and smeared into the floor. It was a mess. It was after I brought the second side of beef in that I realized that the diagram was facing the other way. So, I had to take off my shoes and socks, wipe off my feet and go find a mirror and set the diagram so that it was reflected backwards in the mirror."

Dad had to admit that it was just plain egotism and pride in his wanting to do this. But Mother was at his side the whole time. "It's like any other advancement people make in their lives," he said. "You venture and you succeed. You are happy to know that you have that in your mental bank. You can do it! We already had butchered pigs stored in our freezer locker. The locker people took on the job of picking up the pigs, then processing the meat and freezing it for us. But that wasn't my idea of farming. There was nothing to doing that. We had experienced farm life at its fullest. We knew what we could accomplish. Our lives were rich and full."

Mother's love and admiration for Dad seemed to overshadow any hardships she might have felt living this country life. Seeing him happy brought her great happiness.

Dad recognized Mother's inner strength and beauty and her ability to always see the positive side of life. That is why he loved her. Their marriage was built on a strong foundation of love and respect for each other, as you can see in a segment of a letter written by Dad in 1936 to his eighth-grade school teacher in Pawnee, Oklahoma:

> Perhaps you wouldn't know this thin-faced kid that used to answer to that roll call by the name of Gould. I weigh one-hundred-seventy pounds, have some double chins (two they say) am happily married (since 1926) to the most wonderful woman on God's green earth, a Chicago girl.
>
> I have a young daughter, Jean and a whole armful of happiness and good luck. Although I work in Chicago everyday at the Tribune Tower, we live on a farm near Woodstock, and I ship two cans of Grade-A milk to the Chicago Market everyday. Have four horses and hold a deed to sixty of the prettiest acres around here. I have a man attending the farm on a straight salary basis, and life is very busy, but *very* happy.

That was Dad's outlook on life ever since I could remember. He loved life and loved his family. Each morning was a new beginning, a fresh new day, whether it was rain, snow, sleet or sunshine. It didn't matter; he loved it all. Even on the worst snowy days, he would be up before dawn clearing the driveway of snow; then down he'd go to the garage and out to the barn with a contraption he rigged up to the tractor. Coming in an hour or so later, covered with snow and icicles, cold, runny-nosed, ruddy-faced and glasses steamed up, he would be the most cheerful person and ready for breakfast.

There was one exception: some Monday mornings weren't so cheerful. If over the weekend he hadn't reached a satisfactory story plan for his upcoming Sunday page, he was pretty tense. Mother and I didn't say too much on those mornings; we kept things light and cheerful.

One Monday morning in 1945, Dad came down to breakfast in a peppy sort of manner. He had already been working at his drawing board for several hours. Mother and I knew right away that this was a really good Monday. We sat down to scrambled eggs (fresh from the chicken house), bacon and toast with peanut butter and homemade jam. Dad couldn't wait. "I have a new character," he burst out. "What do you think of the name 'B.O. Plenty'?" Back in those days, a phrase like "B.O." was never used though everyone knew it existed. My immediate reaction was shock, and even before Mother could answer, I hurriedly asked, "Daddy, you wouldn't really use that name, would you?"

He looked at Mother and me and smiled as he said, "Can I help it if his name is 'Bob Oscar Plenty'?"

So old bewhiskered B.O. Plenty made his debut and became one of the strip's most lovable and popular characters. He was Dad's favorite above all other characters he had ever created, except for Tracy. B.O., with all his backwoods personality, became what is known as a relief character in comic strips. On occasion, the main story would switch to Sunny Dell Acres at the corner of Ecstasy and Rainbow Drive, where B.O. lived in a tumbledown shack. (Those street names always seemed to change.) Any day Mother and I heard laughing coming from the studio, we knew Dad was working a sequence involving B.O. Plenty, and I was glad — B.O. had become one of my favorite characters, too.

Top: The meeting of B.O. (Bob Oscar) Plenty and Gravel Gertie, 1946. *Bottom*: The marital bliss of B.O. and Gertie, 1954.

Careful thought went into creating new characters before putting them into *Dick Tracy*. Dad tried to get a character whose name would be easy to remember — something simple and as common as you could get. "I tried to avoid being historically smart, grammatically smart and smart in a literature way," he said. "That bores people to death. I drew for the man on the street, as Patterson instructed me to. That's the man that doesn't want to deal in big words and doesn't use them. He likes it when a spade's a spade."

Speaking of humor, Dad continued, "Humor doesn't have to be jokes and gags. B.O. Plenty is an image of pioneer characters I knew in Oklahoma as a boy.

"These characters were uneducated but smart, cunning and tough with a ready, built-in funny bone. The incongruity of the rough exterior with these subtle qualities was humor in its richest form.

"I tried very hard to use that subtle formula throughout *Dick Tracy*."

"Serious writing must be seasoned with humor to be complete. Excruciating suspense of a mystery story is enhanced, in fact, by the nervous laugh and quip of a finale that says *all's well*!"

Spontaneity, too, was a driving force in Dad's work, the element of surprise and irony. The character Flattop, for instance, was inspired by radio newscasters who referred to U.S. aircraft carriers as "flattops" during World War II in 1943. That is when Flattop first appeared.

I even saw Dad create a character right before my eyes. He was doodling with a pencil on a small pad of paper — one page, then another and another, I asked, "What are you doing?" He answered, "Trying to get a new character," as his pencil continued these scraggily up-and-down lines that converged at both ends. Making some adjustments on this doodle and adding two eyes, nose and a mouth, Dad looked up at me and said, "Meet Pruneface." It was just like that: another one of those unforgettable characters, right out of the blue. (I always thought Dad gave Pruneface very kind-looking eyes for a criminal.)

Pruneface was created in 1942. He turned out to be a foreign spy working against the United States in the war. Toward the end of a fascinating story, Tracy discovered where this horrible villain was hiding, in an old abandoned house on the edge of town where he could set up his radio equipment. It was one of those windy, below-zero days when Tracy discovered his whereabouts. He and his backup-men, after giving Pruneface a chance to turn himself in, shot out all of the windows of the house, hoping that would do the trick. Pruneface remained inside and finally froze to death.

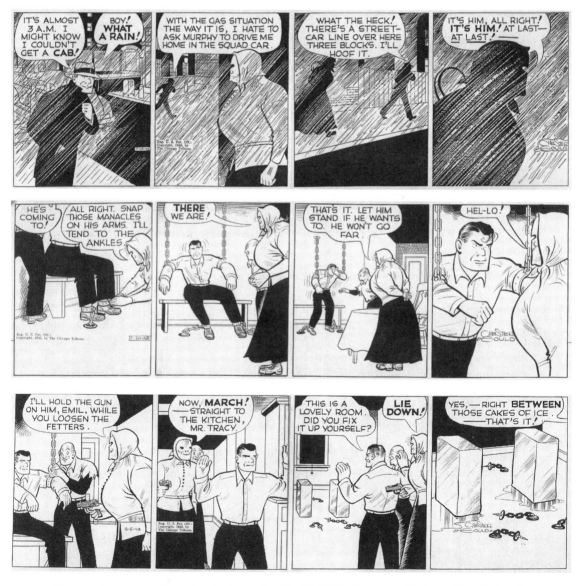

Above and next page: Pruneface had an evil wife. Of all his characters, Dad considered Mrs. Pruneface his most vicious. In this series of strips (1943), she is seeking revenge for the death of her criminal husband, who was an espionage agent during World War II.

The Entertainer

If anyone could laugh at himself, it was Dad. Since childhood, he had had the ability to "ham it up" quite a bit. He loved to make people laugh.

He went so far as to clown around, of all places, on the roof of our house, where he was doing some repair work. It was very impromptu. When he saw Mother with our new movie camera that was all he needed. Suddenly he was going through some silly antics while straddling the ridge of the roof. Mother and I held our breaths. He lost his hat but that was all, thank goodness. And Mother got it all on film.

An early photo of Grandma and Grandpa Gould and me, taken on one of our family trips to Stillwater, Oklahoma. Dad would have to get a week ahead in his work, and our visits never seemed long enough because Dad insisted on driving rather than flying.

One of his specialties was running into a door and knocking out two, sometimes three teeth. He did it many times. He had mastered a technique that made it seem he had hit the door hard, because his hand hit the side of the door away from the viewer to make a "bang!" That was the impact. Then as he grabbed his jaw in shock and pain, two or three teeth would come flying out of his mouth, to the horror of my little friends—who would then discover that Dad was a cut-up, and the teeth were only kernels of corn.

Taking off his thumb was another trick, all done in the way he held his two fists side by side. With the twisting of his fists, it looked like the real thing.

While entertaining his little five-year-old nephew, Dean, back in the late 1930s, when we were visiting his family in Oklahoma, Dad tried this trick, thinking Dean would giggle and carry on. Dean cried his eyes out. He just couldn't be convinced, even when his Uncle Chet showed him that his thumb was still on, that it was just pretend. Dad felt pretty bad about that. Finally, Dean gingerly took hold of his thumb and found it was still attached.

Another of these tricks that Dad pulled off really well was to pretend that someone was trying to pull him by the neck. Positioning himself behind a door or doorway opening so that the viewer could see only his head, neck and one hand that was holding onto the edge of the door or doorway, he would put his other hand around his neck and act as if someone was pulling him. Hanging onto the door Dad would growl through gritted teeth, "Let me go! Let me go!"

Dad's repertoire of these tricks seemed unending, and I thought they were remarkably done. But for an outsider, they might have looked a bit macabre, until that person saw that it was all in fun. My school friends, who were his primary audience, had to see every trick as many times as Dad would do it, and probably went home and tried it. My school girlfriends would spend the weekend with me once in awhile. They all thought I had the greatest Dad.

On those weekends, besides Dad's clowning around, there was plenty to do. My school friends and I rode horses and played in the hayloft, looking for litters of wild barnyard kittens between the bales of hay. We followed imaginary trails through the woods to the rocky gully where we thought we found precious stones. The gully led to the brook where we'd step from stone to stone crossing the water, then across again in a different spot to get to the bogs. Bogs are little spongy mounds of grasses in a marsh area. We found that if we stepped lightly on them, we wouldn't sink into the wet mud — usually. There was always something to do. In the winter, Dad would hitch up the toboggan on to the back of the tractor and take us all over the fields, curving every which-way.

No matter what other entertainment my friends and I found on the farm, Friday afternoons were always the same: We said our hellos, greeted the dogs, and headed upstairs to my room to listen to the radio serials— including *Dick Tracy*, which had found life on the Mutual Radio network in 1935. The program moved to NBC in 1937 and continued in 15-minute segments through 1939. The sound effects of squealing tires, explosions, and gunfire added great excitement to the already thrilling stories. Like the heroes of the other programs— including *Captain Midnight*, *Little Orphan Annie*, and *Jack Armstrong*— by Friday afternoon of each week, Tracy was up to his neck in trouble. Thank goodness for my "Dick Tracy Secret Patrol Code Book," which I, like every other child listening to the program, just had to have in order to decode the secret messages given out on the show. The codebook was a premium offered by the show's sponsor, Quaker Oats. With just two box tops from either Quaker Puffed Wheat or Quaker Puffed Rice cereal, you could get this book and use the code to send messages to your friends. This was pretty exciting stuff before television.

The codebook had enticements within its pages; five separate *Dick Tracy* badges were available, each more important than the other, and each requiring a handwritten note to Dick Tracy telling him of a good deed you had done at home, along with, of course, the proper number of box tops. The most important badge, the fifth, was a 14-karat gold-plated "Inspector General" badge. Beyond that, if you recruited five new members and two box tops from each of them, plus two more from you, you received a 14-karat gold-plated "Patrol Leader" bar from Dick Tracy himself. Then you had a club. If you got that far, your mother had to have bought thirty-nine boxes of Quaker Puffed Wheat or Quaker Puffed Rice cereal. Me? I was happy with my codebook and my five-boxtop "Officer" badge.

Many of these fifteen-minute radio serials had offers similar to this one, using box tops or labels. These offers had to have been great marketing tools. Today, these premiums are costly collectors' items.

As for *Dick Tracy* merchandise, Dad was sent samples of toys, books and games as they were introduced on the market back in the l930s and early 1940s. He would give them to me as they were sent to him, and I would play with them until I wore them out or used up the special papers or materials that came with them, such as the invisible ink or the fingerprinting ink, among other things. The rubber stamp set of *Dick Tracy* characters and several other

This is one of my favorite premiums, the Dick Tracy Secret Service Code Book, from Quaker Oats. My friends and I could now send messages back and forth!

Tribune cartoon characters I just loved. You could line up your own characters, put in your own dialogue, even color them, making your own comic strip.

Whenever I grew tired of any of these games or toys, and as long as they still looked okay and worked, I took them to school and gave them to my classmates. Neither Dad nor I had the foresight to keep much of anything. I did keep several Big Little Books from those years. In recent years, Larry Doucet, an avid *Dick Tracy* collector from New York, sent me a number of *Dick Tracy* collectibles. I have them displayed in a special case in my home. The irony of it all!

A Test of Faith

How blessed I was to have had such wonderful parents. I always marveled at how Dad could be whatever the occasion called for. He could be a shrewd businessman staying on top of every situation with a keen eye for detail. He was an expert in the stock market and in investments, methodically studying his monthly investment books. He knew in detail practically any company's past and present performances, its prospects and its president, anything that would help him make the right decision about an investment. He was a problem solver, able to push aside unimportant distractions and get to the heart of the problem. He was such a fun father, always happy, and he dearly loved his family and his home. In later years, he would be down on the floor with his grandchildren, Tracy and Sue, where he was instigating all the fun. I used to wonder how one man could have mastered so much in life.

However, in 1943, I saw Dad as I had never seen him before: vulnerable. I was a freshman in high school when Mother became desperately ill as a result of an infected gall bladder. This led to grave complications. One evening at the hospital, Dr. Sandeen told Dad and me that he had done everything he could do, and prayed that mother was strong enough to pull through. He was trying desperately to obtain a scarce new germicide we know today as the antibiotic called penicillin. The difficulty in producing this new germ fighter was that as fast as it was produced, it was sent overseas for American soldiers. Considered a miracle drug, it was like nothing our country had ever seen before.

Dad and I went home in silence that night. I remember how scared I was as we sat in the library. Never had I seen Dad so shaken. I couldn't hold back the tears. He was the strongest, most courageous man I had ever known, but not tonight. He took his Bible off the bookshelf and we took turns reading passages we thought would help us, and we prayed for Mother to be strong. Then, going to bed, we held those thoughts and knew that tomorrow Grandma and Grandpa Gauger would come to stay with us.

Early the next morning the phone rang. It was Dr. Sandeen, saying that the penicillin had arrived and Mother had just had a prolonged-action shot. Although it was a school day (my high school was right next door to the hospital), I didn't go to school. Instead, Dad and I drove right to the hospital. Suddenly bursting with happiness, I turned on the radio, but I then I switched it off, realizing this wasn't the time.

Dad and I hurried inside the building and up the elevator heading for Mother's room, only to find nurses bustling around. Dr. Sandeen met us with the words "Mrs. Gould has had an allergic reaction to the penicillin."

It was hard to believe. I couldn't go to school. Dad couldn't go home to his drawing board. We sat for hours in the waiting room checking about every fifteen minutes, and finally, the nurse let us in for a few minutes after they had finished their duties in the room. Mother's face was all swollen. She was asleep. Her private nurse assured us that she was out of pain and in the best of care, and that right now needed to sleep. She said it would be best for us to go home; we would be called the minute there was any change. I wanted to sit right outside her door in the hall the rest of the day and all night and I know Dad did, too, but we went home, just drained.

At home we were greeted by Grandma and Grandpa Gauger, now at our house. What a welcome sight they were. Such comfort all of us had being together, suddenly realizing that mother had already come through so much and that she was still with us. She *was* strong.

The next day, we arrived at the hospital early and walked right into Mother's room. She was still sleeping. Her cheeks were still puffy, but rosy. Several tubes were directed into bottles set on the floor beneath her bed to catch the drainage coming from her body. I remember one was an awful yellow-greenish color. Dad took one of her hands and I took the other as he spoke to her. Just like a miracle, she began to open her eyes and gave a little smile, then went back to sleep. Dad's release of anxiety was so great that he started telling her how much our dogs missed her, and of some of the silly things the dogs had been doing. Then I started in. The nurse gently touched Dad's arm, suggesting that we go home for a while. As we turned to leave, Dr. Sandeen came in. I will never forget his words as he put his hand on Dad's shoulder: "She is one strong woman. She has passed the crisis."

All the way home, we were basking in the good news. Dad started singing some bouncy song, and we sang and sang together. Dad was returning to his old self; neither of us had been ourselves for days.

While Mother was recovering, I found I could walk to the hospital, which was near the school, during my school lunch hour and spend a good half- hour with her. When her lunch tray was brought in, they brought me one, too. To my surprise one day, Mother looked at the food on my tray and said, "That looks good."

"Would you like to trade?" I asked. When she said, "Yes," I couldn't get my tray on her bed table fast enough. I knew she was getting better.

It was three weeks before Mother came home with her wonderful private nurse and a bottle containing one giant gallstone. I couldn't remember a happier day in my life.

During these stressful weeks over Christmas of 1943, Dad was doing some of his finest work at the drawing board. Flattop was just coming into the picture.

New York, New York

By the middle 1930s, *Dick Tracy* was climbing fast in popularity. Dad was asked to join the circuit of cartoonists giving "chalk talks," which had become very popular with comic strip fans. For a chalk talk, the cartoonist stood at a tall free-standing easel stacked with paper. Using chalk or charcoal (later ink markers came into use), the cartoonist entertained the audience by drawing his characters one by one, bigger than life, and talking about his work. The audience relished seeing his characters come to life right before their eyes. These were characters they saw every day in the comic strips about which they loved to read. After the talk, the drawings would probably be dispersed among the audience.

Some cartoonists could do this with ease, but after doing several chalk talks, Dad found it too difficult and time consuming. He said he could do one or the other: draw his strips or do the chalk talks. He did make a few of these talks, and gladly participated in the Cartoonist's War Bond Drive during World War II.

In the early and mid–1940s, however, he made some radio and TV guest appearances in New York when he was there attending the annual Editors and Publishers Convention. This convention took place every April. Among the shows he did were Arthur Godfrey's radio program, Ed Sullivan's *Toast of the Town* and *The Fred Waring Show*. What a thrill it was to see, first, the shows in rehearsal, and then the real thing the evening of the live television performance. Fred Waring invited just the three of us to join him in his New York apartment for dinner after the show. To this day, I still have a little velvet pouch holding a silver dollar that Mr. Waring gave to me that night.

In preparing for the Editors and Publishers Convention, Dad worked with fervent effort to get a week ahead with his Tracy strip. That was doing two weeks in one week. It was a difficult time for him.

I attended the convention with my parents for about five years, being excused from school for two or three days each year. We had never had much of a chance to travel with Dad's demanding schedule, so when the convention came along, he pulled out all the stops.

From the minute we walked down the rich red carpet runner that ran alongside the 20th Century Limited train (the same train by which, in 1928, Dad had mailed cartoon ideas each day for one month to J.M. Patterson), I could feel the excitement building. We passed porters standing tall at attention in their uniforms at the boarding doors, obviously proud of the train they served and ready to help the passengers. Upon boarding, we were escorted through a plush carpeted corridor, so quiet you could hear a pin drop. With a graceful bow, the porter motioned us into compartment "C," then stood aside as we went in. Inside the compartment we could truly feel the elegance of this silver streamlined conveyance that would take us to New York. Dad had reserved two bedroom compartments that had been opened to make one larger room. We had two built-in seats that opened into double beds; two berths, each with a small window (that's where I wanted to sleep); two spotless, round, built-in stainless steel sinks with "20th Century" monogrammed soaps and linens; two private commodes and two closets. The windows spanned the whole room. I thought it was glorious. Seeing Dad put his shoes into a little compartment near the floor that night and take them out in the morning all polished seemed like a little bit of magic to me, even though I knew the shoe compartment was accessed from the corridor.

With a knock at our door, there was the porter with a silver tray of ice water and three glasses tinkling with ice, along with a carafe of coffee and cups. Raising a built-in table that pulled out from under the windows, he set the tray down, offering Mother and Dad coffee and asking if there would be anything else. As he turned to leave, he said, "In twenty minutes, dinner will be served in the dining car." Sure enough, at the appointed time a porter came through the corridors with a dinner chime announcing, "Dinner is now being served."

I couldn't wait to walk through the moving cars to get to the dining car. I couldn't wait to have dinner while the towns rolled by. I couldn't wait to go to bed in the upper berth with the little window, then to have breakfast in the dining car. I couldn't wait to get to New York.

During the 1940s, Dad's work had skyrocketed to the top of the polls, and he strove to keep his strip the best in his own mind. Like all the best cartoonists, he found that this effort, along with thinking ahead from week to week, occupied tremendous hours of his time.

The convention was very important to him, a chance to meet face to face with newspaper editors and publishers from all over the country. Editors and publishers usually had important questions to ask a cartoonist about his strip. Sometimes they objected to or praised something about the artist's work, proving to be a valuable barometer as to how the strip was going in their part of the country. Dad took their comments very seriously.

The convention was also a chance to meet his fellow cartoonists from all over the country. There was Harold Gray (*Little Orphan Annie*), Martin Branner (*Winnie Winkle*), Zack Mosley (*Smilin' Jack*), Carl Ed (*Harold Teen*), Walter Berndt (*Smitty*), Frank King (*Gasoline Alley*), Stanley Link (*Tiny Tim*), Dale Messick (*Brenda Starr*), Milton Caniff (*Terry and the Pirates*), Bill Holman (*Smokey Stover*), and George Clark (*Neighbors*). These were just the *Tribune* cartoonists.

Dad reserved a beautiful suite in the Waldorf Astoria Hotel or the Savoy Plaza Hotel where he and Mother could talk to some of his colleagues in more personal surroundings.

We dined at the Diamond Horseshoe (where the stage raised right up from the floor), the Copacabana, the Rainbow Room at the top of the Radio City building, the 21-Club and other exciting places that Al Loewenthal, Dad's agent, told him about. All the glamorous floor shows made my head spin. We often sat right at the edge of the dance floor where dancers would swish past us with their billowy costumes. One night I even danced with Jimmy Durante after his piano act, which included a beautiful white grand piano that fell apart piece by piece on the dance floor as he played it.

We saw Broadway musicals including *The King and I* (Yul Brynner wasn't even a headliner yet), *Oklahoma, Guys and Dolls, South Pacific, Annie Get Your Gun*—it was a whirlwind kind of fantasy that I would never forget.

Watching Dad through all this glitter and glamour, I could see his humble, unassuming manner around his peers. Thinking about this after I was grown, I knew Dad had never lost sight of his Oklahoma roots in his struggle to reach this pinnacle. He had retained a level head through these years, never reaching either the depths of despair or the heights of arrogance. It was a great lesson I had learned.

An added bit of excitement on our 1947 trip to New York for the newspaper convention was our trip to Ideal Toy and Novelty Company. It was excitement born of romance: Some time before our trip, *Dick Tracy*'s bewhiskered B.O. Plenty character had met Gravel Gertie, an ogre of a woman who lived in a gravel pit. They were at first repulsed by each other. Then they fell in love and married. When the time arrived that they were expecting a baby, no one could imagine what a baby born of those two characters would look like. At the time of the 1947 convention, Dad was asked to stop at Ideal Toy and Novelty Company to take a look at a mock-up doll of this baby and make any recommendations before it went into production. We thought it looked perfect.

The August 25, 1947, issue of *Life Magazine* carried photos of the *Dick Tracy* strip and the doll, with an article that read:

> In the comic strip *Dick Tracy*, Chester Gould has created a repulsive gallery of characters which includes such figures as Flattop, the Brow and the Mole. Last year, Gould married off two of his unseemly personalities, B.O. Plenty, an unkempt, smelly old criminal, and Gravel Gertie, a banjo-playing dervish who lived in a gravel pit. Two months ago, this grotesque couple amazed Gould's public by producing a beautiful child named Sparkle. Her dazzling eyes and hip-length hair immediately won the hearts of *Dick Tracy*'s 26 million readers. Among them, an All American football player named William M. McDuffee, manager of the toy department at Gimble's, one of the largest department stores in the U.S., took his idea to Ideal Toy and Novelty Company. Forty-eight days later, the production of Baby Sparkle Plenty dolls began. On July 29, 1947, they went on sale. At a stiff $5.98 apiece, 10,000 sold in the first five days. Sales in the next two weeks zoomed to 22,000. At this rate, more Baby Sparkle Plenty dolls will be sold in the last months of this year than all other types of dolls put together. McDuffee, who knows a good thing when he has it, is getting ready to bring out a Baby Sparkle Plenty cradle and a Gravel Gertie banjo.

At home, the Sparkle Plenty, B.O. Plenty, and Gravel Gertie phenomenon was just amazing. Baby gifts were arriving almost every day addressed to "Sparkle Plenty, P.O. Box 191, Woodstock, Illinois." All kinds of beautiful baby clothes were sent from California, Michigan, Washington, Florida, Pennsylvania, Illinois—from all parts of the country.

Gifts of orange bars of Lifebuoy Soap tied together (to help prevent body odor) arrived for B.O., along with mugs of shaving cream with brushes and even razors. Some sympathetic readers even sent plugs of chewing tobacco.

Then, one day, a box addressed to Gravel Gertie was waiting at the post office. It contained a beautifully crafted pair of leather high top boots, just like the ones Gertie wore, wrapped in tissue in their own shoebox, ready to wear. Tracy readers were really swept up in the story and wanted to show it. The *Chicago Tribune* had the same thing happening.

Mother and I eventually packed the baby clothes and toys in a big box, all still in their gift boxes, and delivered them to the Woodstock Children's Home in Woodstock, where they were gratefully accepted.

The Mystery Caller

There is no better example of Dad's ability to weave one story into another than in the story of Sparkle Plenty's birth, which coincided with the beginning of the Crime Stoppers segment of his strip. That segment had a most mysterious beginning.

One early Tuesday morning in 1947, the phone rang in Dad's *Tribune* office. The voice at the other end said, "Mr. Gould, I'd like to come over to your *Tribune* office and see you sometime."

"What about?" Dad asked. "Who is this?"

"I can't tell you over the phone," the caller responded. "I'm under strict orders not to tell you until I see you. I'd like very much to talk with you at your office, at home — anywhere."

"I don't know what it can be that you can't tell me over the phone," Dad responded.

The following week, a second call was made to his *Tribune* office, the same man. This time the caller added, "I think you'd be very happy to know this is good news, but I can't tell you over the phone."

Dad didn't want any part of this, and told him as much, assuming this would put an end to it. Only a few days passed, however, before a third call came — this time to our home in Woodstock. Dad had arrived home about 7:00 that night, having taken the train to work that day because of a heavy snowstorm. Relieved to get home, he built a fire in the fireplace and sat down to dinner with Mother. No sooner had they seated themselves, however, than the phone rang. That same voice was on the other end. "I'm the guy who's been trying to talk to you. I'm in Woodstock, and I'm going to drive out to your place. I *have* to talk to you."

"I have no idea what you want," Dad said, "but this is a terrible night for driving. You've come this far, so come ahead."

Dad got out his .38 snubnose and hid the gun under the cushion of the upholstered chair, facing the foyer. When the car came in, the plan was for Mother to open the door; Dad would be sitting in his chair with the gun.

A fine-looking man in a camel hair coat arrived. He stood in the snow in the doorway. He was motioned to come in. Dad stayed in the chair with the gun still under the cushion.

"My name is Smith Davis," the man said. "I help newspaper publishers find properties to buy and sell. I just sold Frank Knox's *Daily News* to the next owner, Jack Knight. I have a message from Mr. Marshall Field of the *Sun Times*."

Dad gave a sigh of relief. "Well, I don't know you, but you look to me like a very brave guy to have come this far in the snow storm."

"It would never have happened this way, Mr. Gould, if I had my way," he answered, "but I was under orders from Mr. Field. He wants to hire you away from the *Tribune*. Mr. Field is ready to offer you $100,000 guaranteed. We've got Caniff." (Caniff was creator of *Terry and the Pirates* — a *Tribune* cartoonist, but a *Tribune*-owned comic strip.) "He's going to leave the *Tribune*."

The doubling his salary didn't seem to faze Dad. "I'm not going to leave the *Tribune*," he said.

"That's up to you. I took an oath I would follow through with this. Field wants Caniff and you."

"You give Mr. Field a big thank you, and tell him I'm working for the outfit that gave me the only break I've ever had in my life, and a million dollars wouldn't get me away," concluded Dad.

"I love that kind of talk and appreciate it," Davis responded, extending his hand to Dad. "You need a drink."

"Do I need a drink!"

So they went into the little bar, and Dad put out a brand new bottle of Old Grandad and said, "Pour your own drink." He took a big slug from a straight-up glass, a little water, and then another slug. Then Dad started talking about the country around Woodstock and Bull Valley, and how he had started with the *Tribune*.

"You don't know how relieved I am," Smith finally said. "This has been a battle. I tried to convince Field that if I did it my way, we'd have done it weeks ago, but no, he didn't want any word to go out over the phone."

Smith Davis left with a feeling of relief that his mission was finally accomplished, and Dad was sorry that he couldn't have known right from the start what it was all about. He later learned that Smith Davis was a tremendous big shot in brokerage newspapers and bartering papers.

The Unexpected

The physical work that Dad enjoyed outside was something his body craved to compensate for the sedentary job he had at his drawing board. Sometimes just pushing away from his board to stretch out on the maple-framed couch in his studio was all he needed to rest his back ten or fifteen minutes. But in this span of time, he could easily fall asleep.

The first time Mother and I heard moaning coming from the studio, we ran in, and there was Dad, sound asleep and moaning.

Mother awakened him. "Chet! Chet! Are you all right?"

Dad's eyes flew open with a look of surprise and relief. Sitting up suddenly, he took hold of Mother's hand and said, "If you ever hear me moaning, wake me right away, because someone is chasing me."

That was just amazing to me — were his comic strip characters ganging up on him? But he was serious about this, and we never asked him about his dreams. He didn't do this often, but when he did, we always woke him. The fortunate thing was that it didn't happen at night when he and Mother went to bed. It was just during those short naps. But there were times he would awaken in the middle of the night, turn on his night table light, pick up paper and pencil (which he always kept right next to the bed) and jot down a sudden idea that had awakened him. Dad's brain never seemed to rest.

Above and following pages: Dad's imagination is not only seen in unique characters such as Coffyhead, but in his use of diagonals denoting action and carrying the eye from one panel to the next. His use of black and white had become his trademark and was unlike that of any other cartoonist at that time.

Where There's Smoke, There's Dad

What kept Dad going? His answer was his cigars. He had smoked them since he was nineteen years old, and after he and Mother were married, she accepted this as a normal habit for a man. Her father had smoked them ever since she could remember. So I grew up with them too, thinking nothing of it. A common sight was Dad at his drawing board, hard at work, penciling a strip or inking one in, with a blue haze of smoke surrounding him. He claimed that a cigar helped him think. Well, maybe it did. He did very well in that department.

Our honey-colored cocker spaniel, "Cappie" (short for Captain), didn't mind the smoke one bit. Every day that Dad was at his drawing board, Cappie was at his feet — some part of Cappie's body always touching Dad's stockinged foot.

We also had a caramel-colored female cocker spaniel named Miss Pearl. She was very much a lady, but when Dad pushed away from his drawing board and called the dogs in his usual manner—"Come on, men! Let's go out and move the hoses," or "Come on, men! Let's go outside"—Miss Pearl was right there.

Remembering Cappie, Dad recalled, "Well, good old Cappie was quite a clown. He was such a greedy little fellow. When Mother would bring home some knuckle bones, especially cut up for dogs, Cappie would be eating one, then want to take it outside and bury it. Even if it were

A daily sight was Cappie sitting at the feet of Dad at his drawing board. If Dad jiggled his foot, Cappie would answer with a low growl — it was a special kind of devotion.

winter, he'd bury it in the snow. Well, the snow had grown pretty deep, and he had buried four or five of these bones all at different times. When spring came, there was always a little pedestal of snow with a bone on top of it. He was such a self-centered little fellow."

Our dogs, of which there were always two, were a delightful addition to our family life and brought us so much pleasure and many laughs—which, I might add, were often instigated by Dad. Did you ever wonder how a pair of eyeglasses would look on the rear end of a dog, his stubby tail being the nose? Mother, with disgust, but hiding a smile, would say, "Oh, Chet!" But we had to laugh anyway. It was kind of a Groucho Marx look, but his tail kept wagging. Or how a dog would relish a little dab of peanut butter that stuck to the roof of his mouth, and it took a lot of licking to get it off—it was always a circus of fun around our house, and these little pets never lacked for attention. In the winter, after a heavy snow, they knew there would be paths plowed in the high snow and off the beaten path just for them. Dad was like a child with a toy on that plow, and would wind around the chicken house and criss-cross his way out into the field, maybe plowing a half-mile of paths. The plow did make nice paths on which, some afternoons, Dad and Mother would enjoy a winter stroll with the dogs.

Two of the last dogs that lived the Life of Riley with Mother and Dad were Rocky and Cissy, two Schnauzers, in the 1970s and 1980s. Cissy, a little lady, adored Mother; Rocky, a growler at one end and a wagger at the other (you never knew which end to believe), thought there was no one like Dad. I often thought, "Oh, to be a dog in this family!" They were all loved. When they died, Dad gave them a proper burial right on our property. Rocky was buried in a small plot of grass under a tree near our house, where a small pile of rocks would always be a reminder of his rowdy personality. He was the dog that stole Dad's heart.

Mother and Dad had a little game going on with Dad's cigar butts. Mother would quite often find them in her house plants. Dad felt they were good for the soil; Mother didn't. She didn't like to look at her beautiful plants and suddenly see a cigar butt. It was never a big issue, but she must have made her feelings clear, because one day the cigar butts disappeared from the flowerpots, never to return.

The cigars even became part of a silly antic. Dad would take a puff when no one was looking and hold the smoke in his mouth. When he was sure people were looking, he would put his cigar in his ear. Then, putting his hands on his hips, he would give his stomach a quick squeeze and allow a puff of smoke to escape from his mouth. That was my dad!

Dad made numerous attempts to give up cigar smoking, but when he finally succeeded, it was quite sudden. One morning in the middle 1960s, just after he finished shaving, Dad looked at himself in the mirror and said, "You fool. You've had your last cigar." And from that day forward, he never picked up another cigar.

Our Dogs Show Up in *Dick Tracy*

Several of our dogs actually appeared in *Dick Tracy*. The first time was in 1948 when a new character entered the story. Mrs. Volts was a tall, big-boned and matronly woman with cropped curly hair, wearing a pair of old-fashioned pince-nez glasses on her nose. Her left eye was permanently closed and her strange grin seemed to display more teeth than her mouth could hold. She owned a little cocker spaniel that she took pleasure in constantly teasing and tormenting. The dog's name was Flapsie (Dad never lacked for names). "Hy" Volts, her husband, had been killed by gangsters and now Mrs. Volts was running the electrical hijacking racket. As the story progressed, Tracy learned about these ruthless gangsters and was on their trail. Mrs. Volts suddenly had to unload a truck load of stolen goods. Unfortunately, she and her driver, Charlie, dumped the electrical equipment out at B.O. Plenty's Sunny Dell Acres.

B.O. saw what was going on and came running out of the house with his loaded shotgun aimed at the driver. To keep his mouth shut, Mrs. Volts bribed him with a twenty-dollar bill, which B.O. Plenty couldn't resist. Flapsie found her chance to run off. With no time to lose, Mrs. Volts and Charlie sped off without the dog, heading for her cabin in the north woods. When Charlie declared he wanted out of racketeering, there was no alternative for Mrs. Volts. She shot Charlie and buried his body under the stone foundation of the cabin.

Back at Sunny Dell Acres, B.O. Plenty found the little dog, Flapsie. When he saw her, he yelled, "Hey you! Don't go. Come back here. HEY YOU!" When the dog came to B.O., he said, "That must be yo'r name, Hey You." He patted her on the head, and the little dog followed B.O. back to the house. This is how Hey You entered the strip.

We already had a cocker spaniel named Hey You in our family. Dad named him, saying, "All we need to do is open the door and call 'Hey!' and he'll come." It didn't take long before Hey You was known as "Hey Hey." He was such a sweet, gentle dog.

It must have been 1949 when Al Loewenthal, Dad's agent and good friend, gave Dad a boxer. Al loved his two boxers, Queeny and Oscar. He thought that Mother and Dad should have a beautiful, sleek, muscular boxer, too. Dad was of course flattered. Mother wasn't too sure, but thanked Al with sincerity in her voice. Dad, with his endless repertoire of names, was the one to name the dog. Holding the dog's head between his hands and looking at him, Dad said jokingly, "What a mug!" then looked up at Mother and said, "Let's call him Mugg."

I don't think Mother and Dad had Mugg quite a year when Dad apologized to Al and said they felt that breed of dog was just too large and too much for them to handle. They had never had that large a dog and struggled to try and make it work. Al seemed to understand, so Mugg was returned to the breeder.

By now, however, Dad had incorporated a boxer into his next story. It was a great story that started off with Tracy and Sam Catchem entering the house of John Twain, who had been

The Mrs. Volts story where B.O. Plenty discovers her runaway cocker spaniel and names him "Hey You"—just like the "Hey You" that we owned.

dead for at least two days. Twain's boxer was found guarding him. The dog was starving. Sam, as usual, was carrying his lunch in his coat pocket, so he gave it to the hungry dog, who then took an immediate liking to Tracy and Sam. He let Tracy remove a small canister attached to his collar. The canister held a handwritten will stating that the proceeds from John's estate would take care of his dog, Barbel Von Nikelslit Dauber of Purple Woods. John had no family, no heirs. Tracy told Sam that he would adopt the dog, but they had to change that name. "With a mug like that, his name could only be Mugg" said Sam. "Mugg it is," said Tracy.

Mugg played an important role in the story, which involved a character named Pear Shape. (His face somewhat resembled Dad's, but his body looked more like a pear.) To cover his racketeer and killer life, Pear Shape ran a "Reduce U" lose-weight-by-mail scam.

Between the mystery of an old wooden cookstove in the Twain house, the million dollars in jewels hidden on the premises, a hidden message containing the key word that commanded the boxer to dig up the jewels, and Pear Shape and his two cronies who were after the jewels, Tracy and Sam had their hands full.

As the story unfolded, the reader learned how Mugg had several encounters with Pear Shape and his pals when they attempted to break into John Twain's house. Along with Tracy and Sam, Mugg helped capture Pear Shape's two cronies and leaped onto the car as Pear Shape made his getaway.

For the three months that this story ran, Dad's storytelling and his artwork compelled the reader to not miss a day of the strip. Mugg also appeared in several 1950 stories, where he preferred riding on top of Tracy's police car.

Needless to say, Al Loewenthal was always pleased to see a boxer in the strip. As for the two boxers that Al owned, Queeny and Oscar, they were willed to me upon his death.

Al Lowenthal, Dad's agent, was proud to see a boxer dog appear in the strip.

The last time one of Mother and Dad's dogs appeared in the *Dick Tracy* strip was in 1970. This story ran over ten months, from February 22 to December 25, 1970. It was a marvelously faceted story filled with compassion, happiness, suspense, crime, anger, pride and love — it had it all. The dog was a Schnauzer who strongly resembled Dad's beloved Rocky — but this dog's name was Stony.

Stony was a seeing-eye Schnauzer who helped a little eleven-year-old blind girl named Tinky get around in the city. Tracy, having been temporarily blinded when a fire destroyed his home, was out walking and trying to manage his handicap. Tinky heard his cane tapping on the sidewalk and offered to help him cross the street. As they sat in the park together and talked, Tracy learned that Tinky lived in a run-down apartment with a guardian. After several visits together in the park, Tracy decided his goal was to help Tinky get her eyesight back. When members of the police department heard this, they wanted to pitch in and pool their money with Tracy's help. Dr. Irful Charles was the eye specialist in New York who would do the operating. He had been recommended by Tinky's guardian. The operation took place, but to no avail.

Tracy's own eyes gradually improved, but he continued using his cane and glasses for a front, and had small rearview mirrors put inside the corners of his glasses. He had to be careful and have eyes in the back of his head. The criminal gang called "Apparatus" was out to get him, since it failed in wiping him out the night they burned his house down.

The next step was to keep Tinky out of the way. Tracy could feel the atmosphere growing tense. He spoke gruffly to Tinky and told her to keep out of his way and to not bother him in the park anymore. He knew this hurt her.

Anything could happen, any day, and it did. Nick the Assassin, from the Apparatus, chose the park for his dirty work. On the same day Tinky and Stony came down the sidewalk in the park, Nick took his place behind a tree and the park bench where Tracy sat.

Tracy's cane was a hollowed-out loaded gun. In his rearview glasses, Tracy saw Nick taking aim just as Tinky arrived. Tracy stood up, swung around and yelled at Tinky to drop to the ground. She didn't understand why. Tracy shot and killed Nick, but not before the shot that Nick fired at Tracy hit Tinky.

The entire Apparatus membership was in one vehicle to watch the shooting of the great detective. When they saw Nick go down they floored it and sped off until the inevitable happened. An 8,000 gallon gasoline truck was crossing their path. The Apparatus was traveling at high speed when it crashed into the gas tank of the truck. The truck driver was able to jump out in time.

Seriously injured, Tinky was in the hospital for a long stay. Depression overwhelmed her. Tracy prayed for her. Doctors gave permission for Stony to come in and sit on her bed. Nothing seemed to help. Tracy thought of a pep talk as a last resort. He sat down on her bedside and held her hand. He had her feel his eyes without his glasses. He could see. They would find another eye specialist for her. "You're not a quitter, are you, Tinky? Are you a quitter?" he asked. With that, she began to respond with a weak, "No, no, no." Stony's tail began to wag. Tracy's pent-up anxiety was relieved.

As Tinky recovered she was told that she and Stony would have a job working at the police department and a home with police officer Lizz.

Tracy and Lizz searched for her parents and found that her stepfather and her mother had died in a house fire in 1961. Through neighbors' photographs, they were shown a picture of Tinky's father. To their surprise, he was now officer Grove on the police force.

Back in 1958, Groovy Grove, then 21 and a bit of a hippie, had been falsely charged with murder and spent twelve years in the state penitentiary for someone else's crime. He was pardoned when the real killer made a confession on his deathbed that cleared Groovy of the murder. After his pardon, Groovy went right to police headquarters to see Tracy, who had worked on his case and believed him to be innocent. "You were the one friend I had," said Groovy. "I want to be a police officer." When Tracy seemed surprised, Groovy went on: "I studied law for the twelve years I was in prison and I'm going to take the Bar exam next week. I also studied criminals while I was in the 'big-house.' I know how they think — I know how they act — I know their legal viewpoint. I'd make a good cop." Groovy then took out a large, detailed drawing of a policeman in a riot suit he had designed while in the pen. He had meticulously pinpointed every feature a policeman would need for protection and keeping crowds under control. (This uniform was designed for the strip by my dad's staff people, including Al Valanis, who had retired from the Chicago Police Department.) Tracy, Sam and Chief Patton were awed by this drawing. Clearly, Groovy was a progressive thinker.

It was decided not to let Tinky know that Groovy was her father until she was able to see another eye specialist with a chance that she might gain her eyesight back. Then she could see her father when she met him. So they said nothing to Groovy.

The plot thickened when "Diamonds," a jewel thief, who knew Groovy in prison and was now out, tried to con Groovy into becoming an "inside man" since he had joined the police force. When that failed, Diamonds planned to destroy Groovy's career with a deceiving blackmail set-up. This plan backfired for Diamonds, with very positive results for the police department.

These problems and more took place over the next months. Diamonds poisoned Stony. Again Tinky almost lost her life, this time when she was caught in the midst of a final gun battle between Diamonds and Groovy. Groovy was wounded in the arm and it was the end of the road for Diamonds.

Finally, Doctor Iris operated on Tinky's eyes. When the bandages were removed, Tinky was able to see. What a happy day! Stony survived the poisoning. The Christmas bells rang in the season of good cheer. What joy! Tinky got Stony back, but ironically, the poison had left him blind.

The story of "Stony," the seeing-eye schnauzer, who was quite the opposite of Rocky, Mother and Dad's dog.

The story led up to Dad's classic Sunday page on December 20 and is one of my favorites. In finding Groovy and Tinky meeting as father and daughter for the first time, you have to know the whole story to really feel the impact that Sunday page has on human emotions.

Groovy, Tinky and Stony moved into a new apartment and Tinky promised to take care of Stony forever. In a later story, Groovy and Officer Lizz fell in love and married. Now they were a true family.

Gather 'Round the Radio

In July of 1945, when New York was in the throes of a newspaper delivery strike, a remarkable thing happened. The mayor of New York City, Mayor Fiorello H. La Guardia, read the Sunday comics over the radio.

Dad was in his *Tribune* office when he heard that newsreel cameramen had recorded La Guardia reading the funnies over the radio. With *Dick Tracy* on the front page of the Sunday *New York Daily News,* Dad knew that he had to head for a Chicago loop theater to see if La Guardia and *Dick Tracy* might be on the newsreel. La Guardia was a colorful figure and always a delight for the news media.

After lunch, Dad headed for the nearest theater. What luck! As Dad walked in, the news was on, and soon the flamboyant mayor sat in front of a microphone with the Sunday comics propped up on his desk in front of him. The first words that Dad heard were, "Ahhh! Here's *Dick Tracy*! Let's see what Dick Tracy is doing. Now get this picture. Here is Wet Wash Wally! The door of the laundry wagon is open — he's leaning with his back towards the wagon and he's counting the money, two, three, four thousand. Now he's in the hundreds $600, $700, $800. And this picture shows a hand, and it's holding an iron pot ... CRASH! She crashes it on his head — he's knocked out!"

"In the next picture, we see Dick Tracy. You know the fine copper, Dick Tracy. He's been a detective so long and he still has that slender form. Lou Valentine, why do our detectives get fat, I wonder?"

"And say children, what does it all mean? It means that dirty money never brings any luck."

Dad stayed to see it twice, which took all afternoon. When he arrived home and told us about it, we hurried through dinner and drove right into Woodstock's Movie Theater. Mother and I could hardly believe our eyes. There it was! It must have played in theaters all over the country. We drove home that night filled with the excitement about what we had seen.

A Caring Son

Dad often thought about his parents' well being. It was 1945, and they were getting older, with no family nearby. We were making it to Oklahoma just once a year to see them. Helen and her family lived in New Mexico, and Ray had been working in Tulsa as a linotype operator until he was inducted into the Army in 1942. After graduating from X-ray technical school, Ray was sent to the Pacific Theatre of World War II.

Dad honored Ray's service in his strip. It was in the December 24, 1943, *Dick Tracy*, near the beginning of the story of Flattop. One of the daily strip panels showed a view of a house window, and hanging in the window was an armed service banner displaying a star. The significance of this banner was to show that someone in that family had a brother, a son or a husband in the service. These were seen all over America during the World War II, whenever a family member was serving. Some families had more than one star. This particular star in the *Dick Tracy* strip had the name "Ray" below it.

It was while Ray was stationed in New Guinea that Dad discovered Ray's secret talent — along with an answer to Dad's worries about their parents. It happened when Ray sent us a huge coconut with a native face carved on one side and our address carefully printed in white ink on the other. That's the way the coconut arrived in the mail — no box — no wrapping, just the coconut. Dad never forgot the fine lettering job on that coconut and could see that Ray would be a natural as his lettering man.

When Ray was discharged, Dad asked his parents and Ray if they would consider moving to Woodstock. He offered his brother a job on his strip as his lettering man. Ray, a bachelor, didn't hesitate for a minute. It took Grandmother and Grandfather a little longer to consider such a tremendous change in their lives. When they finally agreed to leave Stillwater and sold their house, it was a difficult task saying goodbye to friends and all they had known since 1919. But Dad was relieved knowing they would be near us, and we could see them every day.

A search for a house began. After several weeks, Mother and Dad found just the place they were sure Grandmother and Grandfather would like — a two-story white clapboard house close to Woodstock's businesses on the square. Accented with a picturesque black gambrel roof and black shutters, it stood on a nicely landscaped corner lot. It included a flowering-vine covered trellis that led to the garage, which lent added charm to the already attractive house.

A cheerful, windowed sunroom at the front of the house opened into the living room with a brick and wood paneled fireplace that shared a wall with built-in bookcases. Grandmother would probably put her salt and pepper shaker collection there. It was a cozy and inviting setting. Grandmother and Grandfather were just overwhelmed when they received the photographs of the house, and Mother assured them that the house would be ready for them.

Dad, remembering the well-used furniture they had, told them to bring just a few select senti-mental pieces with them. One of those pieces was a big oak desk that Dad had made in high school in 1918 — not a magazine rack or a step stool, but a big oak desk. It would have been an ambi-tious project for an adult. This desk, later antiqued, stood in Dad's conference room at home, after Grandmother and Grandfather passed on. Now it has an honored spot in my son Tracy's home office, as strong as the day it was built.

Mother worked with a decorator to keep a simple, comfortable look to the house. Plans were that Ray would stay with Grandmother and Grandfather until they felt at home in their new surroundings and had made some friends.

Dad's brother Corporal Ray Gould, home on leave during World War II, standing with his parents, my grandmother and grandfather Gould. Stillwater, Oklahoma, 1943.

Dad had already asked his father if he would take a load off his shoulders by writing his monthly checks for him. Grandfather would be part of Dad's staff. He was more than happy to help his son and would have his own office in a building that Dad owned right on the town square, not more than a couple blocks from their new home.

Grandmother wouldn't be left sitting at home alone. Mother had previously written her about the ladies of the Methodist Church. They would be waiting to meet her to join one of their circles, which she did; all was in place.

They arrived on a Friday, with Ray driving the three of them, followed by a small moving truck carrying their few cherished pos-sessions. I couldn't be there because of school, but Mother and Dad were there. In fact, Dad met them at a designated spot in Crystal Lake at Route #14 and #176, where they followed him to their new home.

I know Grandmother and Grandfather must have been emo-tional and uncertain, but, walking up the sidewalk to the house, they were in wonder and were so proud of what their son had done. That evening we went over with a quick supper, giving them a chance to rest and to get acquainted with the house before emptying their packed belongings. Planning to return first thing in the morning, we could see that they were physically and emotionally tired, but leave it to Ray and Dad to know what to do. Ray just happened to have his old sweet potato pipe (an old ocarina from childhood) in his pocket, and Dad sat down at the new spinet piano. Together they plunked out some bouncy gay tune that suddenly brought laughter and a feeling of relief and closeness to us all.

Everything worked out wonderfully. Grandmother loved the house; Grandfather loved his job on Dad's staff. Before long, *Dick Tracy* publicity clippings, photographs, and interviews of Dad covered the walls of that little office. As for Ray, he did all the lettering on *Dick Tracy* until his death in 1974.

A Dream Fulfilled

It was after Dad's death in 1985 that I found a simple scrapbook, yellowed by the years and filled with pasted newspaper samples of his advertising art, which had appeared in various newspapers. As I looked through this scrapbook with emotion and tenderness, I realized that Dad had sent this to his parents back home in Oklahoma, showing them what he was doing in Chicago in 1921 and 1926: beautiful pen and ink advertising artwork, editorial cartoons, the *Radio Catts* comic strip as well as *Fillum Fables*. They must have spent hours and hours looking through the pages with such pride. Then, turning further, I recognized Dad's handwriting. It was a poem he had written, just in pencil, in between all the samples of his newspaper artwork, titled, "Chester's Poem." As I read it, my eyes glazed over with tears realizing that Dad was only twenty-two years old when he wrote that poem to his parents.

Here is a most loving poem written by Dad to his parents in 1922 after he had settled in Chicago. You can feel the depth of his devotion to his parents, the fervor of his hope to not let them down, and the strength of his need for their love and support.

As I continued further in the scrapbook, I found a special self-portrait drawn by Dad, a marvelous likeness. I had to smile when I saw the Chief of Police star on his shirt. That was nine years before he ever thought of Dick Tracy.

By the looks of the drawing, the star must have indicated to his mother and dad that he could take care of himself and they were not to worry. His fisted hand offering his mother a flower must have had the same connotation.

Dad had a unique way of expressing himself without words. More than once, Grandmother Gould said she would get requests by letter from him asking for an item from home — extra shirt buttons, thread or something he needed. He would never ask for it outright, but he would draw it in a silly "cartoonish" manner. They must have been delighted to see a letter from Chester in their mail box.

Dad's 1922 self-portrait. Note the Chief of Police star on his shirt. This was nine years before he created *Dick Tracy*.

Knowing What to Do

A soft heart, that's what Dad had when it came to his family. We were a very loving, caring family. It was a closeness that had always existed between the three of us. When I started high school, along with that love came a tempered strictness about where I could go and what I could do with my friends. On one of these occasions when I couldn't go somewhere, I was lying across my bed crying. Dad must have heard me from his studio. I heard him come in and start singing and dancing some Scottish jig, in his own silly style. I looked up through teary eyes, just as one of his bedroom slippers flew off and hit the ceiling, leaving a long black mark.

"Wait until Mom sees this," he said, and

we both started to laugh. He came over and gave me a hug and said he was sorry, but we would have fun at home. And we always did.

I remember another time—I must have been a sophomore in high school—when my world had come crashing down on me because there was something else I wanted to do and couldn't. I cried myself to sleep that night. The next morning, I dressed for school, opened my bedroom door to go downstairs for breakfast, and found a beautiful gold star painted on my door. Such precious memories.

The time I came home from a date almost two hours late after a movie (we had a flat tire and no phone to call home) was no picnic for my date. I knew Dad would be waiting at the door, and he was. He gently sent me upstairs. I never knew what he said to my date, but I'm sure that young man had some anxious moments.

Discoveries and Mazes

Across the road from our house, a natural spring in the hill was waiting to be discovered on the seventy acres that Dad bought in 1939. Leave it to him to find the spring and cap it, never realizing in 1939 how well it would serve us in 1947. That's when we built a swimming pool. In Dad's rather crude but inventive way, this icy cold spring water was piped right over to the pool from across the road. Part of the pipe that carried this water ran on top of the ground so that when it reached the pool, it came out a comfortable temperature, having run through some solar-heated pipes. This water ran throughout the summer and was turned off in the fall. With the use of the well water as a supplement, the pool water was always comfortable.

In 1946, on this same property across the road from the house, Dad and Orville, the yardman, cut up fallen trees, limbs and brush on the hills to create some wonderful paths. This was a colossal job at best. Then Dad mowed what seemed like miles of paths in about thirty of the seventy acres. These paths

JEAN 18YRS 1946

That's me standing on the square in Woodstock, 1946. When this picture was taken, the population of Woodstock was 6,000. In 2006, it was well over 20,000.

went every which-way, criss-crossing into what felt like an unending maze. Once you were into it in some places, the growth around you was so high you couldn't see anything but the path you were on. It was a real jungle, and exciting! Dad knew every inch of it and loved taking us for one of his special, sometimes harrowing rides and hearing the "oohs" going around the precipitous curves, and the compliments in his wondrous handiwork. It was just that. He loved taking guests over there in the open jeep for a ride beyond anything they ever expected. It was daring and beautiful at the same time. Years later, he had fun with his two grandchildren, Tracy and Sue, on some of those exciting excursions through his hidden trails.

An Ode to Strained Spinach

One day Dad stood at the kitchen sink eating what looked like a jar of baby food. Uh-oh, I thought, what is he doing? He must have a touchy stomach.

"What are you eating?" I asked.

"It's a jar of strained baby food spinach and it's really good," he replied. "I'll have to have Mom get more of this. Here, taste some."

It was good!

The next day I saw a group of jars of baby food lined up in the far corner of the counter. I had noticed how Dad had been taking some bicarbonate of soda once in awhile, but he made light of it all, and rolls of Tums were always in his taboret. For a 5'9" man weighing close to 200 pounds, it wasn't any wonder. He loved to eat. Soon, Mother had him on a healthful diet of mostly chicken, cucumbers, tomatoes and fruit. That did wonders for his shape, for his indigestion, and for his morale.

Out of this experience, a new character was launched in *Dick Tracy*: Diet Smith, a multimillionaire industrialist. His prodigious stomach was an indication of his passion for food, just as his stature was an indication of his importance. But like Dad, he was taking bicarbonate of soda and belching with as much dignity as he could. On January 3, 1946, the second day of his appearance in the strip, Diet Smith was sitting in his plush office at Diet Smith Industries with telephones and assistants around him, and being served a jar of strained baby food spinach on a silver tray—certainly not standing at the sink!

When Dad was setting up this new character in the strip in 1946, it was to launch an idea which he wanted to put into the strip, a 2-way Wrist Radio. And it was Diet Smith's top engineer named "Brilliant," a blind genius, who created this miraculous piece of engineering. In January 1946 the 2-Way Wrist Radio was introduced in the strip. Did that raise eyebrows! "It's an outrageous idea! It's an impossible idea," people said. Nevertheless Dad considered this one of his greatest achievements in ideas during his career, and he made sure that Tracy was talking into his 2-Way Wrist Radio every day from then on and that it was shown in the heading at the top of every Sunday page.

By October of that same year, Bell Telephone Laboratory in Allentown, Pennsylvania, contacted Dad saying they had produced a mock-up of the 2-Way Wrist Radio. They invited him to be their special guest and examine it. With great curiosity, he graciously accepted their invitation.

Said Dad, "The only wrist about it was the microphone on the wrist; the speaker you carried in your front pocket."

When Dad mentioned that television was coming, someone spoke up and said, "Forget television. Police work on words only. What can they do with a picture? It's going to be hard enough for your readers to believe that you can get a 2-Way Wrist Radio. Television, they'd laugh at." Dad agreed, thinking that would come later.

In 1954 another of Dad's ideas, the Closed Circuit TV Showup (lineup), became a reality, as this 1954 news wire shows:

NEW YORK, FEB. 5 [1954]— The New York Police Department today began experimenting with telecasting the headquarters showup of criminals and suspects, an idea suggested by Chester Gould in his *Dick Tracy* comic strip Jan. 18, 1953, and referred to in *Tracy* strips at least half a dozen times since.

Televising a New York City showup to Chicago and Detroit was being done in the *Tracy* strip of more than a year ago. Sending of the headquarters TV is now a routine part of the mythical police department in which Tracy appears to be chief of detectives and has frequently been referred to in the strip sent by the *Chicago Tribune — New York News* syndicate to 430 cities.

In New York's experimental telecast of the headquarters showup — telecast from there to Brooklyn Police headquarters— detectives impersonated criminals. Twenty-five detectives took part. New York commissioner Francis W. H. Adams, other police officials, and representatives of the telephone company, and Radio Corporation of America, attended.

Doubt as to the legality of exposing prisoners—criminals or suspects— to a telecast led the New York officials to use policemen in telecast experiment. The matter is under study by legal experts.

Asked about his televised showup suggestion in the *Tracy* strip of more than a year ago, Gould told a reporter:

"I'm compelled to do a lot of thinking and a lot of imagining, getting out the *Dick Tracy* strips. This is one of the results, I guess. 'Way back on Jan. 20, 1946, I conceived the idea of a two-way wrist radio— like a watch, you know — and that's been experimented with ever since. It seems to me there's no reason a closed police network couldn't telecast showups from city to city."

New York officials are planning closed circuit telecasts from headquarters to 85 stations in the metropolitan district.

Diet Smith became the catalyst for Dad's fertile imagination for other "outrageous" ideas that he created over the years. But here today, forty and fifty years later, a good many of those ideas that were outrageous are, in some form, commonplace today:

1946 the Atom Light
1948 the Portable Teleguard (predecessor to the surveillance television camera)
1954 the Electronic Telephone Pick-Up (predecessor to caller ID)
1956 the Floating Portable TV camera (predecessor to the camcorder)
1962 the Magnetic Space Coupe
1964 the 2-Way Wrist TV
1968 the Magnetic Police Space Car

If ever a cartoonist was careful about his ideas and characters, it was Dad. On the day he created a new invention or major character, he made a drawing of it, sealed it in an envelope and mailed it to himself that very same day. The postmark was the proof that the enclosed idea within the envelope was created on that date. Its purpose was to protect his idea in case a casual comment about one of his ideas was overheard in the engraving room at the newspaper and, subsequently, used by another cartoonist. After his invention or character appeared in the paper, he would discard the unopened envelope.

In 1962, a controversial idea entered the strip: an atomic powered Magnetic Space Coupe. It would take Tracy to the moon. It was developed through Diet Smith Industries, and, like all the other inventions that Dad had in the strip, the Magnetic Space Coupe seemed impossible. But Dad's explanation of this invention at the breakfast table had Mother and me spellbound and convinced it could happen. It all depended on atomic power and sixteen atom-powered energizers built into the hull of the vehicle. They would propel the Space Coupe by multiplying the mag-

The four strips above, which appeared in the Tracy story in 1953, caused the New York Police Department to experiment with Dad's idea for a closed-circuit TV "showup" (lineup) in 1954. The photograph opposite shows the experiment in progress (*Chicago Daily Tribune*, Feb. 9, 1954).

netic attraction millions of times through its projecting "ears" (so Dad called them). This would enable the Space Coupe to rise silently in the direction those "ears" were pointed. Dad was convinced that magnetism was here to stay. "It is silent, vibrationless and the speediest power known to man." As he went on to explain further, he had Mother and me hanging on every word and envisioning the whole thing until he brought us back to reality and said, "You can do anything on paper." But never did he waver in his belief that this would someday change space travel.

The September 1983 issue of *National Geographic Magazine,* devoted to the United States space program, includes a photograph of Dad sitting at his drawing board at home. Referring to the Magnetic Space Coupe, the caption beneath Dad's picture reads, "A Visionary Genius." It was a thrill seeing him get such recognition.

April 30, 1947: The Origin of the Crime Stoppers

One day Junior, Tracy's adopted son, and three of his friends hurriedly entered police headquarters anxious to talk to Dick Tracy. Junior handed Tracy a piece of paper on which he had drawn a shield inscribed with the words "Crime Stoppers," saying, "We want to start a club. We're going to call ourselves the Crime Stoppers." And that was the beginning of a term that first appeared in the *Dick Tracy* newspaper comic strip on April 30, 1947, and is still well recognized today.

Junior Tracy, Dick Tracy's adopted son, created the idea for a Crime Stoppers Club in the April 29, 1947, daily strip.

Junior and his friends told Tracy they felt they could do a lot of good helping kids who might go wrong before they got started, by finding odd jobs for them to do after school and by being friends with them. Junior could see that idleness made trouble for a lot of kids. He and his pals' idea was to be a sort of detective club with helping hands.

A boy they had in mind was Bronk, who was already in trouble. He had stolen a bike and was getting involved with the criminal element.

So impressed was Tracy with their idea that he offered to have Crime Stopper badges made for them. Then, taking these eager young boys into the police crime laboratory, Tracy showed them where many clues were discovered through scientific crime detection and offered to meet with them in the lab once a week to show them how some of the equipment was used. Above all, he would teach them to be keen observers. They befriended Bronk, helped him turn his life around, and eventually helped him become a Crime Stopper.

Above and following page: Some examples of forensics used in the strip.

One of Tracy's many forensic investigations

These enthusiastic Crime Stoppers learned well and played an important part in aiding the police in a number of Dad's stories, but unfortunately, few references were made to the Crime Stoppers Club after the first year.

Out of the Paper, Into the Community

The same year that the Crime Stoppers Club appeared in *Dick Tracy*, a real Crime Stoppers Club was developing in my hometown of Woodstock, Illinois. This quiet little farm town, population 6,000, had one police car and no police radio. Policemen patrolled the Town Square on foot. However, a stranger would think twice about confronting Woodstock's four hundred pound Police Chief, Emery "Tiny" Hansman. Impressive in stature, yet able to ride a motorcycle with the greatest of agility, he was also a man who cared about Woodstock's youth.

Getting together one day, he and Dad came up with an idea that developed into a Crime Stoppers program for Woodstock's youngsters. This program was filled with direction, inspiration and activity. As it was, there was no outside activity available for young people, and Tiny knew they needed something. Besides, while children were having fun and learning the importance of being good citizens, they would have a chance to get to know the policemen on the beat.

Tiny and three policemen from the department laid out the plans for meetings to be held every Saturday morning. When the news got out about a Crime Stoppers program, with a

After the Crime Stoppers Club was introduced in the *Dick Tracy* strip, police chief "Tiny" Hansman started a Crime Stoppers chapter in Woodstock, the first of its kind. At this session, Dad joins "Tiny" in the Woodstock Opera House to discuss gun safety. (Early 1950s photograph courtesy Don Peasley.)

Crime Stoppers badge to be earned and prizes to be won, the Opera House auditorium suddenly became packed with youngsters who attended each Saturday morning. They were so eager that at the height of the program, some seven hundred youngsters filled the Opera House.

The local Moose Club, the American Legion, the VFW, the Elks Club and the Jaycees donated prizes that were presented at the meetings. Tiny, having been a lineman for the Chicago Cardinals in 1935, had footballs and other sporting items available for the program. From time to time, he saw to it that a group of Crime Stoppers could attend one of the big league baseball games.

Not only were these young people asked to be responsible in being good citizens, their parents were asked to be the same. The police felt the parents would be curious about what their youngsters were learning.

Meetings were filled with fun, interspersed with safety films, talks on safety prevention, and movies. Once in awhile a member of the FBI or the state police spoke on the importance of safety. Dad even did his part.

George Meyers, a Woodstock police officer who became police chief when Tiny retired in 1961, today recalls the Crime Stoppers with a smile. "Kids who joined the program received a badge," he says. "It was a prestigious thing to have a Crime Stopper badge. It showed you were a good kid. Not to have one — some might think you weren't so good."

Phil, an original Woodstock Crime Stopper and now a businessman, remembers going to see the fire trucks in the fire station. "Tiny was big on safety and always educating us in this regard."

Larry, another childhood Crime Stopper, was impressed with a tour of the jail cells. "Tiny took us back to the area in the Opera House and locked us in a cell. We got an idea of what it would be like, and it impressed us with the bleakness of jail cell life." (The Opera House, originally built in 1890 as the City Hall, housed the police department for many years, as well as the fire department, all of the government offices, the council rooms, the justice court and the Woodstock Public Library. The term "Opera House" referred only to the impressive 400-seat auditorium in the building.)

George Meyers saw Woodstock become an All-American City in 1963. Meyers never failed to stress the importance of the Crime Stoppers because he saw youngsters and police brought together in a friendly fun and educational way. It was never meant to be a monetary reward system as it is with adults today. The Crime Stoppers was a remarkable labor of love for eighteen years until Meyers retired in 1965.

Other communities picked up on this idea, even the National Police Hall of Fame in Port Charlotte, Florida. They organized a Crime Stoppers Club, and children who wrote in and promised to avoid strangers, obey their parents, attend school, always tell the truth and make friends of their neighborhood policeman received membership cards in the club. Ten thousand cards were sent to youngsters in the first three months.

Woodstock police officer George Myers holds up a Crime Stoppers badge, a prestigious accomplishment for a young boy to earn. After "Tiny" Hansman's early retirement due to illness, George became Woodstock's official police chief. (Photograph courtesy Don Peasley.)

Letters were coming in to the *Chicago Tribune* newspaper syndicate on a daily basis requesting Crime Stopper program information. When the syndicate approached Dad about taking part in this amazing phenomenon, making personal appearances and so forth, he declined. He knew his limitations and the time it would take away from his already tough schedule. Nevertheless, communities successfully pursued their own Crime Stoppers programs.

The Adult Crimestopper Program

In 1976, George MacAleese, a police officer on the Albuquerque, New Mexico, Police Department, contacted Dad to get permission to use the name Crimestoppers instead of Crime Stoppers for an adult program that he wanted to organize. The result was the beginning of one of the most effective citizen–law enforcement, anti-crime programs in existence. By 1982, more than 300 communities in the United States had similar programs, and that same year Crimestoppers went international.

Now there are thousands of similar programs throughout the United States and world, reaching as far as Australia.

The Crimestoppers program uses a brilliant reward system: it gives a cash reward for information leading to the arrest or indictment of a criminal. Each caller is guaranteed anonymity with the use of various codes and key words used for identification. Caller ID is never used in this program. These calls can come from concerned citizens or paid informants. The program was well planned and has had great success since its inception. Crimestoppers has been praised by all levels of law enforcement as a major deterrent to criminal activities and a positive force in making communities a safer place to live. Such a program is funded strictly by monetary donations from citizens.

In some areas, Crimestoppers has established programs in elementary, junior high and high schools, where students have submitted information on crime in and around their school with enormous success. Vandalism and locker theft in those schools has been greatly reduced since the program started. Concealed weapons have been reported and confiscated. Here, it is the young people who play an important part in the Crimestoppers program.

From the day Crime Stoppers was introduced in the strip in 1947, it has played a useful part in our society.

50th Anniversary of the Crime Stoppers

In celebration of the 50th anniversary of Crime Stoppers in 1997, Woodstock's police chief Joe Marvin created a Crime Stoppers Junior Police Academy. Developed in an effort to resurrect some qualities of Woodstock's old Crime Stoppers program, it was designed to meet the needs of today's young people. The goals were to give students the skills necessary to become active members of the community, to help them develop good citizenship, and to provide them with crime prevention and personal safety techniques.

Taught in a fun, hands-on, yet serious approach to law enforcement, the Junior Police Academy program gave sixth, seventh and eight grade students an introduction to law enforcement with instruction in crime prevention, methods of fingerprinting and evidence, traffic accident investigation and enforcement, police report writing, suspect identification, and arrest and booking procedures. Woodstock police officers, each in his area of expertise, taught the sessions. The last day, a guest from the United States Department of Justice spoke, concluding the eight-week program with a graduation ceremony and certificate presented to each student.

Said students in response to this program: "The instructors were terrific." "I found the fingerprinting interesting." "I liked the hands-on portions of the program." "I really liked the Academy and hope you do it again."

The *Crimestoppers Textbook* Tips

An outgrowth of the 1947 Crime Stoppers was the weekly *Crimestoppers Textbook* tips, which were a natural extension of Tracy's promise to teach young "Crime Stoppers" how the police laboratory worked in helping to detect clues in solving crimes. The *Crimestoppers Textbook*'s first appearance in the strip was on Sunday, September 11, 1949. It appeared opposite the "Dick Tracy" heading at the top of the Sunday page on the right, a spot that had always bothered Dad because it was too small to fill with much of anything. This 2" × 3¾" space was perfect for a small rectangle drawn to look like a page for a loose-leaf notebook, with an indication

CRIMESTOPPERS
TEXTBOOK

Oct. 7, 1951

Dec. 23, 1951

May 1, 1966

June 25, 1967

May 14 1967

June 12, 1970

Jan. 30, 1972

Nov. 2, 1969

A sampling of *Crimestoppers Textbook* tips.

for holes to be punched out on the left side. The idea was for youngsters to clip each textbook tip and make their own collections. Topics appeared in no particular order and included tips on safety and fire prevention; information about blood tests, bullets, cars, and fingerprint identification; suggestions for finding clues and being a keen observer; and so forth. There was even a recipe for invisible ink. Dad's sources were his many books on crime detection, his police manuals, his law enforcement magazines, and material from police departments and the FBI.

In 1953, Al Valanis, a retired Chicago police officer, played a large part in this feature when he joined Dad's staff. In 1960, some of the *Crimestoppers Textbook* tips were directed toward police rookies, giving them tips on how to become competent officers. Aided by Al's vast knowledge of police work, Dad hoped to attract youngsters who had grown up reading *Dick Tracy* and the *Crimestoppers Textbook* tips to careers in law enforcement.

The *Crimestoppers Textbook* had tremendous response from police chiefs and law enforcement agencies all over the country. They hailed this addition to the strip as an invaluable way to reach millions of people everywhere to inform them of the importance of safety and crime prevention. This feature was equally helpful to police rookies and to the man on the street. At one of the police dinners Dad attended, a chief of police at one of the Chicago suburbs said that he had been telling his men to clip out those *Crimestoppers Textbook* tips. Another police chief said, "You'd be surprised, in spite of the training, how many subjects that are touched upon in *Crimestoppers Textbook* that the average rookie doesn't know about, or if he was told about, he forgot." Ordinary citizens were also writing Dad and commending him for this instructive addition to the strip.

Today, a few of the *Crimestoppers Textbook* tips have been made obsolete by new technology, but most are as valid as they were the day they were written. But it should be noted that, in their entirety, the *Crimestoppers Textbook* tips should be considered a historical record of Dad's contribution to America's youth.

More Farm Life

In 1947, "the farm"—which was never known by any other name than "the farm"—was about to get a facelift. Though the barn and outbuildings still stood void of any farm life, as they had since Dad sold the dairy operation in 1941, a local landscape architect had created an extensive plan for the perimeter of the house. Since 1936, our yard had just blossomed forth as a result of Mother's hard work and the gardener's help. It was going through a transformation and was looking beautiful, while still maintaining a country look. After months of putting up with mud, machines, trucks and dust, the end was in sight. Before, Mother and Dad had been walking on boards to get to the garage and to get out any door. Now, blue stone walks replaced the boards and a blue stone stairway led to a lower terrace to the east part of the back yard. This terrace was framed with low, forty feet long, stone walls facing one another about thirty feet apart on the north and south sides, with a wide expanse of lawn between them. Along the inside of these walls ran colorfully designed flower gardens, each with its own sprinkler system. The low walls and lawn between the gardens circled around a fish pond at the far east end of this terrace, and a blue stone step led to the open acres of lawn, beyond which had once been corn and alfalfa fields.

At the west end of this terrace, a wide stairway led up to another level. Here an umbrella table and chairs overlooked the terrace to the east, the picturesque countryside to the south, and to the west, a swimming pool. Wide blue stone walkways surrounded a 25' × 50' reinforced concrete swimming pool. Low lannon stone walls bordered the wide walkways where planting areas supplied rich greenery, ending at the west end of the pool in a lannon stone and screened-in area. Here stood a fireplace and a barbecue of the same stone, a sink, cabinets and refrigerator, making a complete little kitchen. One could get warmed by the fire, then refresh oneself with a drink and enjoy a barbecue after a swim. Of course, Dad supplied the entertainment, showing off his culinary duties as chef with a little clowning around, which he loved to do. Whether it was just our family or other family and friends, those summer days hold so many happy memories.

On a sunny day, the brilliant aquamarine pool, with its bright coral potted geraniums at the corners, looked like a jewel from our dining room, kitchen and patio.

(Dad found swimming great therapy for his back and in warm weather swam every morning and every evening, without fail. The slow Australian crawl, ten lengths in the morning and ten lengths at night before bedtime, became a part of his daily routine during the summer. It not only helped his back, he loved the exercise and sense of exhilaration it created.

The dogs had a workout, too, following him back and forth. It was a funny thing to see. One time Rocky even fell in, not been paying attention to anything but Dad. Finding himself bobbing up from under the water, he quickly did what dogs do, the dog paddle, until Dad lifted him out. Swimming was a daily routine for Dad until he reached eighty years of age.)

Old Chicago paving bricks, worn from years of use on Chicago streets, picturesquely became our courtyard. Meticulously setting those bricks in a huge pattern that converged at the center, spanning the full length of our house, proved to be a major job. Weighing twenty-five pounds apiece, these paving bricks were originally cut and shaped by Minnesota prisoners.

Surrounding this brick courtyard was an eight-foot span of grass with 30" high lannon stone walls beyond, forming a U-shape around the courtyard and leaving an opening for the driveway to the west and to the east of the courtyard. Twelve flowering crab apple trees were planted around the outer edge of these walls and were meticulously trimmed. During blossom time in the spring, they looked like trees of popcorn. It eventually took the snorkel truck with a hydraulic bucket to reach the tops of the trees, which made trimming a time-consuming job. But the result was breathtakingly beautiful.

This grand landscape project looked bigger than life while it was in progress, with truckload after truckload of lannon stone, blue stone, lumber and other materials delivered on a

A view of the back of the house looking toward the pool and the screened-in area with the fireplace and barbecue, where many wonderful times were spent swimming and eating (1947).

Top: The pool, built in 1947, became not only a wonderful gathering place for fun and entertaining, but important therapy for Dad's back. *Bottom*: A view of the house after the landscaping and swimming pool construction were completed. Dad's studio is on the second floor across the front of the new section of the house. The original farm house is on the left side of the house. (Photograph courtesy Don Peasley.)

daily basis. Machinery, noise, dust and workmen were enveloping the whole place. At least once, the giant bulldozer digging out the vast cavern for the swimming pool teetered dangerously close to the edge. Dad was getting extremely anxious. He wanted to get the whole thing over with. Months went by.

One night in the wee hours of the morning, I awoke to see a light under my door. Dad often sat at his drawing board when an idea struck him in the night, but this time I heard Mother talking to him. Something was wrong. I quietly tiptoed to the edge of the studio door and saw Dad with his head in his hands and Mother sitting with him with her arm around him. This was a frightening sight, because Dad was like the Rock of Gibraltar to me. Something was very wrong. I was scared and couldn't help myself. I went in and hugged them both, wanting to know what was wrong. Mother immediately said, "Everything's all right." Dad blew his nose with a honk, as he usually did, and put his arm around me and said, "Everything's all right, honey. I woke up with a bad dream about all this construction." Dad suddenly seemed more like himself. "Let's go to bed," he said. It will be time to get up before we know it." The immensity, the noise, the interruptions, the inconvenience, and final expense of the job, I'm sure, had taken their toll on Dad.

When the construction was completed and the gardens were planted, it was just beautiful. Mother and Dad looked upon it with great pride. The first party to take place was for all the workmen, their wives and Barton Austin, the landscape architect. The year 1947 was a big one on the farm.

The Drawing on the Wall

After graduating from high school in 1946, I left for college in the fall, choosing Stevens, a junior college in Columbia, Missouri. It was a marvelous place to begin my higher education. Stevens was a small college with a beautiful campus, and though it was a girls' school, we didn't lack for fellows, with the University of Missouri in the same town.

In 1948, Mother and Dad arrived in Columbia, Missouri, for my graduation. During all the activities, I wanted them to taste Ernie's "Chopped Cow." Ernie's Steak House was one my favorite restaurants, and I had raved about it in my letters. My friends and I classed it as AAA. Ernie loved the college students. Although famous for steaks, Ernie was equally famous for his "Chopped Cow," a deluxe hamburger (this was before fast food restaurants). Mother and Dad ordered these wonderful burgers and agreed they were the best. Ernie came over, introduced himself and asked Dad if he would autograph his wall, and Dad obliged. Today, more than 50 years later, that drawing still remains in Ernie's Steak House.

The Party Givers

August of 1948 was the first of five annual *Tribune* parties at the farm. Mother and Dad's guests were *Tribune* executives, editorial writers and editorial cartoonists as well as feature writers. The planning took all summer. Mother had a talent for planning parties that kept the country look, but added a touch of elegance. She and Dad were wonderful hosts, always upbeat and happy. One couldn't help getting swept up in their enthusiasm and good conversation. And, luckily for me, I was home from college for the summer to help with the plans and to meet these impressive people.

The day of the party, Mother and I set the tables that had been placed around the pool, colorfully and beautifully appointing each with a fresh floral ring surrounding a tall hurricane

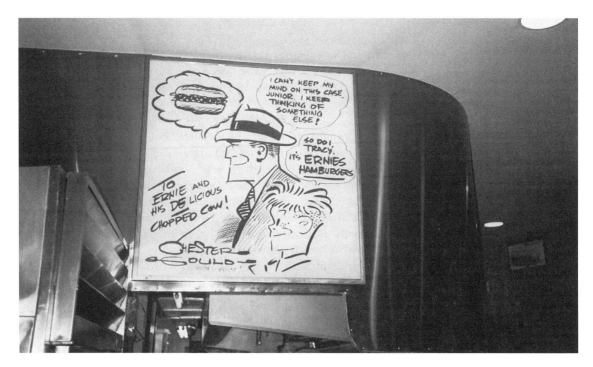

In 1948 while in Columbia, Missouri, for my college graduation, Dad decorated the wall at Ernie's Steak House with this autograph and drawing. When the restaurant was remodeled, that section of wall was preserved, and it is still displayed at Ernie's today. The same drawing adorns Ernie's menu.

lamp. We were pretty impressed with the overall look we had created. We had already finished decorating the dining room table. It would be a buffet table this night, and it looked grand with its large wildflower arrangement flanked by candelabras. Later that afternoon, the bartender came and set up his bar at the west end of the pool. Dad had hired strolling minstrels to play and sing during the late afternoon and evening. The kitchen was buzzing with activity. Hundreds of hors d'oeuvres were in the making, along with the meal itself. With dinner, then entertainment, it would be an evening to remember.

The guests all found their way, thanks to Dad's hand-drawn map with his clever cartoonish landmarks and comments. Though the distance may have been longer than they had anticipated (many drove an hour or more), they seemed to enjoy the relaxed atmosphere. The cows mooing in the distance and the gentle breeze filled with the fragrance of clover and other country smells were certainly unknown in the city and suburbs. Some of the husbands and wives brought their swimming suits and trunks. There they were during the evening, some swimming, some just standing in the water talking and laughing, while others, with their drinks, sat on little floating cushions. There was even some singing of old time songs with the hired musicians.

One of the first people I met was Reuben Cahn, Dad's 1922 business and economics professor from Northwestern University. Now, he was business and economics advisor to Colonel McCormick, head of the *Tribune*.

What a thrill to meet these people, especially the ones whose work I recognized in the paper. There was Cary Orr, whose editorial cartoons, usually in color, appeared every day on the front page of the *Chicago Tribune*, delivering a biting political message. He pictorially stated the *Tribune*'s political views in no uncertain terms. Daniel Holland's editorial cartoons were toned down somewhat but still carried a stinging message. Joseph Parrish, in his humorous ridicule of national and international situations, sometimes used Dad's favorite characters, including bewhiskered B.O. Plenty. In one cartoon, Mr. Parrish drew four "solutions" to New York's 1949 water shortage. In one corner of the cartoon, the unwashed B.O. nonchalantly tipped back in a chair as three impeccably dressed New York City officials anxiously leaned toward him, saying, "Frankly, sir, we want your advice on how to get along without the use of water!" Dad just loved it. He received the original drawing from Mr. Parrish and, over the years, received several others that involved *Dick Tracy* characters.

Then there was Dr. Theodore Van Dellan, not only one of Colonel McCormick's medical advisors and an associate dean in the School of Medicine at Northwestern University, but a *Tribune* writer as well. His popular "How to Keep Well" column ran every day on the editorial page, answering medical questions asked by readers. Though his answers were short, they were to the point, as was his answer to the woman who wrote asking for a magic formula on how to lose weight. His response was, "Just remember, it's in your mouth a few seconds and on your hips forever."

I found it staggering to realize that the people at this party directed the operation of the *Tribune* and created all its editorials, cartoons, and features. Here they were, all these important people, completely loving the fresh country air, the starry night, the night sounds of the owls and crickets, the sounds of cattle in the distance, the absence of daily pressures. By the end of the evening, Mother and Dad knew they would have another *Tribune* party the following year.

Dad treasured this editorial cartoon that Joe Parrish gave him, after it appeared in the *Chicago Tribune* and, undoubtedly, in many other newspapers in 1949.

Missing from the party were Colonel McCormick and his wife. Dad and the Colonel were friends—Colonel McCormick had invited Dad to join his Overset Luncheon Club, made up of executive and policy setters from the paper. (Head of the *Tribune* since 1914, the colonel had shared the responsibilities of editor and publisher with his cousin, J.M. Patterson, when Patterson moved to New York to take over the operation of the *Chicago Tribune*. From 1925 until his death in 1955, the Colonel was one of the most powerful journalistic figures in the country, with definite conservative views. There was no mistaking where the Colonel stood.)

Though the McCormicks had been invited and sent their regrets, the Colonel contacted Dad the following week, undoubtedly having heard about the party. He suggested that if Dad were to have another *Tribune* party, he should create a small cemetery for the villains that Tracy had outwitted. Dad was highly flattered by the Colonel's suggestion—and of course it was the sort of idea that hit Dad just right. He said he would do that.

The following year on the late afternoon of the second annual *Tribune* party, there stood a small-scale villains' cemetery in a partially shaded plot of grass, just east of the pool. Framed on two sides by low lannon stone walls, it made a perfect setting for the crooks that had caused Tracy sleepless nights. With a few clusters of flowers here and there, it looked very proper and very funny indeed.

What Dad had done was craft simple grave markers out of plywood, with a pointed end that stuck into the ground. With the help of his brother, Ray, and Coleman Anderson, both assistants on the strip, he painted them white; then he inked in the heads of sixteen of Tracy's worst villains and the dates they died. There was Stooge Viller, 1933; Spaldoni, 1933; Doc Hump, 1934; Nuremoh, 1939; BB Eyes, 1942; Mrs. Pruneface, 1943; Flattop, 1944; Brow, 1944; Breathless Mahoney, 1945; Gargles, 1946; Itchy, 1946; Shoulders, 1946; 88 Keyes, 1947; Mumbles, 1947; Mrs. Volts, 1948; and Sketch Paree, 1949.

Out of these sixteen characters, Tracy shot three: Spaldoni, who was going to shoot Tracy's adopted son, Junior; Itchy, who went for his gun; and 88 Keyes, shot in a railroad workman's shed. The other thirteen died through carelessness or by the hand of someone else.

It made a big hit with the *Tribune* guests, this cemetery for the scoundrels—all the Colonel's idea and such a simple one that created so many laughs.

There was plenty of mischief afoot that night, thanks to a special guest Dad had hired. Although Dick Tracy would have been on this man in a minute, no one else knew that he was a professional pickpocket. This very finely dressed gentleman milled around with the guests, listening to their talk. When there was an opening in the conversation, he would insert a question, as he did to Mr. Wood, asking, "Are you missing your watch?" Mr. Wood looked down to see only his bare wrist. As he stood there in disbelief, the sleight-of-hand artist held up an object between his fastidiously manicured fingertips. "Is this your watch?" And it was. He performed the same trick with the ladies, removing bracelets, watches, and even earrings. All night the conversation went something like this: "Did you feel that?" "Did you see that?" And through the hour of mingling with the guests, this master artist continued to amaze them.

Dad's ability to find unique and fine entertainment brought magicians, hypnotists, dancers and singers to the parties, making each party a memorable occasion.

That night, after everyone had left, Dad pulled up the markers, fearing that Cappie, the dog, might find them a convenient place to take care of his business. As he put them in a cardboard box in the garage, he couldn't help chuckling over the commotion they had caused.

The following week, a little before noon, the phone rang; it was the *Chicago Tribune* calling. They wanted to send a photographer out to get a shot of the cemetery for their Sunday rotogravure section. On the day the photographer was to arrive, Dad went out and set up the cemetery markers thinking it was a good thing he had saved them.

After getting his photos, the photographer, with a chuckle, wrote out the explanation

Dad's little cemetery plot of Tracy's foes made national news in 1949.

that Dad gave him and then left. It always amazed me how our little farm, tucked down in a valley, could be found by reporters and photographers.

The following Sunday, September 11, 1949, there it was, a picture of Dad tending to his villains' cemetery. Other newspapers began calling and wanting to get a photograph and the lowdown on the cemetery, which had all been just a spoof for a party.

Mrs. McCormick attended the fifth and last of the annual *Tribune* parties, being chauffeured from the Colonel's "Cantigny" estate in Wheaton, Illinois. As Mother and Dad welcomed her, she stated that the Colonel was in Europe. But she came, and Dad felt this was an honor he had hoped for, but never expected.

Recognition

The 1940s were remarkable years for Dad. Dick Tracy had become a household name. Radio, television, books and movie scripts used the gag line, "Who do you think you are, Dick Tracy?" Popular radio shows like Jack Benny, the *Kay Kyser Show* and others had *Dick Tracy* characters involved in their skits. The popularity of the strip was soaring. I often wondered if Dad really had a chance to bask in the glory of it all, since he worked so hard to keep on top.

The greatest compliment from one of Dad's peers come from Al Capp, the creator of *Li'l Abner*. He had one of the top strips of the day. In a letter he wrote Dad, he jokingly called him "King," referring to his ratings.

Colonel McCormick is congratulating Chester Gould upon receiving his new Cadillac. The Colonel's faithful bulldog, Buster Boo, is looking on from the front seat.

Although they had never met (only talked on the phone), in the early 1940s, Al suggested that they do a sequence in their strips where Dad would use a hillbilly character from *Li'l Abner* and Al in turn would use a *Dick Tracy* character. Dad told Al that his kind of strip just wouldn't adapt to Al's kind of burlesque humor. Well, Al took on *Dick Tracy* anyway. An expert at lampooning anything or anyone, he had already lampooned Orson Welles, *Gone with the Wind*, Frank Sinatra and others. Now it was "Lester Gooch" and "Fearless Fosdick," a take-off on Chester Gould and Dick Tracy. It was cleverly done, humorous and lighthearted parody that over the years turned to bitter satire. The popularity of this addition to Al's strip went on for years.

Said Dad, "I told Al I was the only cartoonist who had another famous cartoonist working full-time for him without pay."

The Black Bag Mystery Contest

Who doesn't like a mystery? In 1949, Colonel McCormick thought a mystery contest would be a great way to increase his newspaper's circulation. His goal was to get 100,000 new readers.

The Colonel contacted Dad and asked him if he would write a *Dick Tracy* mystery story in a contest form for this purpose. It was to run for thirty-six consecutive weekdays and would appear each day in color on the back page of the paper. Dad accepted the job with the understanding that he would write the story, pencil in the characters, rough in the backgrounds, and then hand it over to another artist to do the inking and coloring. With the Colonel's okay, Dad took on this job with his already busy schedule.

He created a story that involved the mysterious disappearance of a black bag containing one million dollars. Woven into the plot were a host of characters, including some old favorites as well as some new ones. But it was Tracy himself doing the detective work, finding perplexing clues upon which readers could build their conclusions. Finally, it was up to the reader to send in his or her solution to the mystery. Cash prizes totaling $25,000 awaited the best answers. Prizes ranged from $5,000 down to $50.00.

The contest didn't gain 100,000 readers, but it did pick up 50,000. The Colonel's intent was to reward Dad handsomely for creating the contest, but Dad wanted nothing for his efforts. He had tremendous pride in helping to increase the circulation of his paper without compensation.

Not long after the contest was over, John Parker, the production manager at the *Chicago Tribune*, called Dad's office and said that Patterson wanted them to come to the *Tribune* garage at 11:00 A.M. to see some equipment. "Why would Patterson want me to see equipment—an idea for a story?" thought Dad. To his surprise, when they arrived at the garage, there stood all of the *Tribune* directors. What was going on? It was fairly clear something was afoot.

Gradually, as his eyes adjusted to the darker interior, Dad heard a loud revving of a motor coming from the back of the garage. Then through some big black tar paper an object burst — a car. It happened just like that. Moments later, the shape took form. The black tar paper was shaped into a giant black bag, like the one in the Black Bag Mystery Story that contained the one million dollars. The car—with the Colonel in the driver's seat—was a beautiful, sleek, black Fleetwood Cadillac. If ever a gift presentation had been made with imagination and surprise, this was it. The impact of the Colonel himself behind the wheel was overwhelming to Dad. It was one of his most cherished memories. The framed photographs taken that day found a place of honor on Dad's studio wall. That night, the train was forgotten as Chet and Ray drove home, a bit dazed, but in luxurious style.

9

Dick Tracy and His Public

In April of 1950, Blowtop, a hot tempered crook who happened to be Flattop's brother, decided that it was time to get even with Tracy for Flattop's death. He carefully planted a bomb at Tracy's house to go off in the middle of the night. His plan worked, and the explosion nearly cost Tracy and Tess their lives.

After saving Tess, Tracy went back into the burning house to find Junior, who, unbeknownst to him, had been kidnapped by Blowtop. Tess was frantic until Tracy came out of the fiery inferno with his hair completely singed off his head and his face badly burned. He hadn't found Junior. The house was a total loss.

As the story took on unexpected twists and turns, and as Tracy healed and eventually regained his eyesight, Dad asked me if I would design a floor plan for Tracy and Tess's new house. At that time, having graduated from Stevens College, I was attending the Chicago Art Institute. I was in my second year, majoring in Interior and Architectural Design. I think Dad was subtly testing the waters as to my interest in working on the strip. Anyway, I was flattered to be asked to create a floor plan. Never giving a thought to the cost of a home that a detective could afford, I presented Dad with something rather palatial. Looking at it, he must have thought, here we go again, because Tracy's first house looked somewhat beyond a detective's price range. (I later figured that was probably why he had Blowtop do the job for him and eliminate the house.) Nevertheless, Dad, undoubtedly short on time, said, "Honey, that's great. Why don't you pencil it in right here in this panel and then ink it in." I nervously did, having never worked on the strip before, and Dad thought it was wonderful.

Nine weeks later, in July, when that Sunday page appeared in the paper, there was my overly grand floor plan. Further down, in another panel, was Tracy looking at my plan and saying to the designer, "Jean, you and your ideas are going to ruin me." Oh boy, Dad couldn't even imagine. Soon letters began to arrive at his office, at home, at the *Chicago Tribune*'s "Voice of the People" column and at other newspaper offices around the country, all wanting to know the same thing. "How can Tracy, on his salary, afford such a large home?" Police officers, in particular, were wondering. Poor Dad — what had I done?

Some letters were a bit tongue-in-cheek, like the following:

The New York Daily News: *Voice of the People*, November 14, 1949. Brooklyn, New York:
  For some time now, I have suspected that Dick Tracy was taking graft. How could he have afforded his big car and ranch house with his present salary? He probably was paid off by Flathead, Pruneface and the kingpin of them all, Shaky. I have full confidence in Chief

Patton as to the apprehension and conviction of the once great detective. As a result of the shakeup, I predict Gravel Gertie will take over Tracy's vacated place.

The New York Daily News: Letters to the Editor:
   Let me advise you *News* people that Arthur Godfrey knows where Dick Tracy got all his money. Godfrey says that Daddy Warbucks character from *Orphan Annie* gave it to Dick as a wedding present.

Time Magazine: *Letters to the Editor* December 17, 1951
   Sir: How can you question the high standards and honesty of Dick Tracy when for the last twenty years, he's worn the same suit?

Cook County's state's attorney, John S. Boyle, suspected there was dirty work afoot, and he put his suspicions in a letter to the *Chicago Tribune*. "I have received many letters from police officers," wrote he, "concerning the manner in which Richard Tracy lives. They refer to his $100,000 home and 1951 Cadillac convertible. They are sort of hinting that a Grand Jury investigation might be a very helpful thing for the community."

Boyle was not alone. Many other readers had written to the newspapers to complain about Detective Tracy's suspiciously high standard of living. Their question: "Has the nation's favorite funny page detective been a grafter all these years?"

Dad knew he had to do something. He decided to have Police Chief Pat Patton, Tracy's boss, question him.

"Where did you get the money to build your house?" the chief asked.

Even from the great Dick Tracy, the nemesis of criminals, the reasoning sounded thin. Said Tracy, "I've had a steady job here for twenty years. I was a bachelor for half of those years and I saved my dough! I bought that old corner property during the real estate depression for $3,600. There's a nice little plaster — a mortgage." And as for the big car, "Well," said Tracy sheepishly, "I had made a little deal, which I had kept a secret. An auto manufacturer sold me the car cheap, so I could use it to test special police gadgets."

But the explanation still ran pretty thin, and Dad knew he was in trouble. So he decided to add fuel to the fire. Five hundred thousand dollars in cash and jewels was being held in the police vault in two safety deposit boxes as evidence in investigations. The boxes' contents were missing, Tracy was a suspect, and he had only twenty-four hours to clear himself. In Dad's comic strip world, that took six weeks to explain, with a plot that took fascinating twists and turns. Tracy used his keenest investigative and laboratory skills. Using a spectroscope to study paint scrapings taken from the two safety deposit boxes held at the police department and then paint samples taken from the bank's other safety deposit boxes, he found they didn't match. The boxes had been switched. Now the bank custodian was under suspicion, which led to Spinner Record, another unsavory character — and the plot thickened. But in the end, Tracy cleared himself, innocent beyond a doubt. Said Dad, "Utmost faith, that's exactly what I love in old Dick. There's no mystery about his finances. He's an honest guy."

Fan Letters

What a special time it was in 1985 when I came across Dad's fan mail after his death. Hour after hour, mesmerized, I read what people from all over the country took time to write: letter after letter, spanning a period from the last half of the 1950s into the 1980s (he retired in 1977). Hundreds and hundreds. Sadly, there were no letters dated before the middle 1950s. They must not have been saved. It's a shame, because they would certainly have encompassed a great time in his career.

I did find two short telegrams. One was dated May 18, 1944, and was sent from Beaumont, Texas. It read simply, "Want to claim Flattop's body — letter will follow." (I never found the letter).

Another, dated May 14, 1944, from Hackensack, New Jersey, just said: "Tracy must rescue Flattop. Send him after Tojo." (Meaning Japan's war minister, Tojo Hideki, during World War II.)

Young people from grade school through high school and college sent fan mail. These were wonderful letters. There were letters from principals, teachers, professors; from colleges and universities; from private citizens and companies; and many from police departments and law enforcement agencies. Letters came from the army, navy and air force and from every facet of life. *Dick Tracy* fans were everywhere, some as far away as Brazil, Switzerland, Sweden, England, France, Germany, Spain, and Italy. For Dad, these fan letters were the bread and butter of his career. Good or bad, he read them all.

"You love to get fan mail when you're a cartoonist," said Dad. "I have never written a cartoonist in my life, and I loved a lot of strips just as much as anybody, but I never took time to write a letter to the cartoonist. So, I know that when I would get fan letters, there were perhaps for each letter fifty or one hundred people that would do the same if they weren't quite so lazy. I was very lazy that way myself."

It was an impossible task to answer each request for an original drawing. About twenty-five was all Dad could do each week. The others he answered with a card printed with a drawing of Tracy's head on one side and a space for a salutation and signature on other. Tracy had himself watercolored on some cards if time permitted. Grandfather Gould took on the job of addressing and mailing this multitude of answered mail after he and Grandmother moved to Woodstock in 1945.

There were some pretty outrageous requests too, like, "Please send me a drawing of every character that you have had in the strip as soon as you can. I am writing a paper about Dick Tracy for a school project." Or, "I missed the whole story of the Pouch. Could you send it to me?" Those were answered with just a card.

An eight-year-old boy from Bettendorf, Iowa, who had already corresponded with Dad sent him a remarkable 8" × 10" "word find" puzzle he had created. Twenty-five names of characters and words such as "wrist radio," "aircar," "jail," "apprehend," and so forth were hidden in this checkered maze of letters, and at the bottom was "Merry Christmas, John Salkeld."

Children's letters, although sometimes unreasonable, were delightful. Many included drawings of characters that the young artists said they would permit Dad to use in his strip. Young people wanting to be cartoonists wrote asking how to get started. Boy, did Dad know that answer! "Draw, draw, draw and keep drawing," he would say. How little young people know that, when something looks easy to do, it doesn't come without hard work. Their only thought as they watched Dad draw was, "You're so lucky."

A unique letter written in the 1970s by a fan from Sandusky Community Schools in Michigan read:

Dear Mr. Gould,
    I am very concerned about Dick Tracy. Apparently, he is blind and this is a state of emergency. If you cannot locate a specialist immediately, I would like to know in the shortest possible time.
    This strip has long been a favorite of ours and this present situation must be solved.
    I can readily reveal the names of two outstanding physicians who I am sure can do something about Dick's catastrophe, but we MUST NOT DELAY ACTING. Advise!
                    Very truly yours,
                    [sender from Michigan]
P.S. Poor Tess

Another fan from Chicago, concerned about the young girl Tinky and her seeing eye dog who had been cruelly poisoned, wrote the following in 1970:

RE: PLEASE SAVE STONY AND TINKY-HELP!

Dear Mr. Gould,

Please, please save Stony, Tinky's faithful seeing eye dog. I purchase the Tribune newspaper every morning just to read the *Dick Tracy* comic strip, and that is the first thing I read. I enjoy your comic strip very much, but right now I am very sad and unhappy. Please don't let anything happen to Stony. Tinky is just great, and I am happy for her and the fact that she will see once again.

I am not a dog owner, but a dog lover, and I get sick all over when I read about people mistreating dogs. Please don't let me down as well as millions of other readers. I am not alone in asking this favor. Believe me, when I tell you that after reading the *Dick Tracy* comic strip, which is so true to life where the bad men are always beaten, that I am in a good mood and set for an all-day job at the office. *Dick Tracy* first, then the rest of the paper.

Thanking you in advance for at least reading my letter and hoping that I will read good news about Stony, Tinky's faithful dog.

Tinky, who gained her eyesight after an eye operation, happily saw Stony's life spared, but he was left blinded by the poisoning. The irony of this involved and touching story, and the fan mail that followed, let Dad know he had hit the mark.

Concerning fan letters, there was the other end of the spectrum, from the mild to the very critical, sometimes objecting to the violence of a crime. Readers also enjoyed finding mistakes in the strip and writing Dad about them. There were plenty of those letters, and Dad especially liked them, since they proved that the strip was being not only read, but scrutinized carefully. It might be something as minor as Tracy wearing a yellow hat in one panel of the Sunday page and a green hat in another; or it could be a technical error. An example is a letter written in 1950 by a captain in the navy:

Dear Mr. Gould,

Your technical advice is slipping. For two days running, you have showed a Colt automatic, model of 1911A1, with a hammer at half cock and the thumb safety on.

You can have either, but not at the same time.

Dad once described going to see Patterson and telling him he was worried about a certain story.

"Well, what about it?" Patterson asked.

"I've had some pretty nasty letters."

Patterson laughed and said, "Remember, you don't count for anything if you don't make enemies. The people that hate your strip will talk about you and the people that love your strip will talk about you. So you have everybody talking about you. If nobody talks about you, or if they say, 'I think it's a good strip, but I don't read it every day,' you might as well look for another job. You've got to have enemies."

This valuable advice carried Dad through his career with confidence and assurance.

A student from the University of Pennsylvania wrote:

Dear M. Gould,

Pruneface is disgusting. Flyface is disgusting. Fresh is disgusting. Fresh's mother is disgusting and so is B.O. Plenty, Sparkle Plenty, and especially that little brat with a beard. Maybe the comic strip should be called "Disgusting Plenty."

A letter from Norfolk, Virginia, appeared in the *Virginia-Pilot*'s "Letters to the Editor" column on April 25, 1962:

Editor,

Chester Gould creator and producer of the comic strip *Dick Tracy* has in the past, asked his readers to go along with some pretty fantastic goings-on.

But now, Mr. Gould has gone a bit too far. Currently his character, The Brush, is pictured carrying on his shoulder a sack containing over a million one-dollar bills. Does Mr. Gould realize how much one million one dollar bills weigh?

The dollar bill measures 2⅝ inches by 6½ inches. A piece of paper that size will cut 18 out of a sheet of paper 17 by 20 inches. Dividing one million by 18 gives us (in round numbers) 55,500 sheets of 17 by 22 inches. Dividing 55,000 by 500 (a ream) gives us 111¹⁄₁₀ reams of paper. Each ream weighs sixteen pounds. Thus 111¹⁄₁₀ multiplied by 16 equals approximately 1,787 pounds.

I doubt if Dick Tracy himself could tote such a load.

Really now Mr. Gould.

Many people were intense about what they wrote. There was one crook especially who created a lot of flak because he was careless about cleanliness and consequently had flies buzzing around his head and face whenever he was pictured. This character, known as Flyface, had a mother who had the same problem. At least a dozen complaint letters were written about this "repulsive" character whose cronies were seen swatting flies or spraying bug spray whenever Flyface was around. Dad's humor wasn't always appreciated, but one thing was for sure: he never let the reader forget the seriousness of crime and that crime doesn't pay.

Judging from the letters Dad received, the readers who looked beyond characters they didn't like, or minor errors in the strip, always found much to praise and gained much in entertainment and in food for thought. On the score, Dad fulfilled his dream ten-fold.

The Disturbing Years

With the unrest of the 1960s and 1970s came a different tone to some of Dad's stories. Said Dad, "You reap what you sow. I think we're sowing a bad seed in America right now [1974]. We're not instilling the kind of character that made America. We have removed religion. Moral values have deteriorated."

The society of the day was very unsettling to him: the "flower children," the hippies, and the problems of decreasing morality and respect for others. He wrote some stories emphasizing these beliefs, and he received letters commending him for taking a stand. One from a fan in California read:

Dear Mr. Gould,

My family joins me in commending you for interrupting your exciting *Dick Tracy* comic strip and interjecting a spiritual message on Christmas Day.

May the Lord bless you for your stand.

A letter from a minister read:

Dear Mr. Gould,

In your *Dick Tracy* color comics (the Sunday page) in the *Clarion-Ledger* for September 9, 1973, you show Police Detective Tracy talking with a young man arrested for a crime.

The young man Jim, says, "I hate the world."

Dick Tracy says, "Jim, your trouble is the world's trouble. Somewhere in your bringing up, they forgot your compass. They neglected to give you a sense of direction. They left out one important ingredient — God's Ten Commandments. You got short-changed. Family faith that teaches reverence and respect and peace within, that's your real shortage."

Thank you for including this in your Sunday page, and certainly it is a serious and helpful teaching.

People from all walks of life responded to this Sunday page. Letter after letter from church people, from ordinary citizens and professional people arrived in the mail. One attorney wrote that he took this comic strip to Sunday school the day it appeared and read and discussed parts of it with his class. Any number of other letters professed the same thing.

"Coddling the Criminal"

Through *Dick Tracy*, Dad also voiced some of his beliefs about the nation's growing crime rate. He was concerned, he said, that America was "coddling the criminal." An example of

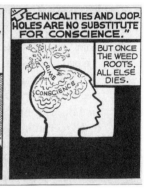

Dad often showed Tracy's disgust and the problems he faced with our changing times.

Dad's frustration showed up in a 1975 story when Policewoman Lizz saved a woman's life by stopping the would-be killer. Instead of stabbing the woman as he intended, the criminal inflicted only a flesh wound. Said Tracy, "After Lizz stopped the red-handed killer and got him into court, he was released on bond."

Another story in 1975 showed the frustration was growing. Tracy said, "Some way to end the year, a double murder, bank hold-up. Two employees dead, a third wounded, has been hospitalized." Then, looking out at the reader, he said, "Crooks engage in capital punishment *anytime they want*, no court decision necessary!"

These strong feelings continued when, in the police department, Tracy said to his colleagues, "With the end of the year, you do a lot of thinking. With the milksop backing the cop gets, should he quit his profession? Would we be justified in walking away from law enforcement?" After a thoughtful few moments, Tracy turned to his cohorts. "For myself, I'll stick around till these 'kiss-the-crook' and 'kick-the-victim' thinkers are banished from high places. That's my New Year's vow." With that, Chief Patton, Sam Catchem and Policewoman Lizz clasped hands with Tracy, joining him in his decision. They knew they couldn't turn away, either.

There was some pretty powerful material in the strip during the 1970s, and some negative letters about it, too. But the positive responses were remarkable in number, and Dad carried on with his campaign for the police. Departing from the main story once in awhile, Dad had Tracy holding town meetings and speaking to concerned citizens about law and order and the policeman's dilemma. In one panel, Tracy was saying, "Fettered as he is with restraining rules and regulations, the policeman needs *EVERY CITIZEN'S HELP!*" At another of these meetings, Tracy spoke so candidly about law and order that one *Dick Tracy* fan in particular wrote to the *Chicago Tribune*:

> The words of Chester Gould in *Dick Tracy* of February 16th were:
> "When the law and courts back up the trained policeman in using his gun, whenever and if he deems necessary, without fear of being censured, harassed or indicted, street crime can be reduced 50% in thirty days."
> This should be boldly re-printed on the front page of the newspaper until the law and courts get the message. This needs pursuing!

Backing up his statements, Dad said, "You're either going to have some authority in this country in the form of first-class policemen or you're going to have no place to turn. Who do you turn to for help? Can you tell me? The policeman should be given a carte blanche authority to do what his judgment tells him to do."

Above and following page: Dad's design for the metered stamp machine that he used in his home, beginning in the 1970s.

The words "Law and Order FIRST!" next to the head of Tracy were seen on every piece of mail that left our house from the 1970s until Dad's death in 1985. The metered stamp machine he rented from the post office held this specially designed canceled stamp that announced each time a letter went through it, "Law and Order FIRST!" with Tracy's profile.

A retired detective from the New York City Police Department wrote Dad in 1970, stating that he had had bumper stickers and door stickers printed that read, "Law & Order FIRST!" As well, he said he had sent many petitions to the U.S. government and state officials signed by New York citizens voicing their feelings against mass picketing, riots, looting, sit-ins and public strikes. "My theory from years of experience in law enforcement is that all necessary force must be used to keep law and order," he said.

10

Exciting Times and Travels

Dick Tracy's engagement to Tess Trueheart spanned eighteen years, probably the longest engagement on record. On the night they announced their engagement to the Truehearts in 1931, Tess's father was shot down in cold blood and Tess was kidnapped. Tracy, then a white-collar worker, joined the police force the next day, asked to solve the case, rescued Tess and captured Mr. Trueheart's killers. Only in a comic strip could a marriage be put on hold for eighteen years. But faithful Tess Trueheart, true to her name, waited for her man. On Christmas Eve of 1949, they were married, announcing the news to everyone on Christmas Day. Chief Patton fainted, the Sam Catchems and the B.O. Plentys couldn't believe this, and it was remarkably obvious to the reader that Tess and Dick looked younger and better in 1949 than they did in 1931.

I couldn't wait eighteen years. My marriage took place less than a year after my engagement. On May 7, 1955, Dad just put his pen down, forgot about Tracy's problems, donned a tuxedo—looking like the most handsome father in the world—and walked me down the aisle. There were no catastrophes at this wedding.

Dad had even hired police to be stationed at our front gate, something Tracy would do, and Andy Fraine's men directed and parked cars.

The day was beautiful, a bit windy, and the church was so designed that my bridesmaids and I had to go outside one door of the church and walk around to the main sanctuary entrance so as not to be seen by the seated guests. And there was Dad, waiting to carry the train of my dress. I loved him so much at that moment as he tried not to step on the train and yet keep it from billowing in the air.

Mother looked beautiful in an ensemble she had specially knitted of light cocoa brown and gold lamé yarn with a matching sweater covered with pearl beads knitted right into the sweater. My three bridesmaids wore watercolor taffeta dresses in colors taken from a Monet painting, with shades ranging from a bright turquoise to paler shades of greens. Their Bird of Paradise bouquets were a striking complement to the dresses—your conventional wedding colors, but our ceremony was conventional.

I remember seeing tears in Dad's eyes as he did what many fathers do at weddings, when they put their daughters in the hands of a husband-to-be. It was only momentary for both of us. He knew what a wonderful man I was marrying, and when I saw Dick O'Connell smiling at me, all was well.

Following the church ceremony we headed for home to a most beautiful reception. All the living room furniture had been carefully stored in the upstairs of the empty barn for that day, and a breathtaking transformation had taken place. Floral garlands were everywhere and one, intertwined with gardenias, graced the stairway where the reception line stood. Huge vases of flowers and ferns stood in strategic locations adding soft beauty to the room. On the patio overlooking the pool stood the wedding cake on a table festooned with fern and green leaf garlands. Beyond the cake in the lower garden stood a tent where linen-covered, floral-decorated tables and chairs awaited the wedding guests. Mother and Dad had made this day something beyond my dreams. Dick and I felt so grateful for all the love around us that day, for our dear families and for each other.

A New Member Heard From

What a surprise it was in 1956 when our first-born decided to announce his arrival two weeks ahead of time! Dick and I were spending that weekend with Mother and Dad in Woodstock, and on that Sunday, we planned on driving into Chicago together to the WGN radio studio where Dad was to be a guest on Herb Lyon's weekly radio program.

About 6:30 that Sunday morning, however, Mother had to call the doctor. He came to the house, checked my condition and asked, "Do you want to have your baby in Woodstock or Geneva?" (Geneva was where Dick and I lived.) It was that quick. I asked him if I could make it to Geneva, an hour away. He felt I could. Dad, I'm sorry to say, canceled his radio interview with Herb Lyon, leaving the poor man in a lurch, so that he and Mother could be at the hospital when the baby arrived.

"Take our car, there's more room," Dad said to Dick, while Dr. Sandeen, who had taken care of me all my growing-up years, climbed into the back seat with me. On our way to Geneva, Dick must have pressed that accelerator right down to the floor every time he heard a moan or groan, and Mother and Dad probably never drove so fast keeping up with us. By the grace of God, we didn't have an accident and weren't stopped by the police. I don't know how long it took to get to Geneva, but within twenty minutes after we arrived at the hospital door, Tracy Richard O'Connell was born.

Dad called Herb Lyon to give him the news. Herb's "Tower Ticker" column in the next morning's *Chicago Tribune* made the announcement that Tracy Richard O'Connell, the first grandson of Chester Gould and namesake of Dick Tracy, had been born.

Quite a coincidence: On May 6, 1951, five years before our son Tracy was born, Tess Trueheart Tracy had a similar experience, but didn't make it to the hospital in time. Their baby was born in the back seat of the police car. Junior, behind the wheel of a patrol car, sped to the hospital while an officer rode in the back with Tess. A beautiful baby girl was born just minutes before they reached the hospital. Where was Tracy? He planned to be home in time, but had his hands full, having cornered another notorious criminal.

Person to Person

In April of 1957, Dad received a call from Edward R. Murrow's *Person to Person* staff at CBS television saying that Mr. Murrow had wanted to do the Gould and Tracy story for several years, but technical problems had prevented them from doing so until now. Dad was flattered and said, "Come ahead. Do what you have to do."

Though the *Person to Person* interview took place in the home of the honored guest, Mr. Murrow never left the CBS studio. No matter where the guest lived, Murrow was always seated in the same easy chair with his trademark cigarette held between his fingers with the smoke circling upward.

Several weeks before the program was to air, a crew of CBS technicians arrived at the house to assure themselves that a picture could be transmitted from this location. A house sixty miles from Chicago, tucked down in a valley, was more than they had anticipated. It didn't take them long to discover that it was impossible to transmit television signals to even the closest relay station about forty-five miles away in Lake Zurich, Illinois, without erecting a tower (the sending unit). With this unexpected task on their hands, they searched for the highest point on the property, which was a high wooded hill in front of the house. There they erected a seventy-five-foot tower far above the trees, with two saucers at the top aimed toward Lake Zurich. From Lake Zurich, the picture was sent on to Chicago on the coast-to-coast network.

Meanwhile, a special telephone cable was being strung from the town of Woodstock (five and a half miles away) to the tower. All this took ten men two weeks to accomplish. Then a telephone company's microwave truck equipped with part of the microwave sending unit had to be located and was stationed up on the hill next to the tower. The tower truck alone cost $16,000.

The afternoon of the night of the program, an impressive CBS monitor truck turned into the driveway, carrying all the props, cameras and tripods to be used the night of the interview. Back in 1957, the cameras were huge and heavy pieces of equipment compared with what we have today.

Said Dad to a *Chicago Tribune* journalist in an interview before this special evening, "I don't know what they want me to talk about. After all, I keep my nose to the grindstone. I do all my writing and most of my drawing. I don't have any hobbies except mowing the lawn and taking a swim in our little pool, and that's only in the warm weather. I don't collect stamps or anything else."

Dad never thought about the hours of police research he did or his contacts with the Chicago police or the state police. The McHenry County Sheriff even deputized him. Dad was Car #41 with a two-way police radio installed in our car. He confessed that he had never been called to help the sheriff apprehend any men suspected of any crime. But no matter: Wherever we were going in the car, on went the police radio. Dad always picked up the microphone and said "10–2," and the sheriff's office recognized that he was Car #41 and responded accordingly. Upon reaching our destination, Dad again picked up the microphone and said, "10–4," which meant over and out. Then off went the radio. I think he felt like Dick Tracy.

As the *Person to Person* broadcast drew near, excitement was building. When Dick, our one and a half year old son Tracy, and I (pregnant with our second baby) arrived at Mother and Dad's, Ray and his wife, Mabel, were just arriving with Grandmother Gould. Mother and Dad met us in the courtyard looking radiant, obviously swept up in all the excitement. After meeting the CBS staff and seeing all the cameras, floodlights and activity, we felt the same way. I thought of my own father being on national television and just shivered with excitement. No daughter could have been more proud of her father.

Several of the staff people took us through the mobile truck, showing us the monitors that were built in across one side. Monitor operators were already in place, talking to the cameramen in the house, getting the best camera angles and the best lighting, and doing short runs through the evening's performance. Each monitor showed a different location in the house. I could see the living room, the upstairs hall, Dad's studio and the exercise and play room. As we left the truck, I marveled at the amazing technology involved and how far we had come. Twenty-two years before, right where this grand CBS monitor truck was parked, there had been nothing but tall weeds, cockleburs and grasshoppers on an old, abandoned farm.

Going back into the house, we watched the last-minute flurry of activity: cameramen making final adjustments, lighting people double-checking spotlights, set dressers placing flower arrangements on tables to hide the microphones. Each staff member had his or her own duty to perform.

When there were just minutes to go, Mother was seated in an armchair near the fireplace in the living room with little Tracy on her lap and a stick of gum in her pocket, while Dad was standing near her. The rest of us were asked to sit in specified areas. Then the director gave us the sign for silence.

The next voice we heard was that of Edward R. Murrow introducing Dad. My heart was just pounding. How could Dad be so calm as Mr. Murrow introduced him to the audience? He seemed so relaxed answering questions about his youth, then introducing his mother, who said a few words. Dad moved over toward Mother and introduced her and Tracy to Mr. Murrow. By now Tracy was a bit fidgety, so out came the stick of gum, which seemed to appease him. After the family was introduced, Dad took Tracy from Mother and handed him to Dick; then Dad and Mother headed upstairs to Dad's studio. Skillfully, the cameraman didn't catch any spotlights in the large mirror on the landing while filming Dad and Mother climbing the stairs as they continued to talk to Mr. Murrow. After seeing Dad's studio and his work area, the cameraman bypassed the spotlight's reflection again as they descended the stairs and headed for the exercise and play room.

We didn't realize how exciting those fifteen minutes were until we saw the film that *Person to Person* sent to Mother and Dad after the show. The behind-the-scenes complexity of this television show was something the viewer could never have imagined, and the immense cost for this fifteen-minute interview must have been staggering, way over what CBS ever expected to spend.

Each week, Mr. Murrow interviewed two guests during his half-hour program. On this night, Dad was first, and the very dignified Dimitri Mitropoulos, conductor of the New York Philharmonic Symphony Orchestra who lived in the heart of New York City, followed Dad. But there was a mix-up. Mr. Murrow introduced Chester Gould as living in a sprawling country farmhouse in Woodstock, Illinois — but the image on the screen showed Dimitri Mitropoulos's immense New York City apartment building. We were a bit shocked; then we laughed and hoped that Maestro Mitropoulos's sophisticated apartment building in New York City wasn't a sprawling country farmhouse. But it was.

Making a Statement

By 1957, many young people's values had changed. Motorcycle gangs, often rough and violent, were glamorously portrayed in the movies, and that portrayal added to the change. Gang-style dress and attitudes were catching the eye of many schoolboys around the country. Tight pants, sweatshirts (sometimes sleeveless), motorcycle boots, motorcycle caps on scruffy heads of hair — these styles were new to schoolboys, but now many wanted to imitate the look. In turn, their dress was causing a noticeable difference in how they behaved.

Feeling the importance of making a statement about this disturbing trend, Dad interrupted his ongoing story in a Sunday page and had Junior and two of his friends put his point across. The boys walked into the police department looking for Tracy. They were wearing trousers, shirts and sport coats. Seeing the boys, Sam Catchem said, "Junior, I never saw you fellows look so sharp."

"Thanks, Sam," responded Junior. "We guys are dressing *right* these days!"

"You mean no more monkey suits of tight pants, sweat shirts and motorcycle boots?"

"No sir," responded Junior. "They're a laugh, infant stuff. The regular guys are dressing up."

"We feel if a fella's going to be a jerk, he'll dress like a jerk," chimed in Junior's friend. "As for us, we're men and we want to dress like men."

That was the only time Dad mentioned the subject, but it was enough to get the attention of readers. The American Institute of Men and Boys Wear were the first to contact him wanting to create a Dress Right Movement to use as their slogan in connection with that September 1 *Dick Tracy* Sunday page. Many school principals across the country started their own Dress Right program in their schools. It seemed as if America had been waiting for someone to start the ball rolling.

New York's Commissioner of Correction wrote that she was convinced that the clothing a person wore was an indication of that person's self-esteem. Some fifty police chiefs and juvenile enforcement specialists from all parts of the country sent similar messages.

Today, 2006, this all sounds pretty tame and almost laughable to many. In 1957, however, the Dress Right Movement was an important statement for decent American character.

Scotland Yard 1958

Dad had toured the FBI headquarters in Washington, D.C., and felt honored to have met with J. Edgar Hoover. Now he had a chance to visit Scotland Yard, made possible by the *Chicago Tribune* and his friend Arthur Vessey, the *Tribune*'s London Foreign Correspondent. The plan was that he would be given a demonstration of Scotland Yard's methods and techniques. The *Chicago Tribune* thought this would be excellent publicity for the strip.

Mother and Dad had never flown overseas; indeed, they hadn't flown anywhere. Our yearly jaunts to New York for the Editor and Publisher's Convention had been always by train. Now they were to fly overseas, and wouldn't you know, before boarding they were told there would be a day's delay due to technical problems. But the next day, on April 6, 1958, they did leave. Captain Anthony Loraine and Stewardess Jill Pratt greeted them as they boarded the British Overseas Airways Stratocruiser, a prop plane, at O'Hare Airport in Chicago. The kind handshakes and smiles seemed to ease their tension a little.

With a two-hour stopover in Detroit and a stop in Montreal, Mother wrote on a card sent from Montreal, "I hope we reach London — by Sunday." To my surprise, when a telegram arrived at our house, it read:

> LANDED 11:00 AM SUNDAY — ABSOLUTELY
> GORGEOUS OVERWATER FLIGHT — TRACY
> AND SUE'S PICTURES ON SAVOY ROOM
> MANTLE — OUR LOVE MOTHER AND DAD.

They found their flight to be delightful. The Vesseys were waiting for them at the airport, having planned an unforgettable two weeks for them. Scotland Yard, however, was their first stop after checking into their hotel rooms. Their car drove them through the historic streets to 4 Whitehall Place. This venerable old building was Scotland Yard. Dad found that only he had clearance for this tour, so, saying goodbye to Mother and the Vesseys, he was cordially escorted through the doors of this world renowned law enforcement agency that dated back to 1829. Dad learned that the building, which opened onto a courtyard, had once been the home of the King of Scotland. A bit overwhelmed with the history, Dad was further awed when he entered a room of maps covering the walls from the ceiling to the floor. They were maps of Greater London covering approximately 735 square miles. Sixteen thousand of

Scotland Yard's Metropolitan Police patrolled this vast area, and two hundred highly trained Alsatian and Labrador dogs were available to the police, used mostly in the search for lost persons.

The C.I.D. (Criminal Investigation Department), where the most difficult crime cases in all of Wales and England are handled, was the next stop. This is what particularly interested Dad. Here, every investigative technique and technician was available to the police force. This is how Dad envisioned Tracy, knowing all the facets of police investigation. Through his years of studying criminology and lab techniques, Dad felt proud of what he knew, and he found this tour through Scotland Yard exhilarating and very informative. It was something he would never forget.

The Vesseys had planned a tour through the beautiful countryside that led to Stratford-upon-Avon, where the picturesque Shakespeare Hotel appeared like a vision out of a history book. Then it was on to Westminster Abbey, Buckingham Palace, the Wilton House and on and on. It was a whirlwind view of history and architecture that Mother and Dad had only read about in books. On their last day in London, they were driven to the quaint little town of Woodstock (the same name as their hometown in Illinois). Its narrow streets and high-pitched roof top store fronts looked like a backdrop for a play as they strolled along the sidewalk down High Street.

Finally, having to say goodbye to their wonderful friends and hosts, they boarded the plane and were comfortably seated on their way back to Chicago. Dad leaned back and thought about the two back-breaking weeks it took to get ahead in his work. Now it was back to reality—not only to his work, but to stacks of mail that awaited him: bills, business letters and fan mail to be tackled. But for now, he and Mother would reminisce about these wonderful two weeks in London and their visit with the Vesseys.

Noticing the night sky spangled with stars as their plane flew into the darkness, Dad took in its beauty for a moment. He knew that the trip had been a relaxing break for both Mother and him. He also knew that before they landed at O'Hare Airport, he would have the beginning of a new story involving Tracy, Superintendent Whitehall (fictitious name), and a fraud investigation at Scotland Yard.

This Is Your Life, 1958

On an August morning in 1958, a normal summer morning, Dick had left for work, baby Sue was in her highchair watching me make cookies, and Tracy was playing with his trucks not far from the kitchen. The phone rang, and I answered. The caller, whose name I can't remember, introduced herself and said, "I'm calling from Hollywood from the *This Is your Life* television show. We want your father to be a special guest on our program."

"Who is this?" I asked, and she repeated what she had said. I couldn't believe it. *This Is Your Life* was one of the hottest shows on television. Everyone watched it. I couldn't believe my ears and asked if she could call me back in a few minutes. This must have been the usual reaction, because she said without hesitation, "Of course." Then, apparently knowing what I was thinking, she added, "Your father must not know about this." I assured her that he wouldn't.

I immediately called Mother. Dad answered. My heart skipped a beat as we casually talked a few minutes about the family. I hoped I didn't sound too breathless and excited. Finally, I asked to speak to Mother. I heard Dad hang up the phone at his drawing board when Mother answered in another part of the house. All I asked her was, "Is it true?"

"Yes," she answered. She knew what I meant.

We talked for only a minute before saying goodbye. My heart was just pounding. My own father was going to be honored on *This Is Your Life*!

In about twenty minutes the phone rang and it was the same caller, undoubtedly knowing what I had done. She went on to describe the whole procedure, then asked me to think about the most important influence my father had made in my life. She also asked for names and phone numbers of relatives and people I knew that had touched Dad's life in some way. She would gather information from these people, and together, she and her staff would create a condensed biography of Dad. They did this every week with a new celebrity being honored on the program. It had to be a monumental job.

Part of the fun of *This Is Your Life* was the element of surprise. The celebrity guest was lured onto the set with some pretext, only to find himself the guest of honor on the show. Friends, family and colleagues would be there to surprise him and talk about his life.

Obviously, it was of the utmost importance that Dad be kept unaware that all this was happening. His working at home with the phone right at his elbow made it a real problem for Mother. I don't know how she did it.

How would they get Dad to the Studio? George Florey, Dad's friend since their meeting in 1931, had worked his way up the ladder to become a very successful advertising man and knew Ralph Edwards, the host of the show. "Just leave it to me," said George. "I'll get Chet there on October 22nd."

George had a real challenge on his hands. He finally came up with an idea that he thought his pal Chet couldn't turn down. He called Dad one day to tell him that a Hollywood producer friend wanted to use *Dick Tracy* in a series of five-minute mystery shorts, and he thought Dad would want to see them before they aired. (Of course the five-minute mystery shorts didn't exist, nor did the producer.) Dad felt George had learned something that he didn't know and was a bit agitated that he wasn't consulted on this before now. In fact he was pretty burned up about it.

"Well, of course I want to see them," Dad said. "When will they be ready?"

"The producer said he would have them ready by October 20." (That was two days before the show.) "We could catch a morning flight out of O'Hare and come back the next day." In 1957, it took eight hours to fly from Chicago to Los Angeles in TWA's latest and finest prop plane.

Dad looked at his calendar. "The twentieth is on a Monday. That's out of the question." George knew he would say that.

"How about Friday?" Dad proposed. George was ready for that one, too. He agreed to Friday, but called Dad a few days later to tell him that the producer needed a little more time. Now, he said, the films would be ready on Tuesday the twenty-first. That was about as bad as Monday.

George was getting pretty nervous when he called Dad for the third time saying the producer promised them by Wednesday (the night of the show). Dad's impatience was wearing thin. But to George's surprise and great relief, Dad finally gave in and agreed to go on Wednesday, October 22.

Mother, having felt the tension growing over the weeks, was relieved knowing George had pinned Dad down. But now she had to feign surprise about this trip to Hollywood. The morning they took off with the Floreys, Dad didn't have the foggiest idea as to what was in store for him.

Dick, Tracy, baby Sue and I met Grandmother Gould, Ray and his wife, Mabel, at the O'Hare Airport earlier that same day, but our paths wouldn't cross with Mother and Dad until the night of the show. It was on the flight that Grandmother Gould said to me, "I rode in a covered wagon when a child, and here I am flying above the clouds in this TWA Constellation."

When our plane landed in Los Angeles, the same woman who I had originally spoken to on the phone was there to meet us and had a limousine waiting to drive us to the Hollywood Roosevelt Hotel. Her instructions were to not leave the hotel until we were picked up and driven to the NBC Studio that night. We could get settled in our rooms, change our clothes and have time to look around the famous hotel. The other surprise guests were also staying there, but we didn't know any of them.

Mother, Dad, and the Floreys arrived late afternoon at the Los Angeles airport and were met by a car whose driver happened to be the show's top writer. They talked about going to the famous Brown Derby for dinner. But instead, the driver pulled up behind the NBC Studio and asked if they would like to see the studio first before going to dinner. The show aired at 6:00 P.M., and it was just about that time.

"I couldn't have cared less," said Dad. "I was hungry."

But they were led through the back entrance of NBC and were taken on a tour of the behind-the-scenes operation. There they saw how the scenery was painted on long rolls that were raised up from the floor below. To demonstrate this, a man raised a huge backdrop from the slot in the floor and there, to Dad's complete surprise, was a huge drawing of Dick Tracy saying, "Chester Gould, *This Is Your Life!*" At this point, Ralph Edwards, the host of the show, walked out from behind some scenery and extended his hand to Dad, saying, "Chester Gould of Woodstock, Illinois—creator of the famed *Dick Tracy* cartoon strip—*This Is Your Life.*" As Dad shook hands with Mr. Edwards, he shook his head in disbelief. But Ralph Edwards continued: "You thought you were coming out here for a business conference, but actually, our plot to get you here was as involved as any *Dick Tracy* adventure."

Dad was stunned. He looked at his friend, George Florey, with a devilish grin and said a few words about his scheming plan. Then they were escorted into the studio as a Prell Shampoo ad came on.

Still looking dazed, Dad was seated on the stage before the studio audience, something he and Mother had seen happen week after week with other guests. Mother and Dad faithfully watched this program at home.

The first guest to be introduced was someone Dad hadn't seen in fifty-one years: Miss Bertha Kirkpatrick, his first grade teacher from the Pawnee, Oklahoma, Grade School. She had a few words to say about Dad's excuses for being late for school. Other guests followed, people who had touched his life in some way through the years, up to the present day.

Toward the end of the program, Mother and I were introduced. As Mother came out and greeted Dad with a kiss, he shook his head again, realizing that she had cleverly kept this a complete secret. Looking at Mr. Edwards, she said, "It was such fun seeing characters develop through the years, and many of them seem to be living right in our home."

My heart was in my mouth as I kissed Dad and gave him a hug, agreeing with Mother. But then I expressed the great love that Mother and Dad had shown toward each other and to me over the years and what a wonderful example it had been for me.

Ralph Edwards then presented Dad with a book bound in burgundy colored leather titled *This Is Your Life: Chester Gould,* a book that he had referred to throughout the program. Mother received a beautiful 14-carat gold charm bracelet highlighting the life of this remarkable man, her husband and my father. Dad received a pair of 14-carat gold cuff links and a tie clip with a diamond in the day of the month that the show took place. A projector and a film of this memorable evening were also given to Dad.

When Ralph Edwards introduced a young twelve-year-old boy, a member of the Woodstock Crime Stoppers Club, the boy told Mr. Edwards and the audience how the club members had learned to help protect their community. Ralph Edwards responded, "We know that your Crime Stoppers Club has wanted a tape recorder so that you could have a permanent record of the ideas that come up at your meetings. So in the name of Chester Gould, an extra powerful RCA High Fidelity portable tape recorder will be presented to the Woodstock Crime Stoppers Club by Prell Shampoo."

Turning to Dad, Ralph Edwards said, "In your world populated with imaginative characters, there are two who are very real to you — your grandchildren, Tracy and Sue." Tracy went running to his grandfather, and Dick came out carrying Sue.

Holding Tracy, Dad put his arm around Mother, as all gathered around with some final words from Ralph Edwards. My heart was overflowing with pride for Dad and for Mother.

After the show was over, a beautiful dinner was held at the Hollywood Roosevelt Hotel for all the guests who appeared on the show in this unforgettable evening. It was truly a remarkable endeavor and an evening to treasure. Dad couldn't have summed it up better when he said, "It was like old home week. We cried on each other's shoulders and had a wonderful time."

Hawaii

It was a monumental occasion when Mother and Dad went to Hawaii with three other couples in late 1959. Mother was so excited. Dad wasn't. In fact, he just wanted to stay home. Leaving his comfortable house was what he least liked to do. He thought of all the excuses not to go. He had to get ahead in his work, and what was more (as he had many times stated), "No one can take care of this place the way I can." Mother finally said cheerfully, "Well, you stay home and I'll go." This caught Dad by surprise, and he thought things over.

The flight took off from O'Hare Airport for Hawaii that September. Dad was right there with Mother and their friends. Mother knew what a tremendous job it was for Dad to do two weeks' work in one week to prepare for this occasion, and she so loved him for that.

For Dad, however, a trip was never just a vacation. Several weeks before leaving for Hawaii, he had contacted Hawaii's chief of police, Dan Liu, and made plans to meet with him and learn about their law enforcement on the island. Chief Liu was delighted, and Dad thought he could possibly develop an idea for a *Tracy* story.

Even before they landed at Oahu Airport, news had spread that Chester Gould was coming. The Hawaiian people loved the *Dick Tracy* strip and were waiting for him to arrive, hoping he would make a number of appearances — which he did. He also got a story.

As Dad's story developed, a tall, handsome Hawaiian man, Haku, was posing as an entertainer. Actually, he was a Hawaiian undercover man looking for two criminals who fled the United States. (Hawaii joined the U.S.A. as a state on August 21, 1959, and this strip first appeared in the paper on September 21 — but it had been written six weeks previously.) Willy the Fifth (nick-named after the Fifth Amendment) and Flyface, a self-taught lawyer who had a strange affliction for attracting flies, were both guilty of killing a Hawaiian. They were wanted in the United States and Hawaii.

After countless twists and turns in the story, Haku found himself held at gunpoint and was told to fly the unsavory crooks to a safe place. Haku thought of a deserted beach near Kona. During the flight, with a gun at his head, Haku courageously radioed the control tower in Hawaii, and in Hawaiian told them to tip off Chief Liu of their destination. The two thugs, suspicious, couldn't understand a word he said, but were somewhat satisfied when he told them that this was flight policy.

Haku landed the plane on a deserted sand beach where he, Flyface and the Fifth spent the night in nervous exhaustion, each crook with a gun in hand not knowing what to do next.

When Tracy arrived in Hawaii, he and Chief Liu took off immediately by helicopter, heading toward Haku's designated location. As they neared Kona, what they saw from the air was what Haku had been alerted to on his flight radio—a tidal wave was coming. The crooks had a quick decision to make, to either face a tidal wave or be arrested.

"Head for the plane, we're taking off," said the Fifth. "Get this plane going and don't touch that radio."

With a gun still at his head, Haku thought fast. "We have little gas left and have to let the motors warm up or we'll end up right in those breakers.—Okay!—Now!—Pull out those chocks!"

"The chocks?" questioned Flyface.

"Yes," replied Haku. "How do you think I could rev these motors without chocks to hold it back? Pull 'em up now and we'll go."

In panic, both Flyface and the Fifth jumped out of the plane to release the two chocks that held the wheels in place. With them off the plane, Haku yanked the throttle and took off in a spray of blinding sand.

"They're all yours, Chief," came Haku's radio message.

"Now it's either the tidal wave or us. They can take their choice," replied Chief Liu.

Landing the helicopter on the mountainside above the beach, the chief called out with his bullhorn, "Walk up the side of the mountain with your hands up or die in the tidal wave. The first big wave is less than sixty seconds away."

Thinking they were tricked, Flyface looked out toward the ocean. "Hey, Fifth!" he said. "The ocean is receding. Maybe they are right."

"Ten seconds," came the voice over the bullhorn. Turning to Tracy, Chief Liu said, "This is only the first wave. The undertow from that first wave will drag them out almost a quarter of a mile."

"I never knew before how tidal waves operate," said Tracy, watching in awe.

"That's only the beginning," responded the chief. "Number two will be bigger. Wait till you see waves four and five. They will be dashed to death against the rocks. It's impossible to outrun the waves." The two law enforcement men could only watch as another wave came in, more violent than the last.

When the tidal wave finally subsided, there was no sign of either the Fifth or Flyface. Haku returned after refueling his plane and he, Chief Liu, Tracy and additional police searched for the bodies. None could be found.

"No power on earth has the destructive force of a tidal wave, Mr. Tracy," said Haku. "Billions of yards of sand have been moved. We may never know if they're dead. Their bodies may be under thirty feet of sand or washed over the cliff."

What was discovered during the search, however, was a pair of yellow undershorts emblazoned with a red number "5" on the seat, and in another location a mound of sand attracting flies—a pretty sure indication that the Fifth and Flyface had paid their debt to society.

Just a week after Dad's story ended, Hawaii actually had a terrible tidal wave.

11

The Later Years

In 1960, two *Tribune* executives, Howard Wood and Dr. Theodore Van Dellan, asked Dad if he would like to join a men's golf club, the Lake Zurich Golf Club in Lake Zurich, Illinois. They would sponsor him. The club was about thirty-five minutes from Chicago and forty-five minutes from Mother and Dad's house. Although he had never been a joiner and did not even play golf, Dad surprisingly accepted their offer after learning about this club's rich history. Dating back to 1895, it was known as one of the oldest golf clubs in America. Its original slate of membership included professors from the University of Chicago, deans, doctors, lawyers, publishers and other noted men; the great architect Daniel Burnham; the advertising great Leo Burnett; and the bookstore owner Carl Kroch of Kroch and Brentano. The library section in the living room in the old clubhouse echoes its rich heritage; books written by or about former members grace the shelves. One could almost feel the past come alive just by being in the atmosphere.

Members of the club to this day carry out the old Scottish tradition of wearing red coats trimmed with green lapels and cuffs, as the Scots did many years ago. However, the Lake Zurich members wear them only on Saturday nights, when they meet for relaxing conversation over cocktails and dinner. Today, wives are invited to join their husbands (family and guests are invited by members from time to time). They experience some traditions that have been carefully carried on as the club's founding fathers had intended. Singing is one of them. After dinner, while still at the table, each person finds a special song book at their place, full of songs written about the Lake Zurich Golf Club, songs from years gone by, patriotic songs and college songs. Only the members sing the last song of the night, praising Lake Zurich Club with their glasses held high, a truly emotional moment. This club was one of the highlights in Dad's life.

In 1976, Dick and I planned a fiftieth wedding anniversary dinner celebration for Mother and Dad at the Lake Zurich Golf Club. That evening Mother and Dad looked as happy as I have ever seen them, sharing a milestone in their lives among their friends, relatives and family at the club that Dad so loved.

What Now?

It certainly wasn't the "Seven Year Itch," because Mother and Dad were nearing their sixtieth birthdays—Dad's in November and Mother's in January—but they wanted a change.

No, not what you're thinking. Their change was possibly moving from the farm into the city. In 1959, Dad had even contacted a Chicago realtor to see what was available in a small building just off Michigan Avenue where they might convert the top floor into an apartment for themselves. During the next four years, the realtor sent glossy photographs of small buildings accompanied with description and statistics of buildings that came on the market that he thought fit Dad's request. One building in particular, on Ontario Street, had caught Mother and Dad's eye. Yet something held them back. The more they thought about being confined in an area without open acreage that they had grown to love, they realized it was the wrong move, even for investment purposes. Dad already had a number of commercial properties. The more they thought about it, the less they could envision themselves living in the city. So that ended that, and their thoughts turned back to country living.

Sometime later, Dad approached Mother on another idea — to build a house on a beautiful piece of property they owned about two miles from where they lived. It included a hill

An evening Mother and Dad will never forget: Celebrating over fifty years of happiness with close friends and relatives at Lake Zurich Golf Club, 1976.

known to have one of the highest elevations in the countryside, a breathtaking view that spanned as far as the eye could see. They often drove up there just to enjoy its beauty. After some serious thought about this idea, Mother agreed it would be a wonderful place to build a home, and she and Dad decided to go ahead with plans.

With the hiring of a well-known local architect, the wheels were set in motion. Once a week, Mother and Dad met with the architect, hashing and rehashing ideas. An enclosed swimming pool to be used year round was the first consideration. It would not only afford great pleasure year round, it would be soothing, relaxing therapy for Dad's lower back, which was becoming a painful problem, undoubtedly from leaning over his drawing board since the early 1920s.

Building a brand-new home offered lots of chances to have all the latest luxuries. Central air conditioning, for example, didn't exist in 1935 when Mother and Dad came to the farm. Window air conditioners were the only source for cooling a house, and we thought they were wonderful, but now a house could be air-conditioned through and through. As for radiators, they were a welcome addition in the winter, but ours often built up a surplus of steam heat and emitted a very noisy racket. Now all this would be a thing of the past. And at last Mother would have plenty of closet space, storage cabinets and a balcony or two for shaking throw rugs.

Months went by as the beautiful new house developed on the architect's drawing board. But on the final day, when the plans were complete and in Mother and Dad's hands, the strangest thing happened. Whether it was this step or the whole past five years that helped them make their final decision, they knew that this wasn't the answer either. Just as if they had awakened from sleep, they suddenly realized they couldn't find a more beautiful setting than where they were — the acreage, the hills, the trees, the open space, the brook — everything they loved when they first bought the tumbledown abandoned farm on the sixty acres of land that they had been living on all this time. It was right under their noses and they didn't realize it. Dad, at sixty-six years of age, and Mother at sixty-five, finally made a decision about building. They were going to embark on a plan that most people their ages wouldn't have dreamed of carrying out. They would rebuild right where they were.

It's 1966! Here They Go Again

Once again crews of workmen and large pieces of machinery entered the front gate. One by one, each vacated farm building came down. The barn, the cement silo (which took a wrecking ball to knock down), the milk house, the bullpen, the corncrib, the pigpen — one by one, all the buildings that we had watched go up thirty-one years before, this wonderful farm, disappeared from the landscape. Grass would now cover the memories of what had been.

The 1935 house we had loved would have a facelift and become part of the new house. The living room and library would become Dad's new studio. The dining room would become the conference room with a kitchen and bathroom facilities. It would be wonderful.

How the farm looked before the buildings were razed in 1967. Only the chicken house remained (the small building in foreground), to be used as a tool shed.

Over the past year, another well-known local architect, John Anderson, had been working with Mother and Dad and had drawn up a new set of house plans, which included taking
the farmhouse down. After it had been dismantled, we marveled at the square nails that were
used in its construction when it was built over a hundred years before.

Mother and Dad did a remarkable job of living in the existing house while the new addition was being built. Once again, they were living among the bulldozers and truckloads of
stone, the pounding, the pouring of concrete, and the dust, along with workmen everywhere.
Separated from the commotion only by a plastic sheet taped across what would become the
opening to the new house, Mother and Dad took it in stride. They greeted John, the architect, with a cup of coffee each day he came, and the three of them often sat on a pile of lumber or in the conference room with the plans laid out, discussing any questions or suggestions.
Before Dad went back to his drawing board, he took a few stereo-realist (three-dimensional)
camera shots of the progress. During the construction of the house, Mother found the safest
place to dress in the morning was in her closet.

In the early planning of the house, Dad, with his vivid imagination, presented John with
several drawings showing ideas he wanted him to incorporate in the house plans. The first
was a unique doorless powder room that he would call the "grotto." When the grotto was completed, it was quite the conversation piece. Opposite the entry's curved stone wall was a jagged
wall of flagstones featuring a waterfall, which gently fell into a small, lighted pond below floor
level. A curved walkway led into the powder room between these walls. Behind a curtain of
crystal beads was a beautiful sink vanity built in against the back wall. Accented with brass
swan faucets and a mirrored wall with crystal lighting fixtures, the sink was a stunning surprise to find in the grotto. Dad had once remarked that he didn't like going to friends' homes
for the first time and being told that the powder room was the second door on the left or the
third door on the right. It was something he wanted to eliminate in his home, and he did that
in a big way.

If the grotto was not unusual enough, there was another of Dad's unique ideas on the
second floor. Climbing the curved stairway from the foyer, you would find yourself in what
Dad called the "rotunda." This circular room, which was used for entertaining guests, had a
wide expanse of windows on the east and west walls. The bedroom wings were on the north
and south sides of the rotunda.

After the house was completed and Mother and Dad started entertaining, they of course
took their guests up to the rotunda. The lively green carpeting in this circular room set off
the décor of comfortable chairs and chairside tables. Inevitably, after some conversation and
laughter over drinks and appetizers, someone would reach for a drink left on the bar, only to
find that the bar wasn't there. Then everyone would notice that they weren't sitting in the
same place where they first sat down, and laughter abounded. They were on a revolving floor.
Dad really had fun with this, and it became a favorite spot for entertaining, because the revolving floor never became a "ho-hum" experience. It was slow and subtle, taking about forty-
five minutes to make a complete revolution. Everyone found it fascinating.

Tracy and Sue loved the saddles that had been made into novelty seats in the rotunda,
the same saddles Dad and I used when riding Cookie and Danny. Curving around one corner of the rotunda was a bar sink featuring the old hand pump that had been in the original
farmhouse kitchen. It was connected so that all one had to do was to raise the pump handle
to get water. In another area of the room, a coffee grinder that Dad remembered his Grandmother Miller using, had been made into a lamp. (I'm sure that that coffee grinder traveled
with the Miller family when they staked their claim in the newly opened Oklahoma territory
in 1893.)

The nickel slot machine purchased in the early 1940s, and old by that time, was certainly an inviting addition to this room. Tracy and Sue were drawn to it like a magnet and always found nickels in a dish next to the machine. Everyone loved dropping nickels in the slot, then pulling the handle down and watching the three noisy cylinders clank into place. Three oranges, three plums, three bells that spit out six, eight or ten nickels were the best to get, other than the three bars, which was the jackpot. The jackpot was a real celebration, with a sudden rush of nickels spurting forth and flying right out onto the carpet. This impressive-sounding jackpot amounted to a measly $1.00 (20 nickels), but it never failed to deliver excitement. (In all the years this machine has been in the family, some sixty years now, never has it needed any repair work.)

Hanging from the ceiling was the old wagonwheel light fixture that Dad had once hung in his studio. Now it was thoroughly cleaned, and after thirty years it again had a place of honor, hanging over a large rustic octagonal cocktail table in the center of the room.

The east and west views from the rotunda looked out on verdant expanses of grass that Dad had transformed into a golf course, which almost went around the perimeter of the house. The golf course is a story in itself.

The Metamorphosis of a Golf Course

I will leave the building a moment to explain how Dad's golf course came about. It is a story in itself, and started on a spring day back in 1960, even before the idea of this new house was born. My family and I were spending the weekend with Mother and Dad along with Dick Gauger, Mother's brother. After a Sunday lunch, we sat around the dining room table talking and laughing, when Uncle Dick, out of the blue, said, "Chet, why don't you put in a golf tee and green right in front on the other side of the driveway?"

Dad had never thought of anything like that. He didn't even play golf. Dick, however, was an avid golfer, one who always carried his clubs in the trunk of his car, ready at a moment's notice. While Dad was thinking about it, he heard Dick say, "I think I'll go out and hit a few balls." That caused all the men — Dick, Dad, and my husband Dick, and little Tracy, too — to excuse themselves, thank Mother for the wonderful meal, and go outside to discuss the possibilities for placement of the tee and the green.

The next time Uncle Dick drove out to visit, to his surprise there was a professionally executed tee and green. The tee was near where the barn had been, and the green was out near the fence at the road — not a long hole, but a good 168 yards. Dad had even bought himself a set of clubs. With Dick's patience and instruction along the way, they teed off and reached the green. Turning around, they walked back to begin again. At this point, Dad decided that a one-hole golf course was ridiculous. "We need another tee out here," he said, "and a green back there."

Before the summer was over, another green sprang up near the first tee, and another tee near the first green. Now they could go back and forth.

That was great for awhile, but it soon wore a bit thin. The following spring, Dad had a third hole put in that went across the driveway and the split rail fences to the brink of a small hill to the southwest of the house. The green was on the hill. It looked so good, Dad had a fourth hole put in down near the apple orchard to the east of the house. Now the golf course practically surrounded the house. The following year, with Dad getting a little bolder and a little better at his golf, in went a fifth hole, a dogleg with a green down near the brook, about 350 yards. Now, playing all the holes forward and back, you could play eight holes.

That's how Gould's Golf Course (as we called it) came about. Golf was never Dad's passion, but we had endless fun and camaraderie with family and friends. Sue and Tracy were paid caddies until they began to play. We all loved the course. Naturally it was not quite as perfect as a professional course, and sometimes you would see your ball land, roll and disappear right before your eyes on the fairway, having rolled into a small animal hole. Not only that, deer found it enjoyable to walk through one particular sand trap on their evening's trip across the valley.

On the morning of any day that company was coming, Dad would say, "Come on, men, let's go!" meaning the dogs, Rocky and Cissy, who would zoom out to the garage and jump in the jeep. With the red golf flags hanging out the back and fluttering in the breeze, they headed for the greens. The dogs bounced along and never minded staying in the jeep while Dad got out and tended each hole and sand trap. They just loved the ride.

Soon after getting a golf cart, Mother devised a system to keep the dogs from taking care of their business on the golf course. She decided they should have their own established spot, and she settled on a willow tree that was actually on the course, but halfway between the house and the dogleg green to the brook. Dad left a perimeter of longer grass around the tree, and since there were already some big rocks there, it looked very natural and like a hazard, which it sometimes was. Mother trained the dogs to know that when they climbed into the golf cart, they were going down to the willow tree to take care of their business. All she had to say was, "Let's get into the golf cart," and they knew where they were going. Out the door they went, tearing around the corner of the house to the pro-shop, where they jumped into the golf cart, Cissy taking the passenger seat and Rocky the floor. It was a funny sight to see them breezing along. Rocky always leaned out as far as he could so as to no miss anything. They loved the tall grass and rocks to sniff around. They were probably the only dogs that had transportation both ways to take care of their business. The golf cart was used until winter arrived. Then the dogs had plowed snow paths.

The reality of a golf course was no laughing matter. Dad had professional help on the greens when he needed it, and more than once he burned the greens with an overabundance of fertilizer. "If a little is good, a lot is better," was often his belief. He ate those words several times and almost lost the greens keeper. The course required a special watering drainage system, which meant a third well had to be dug. A three-car garage was needed to house two greens mowers, an approach mower, a Park Master for the fairways, a big Toro rotary mower for the fields, and two small rotary mowers. They filled the garage to capacity. It just boggled my mind to think how many responsibilities Dad could take on. Amazingly, he always seemed to have everything under control, unless something unexpected happened to a mower. Then, sometimes out of frustration, he would take a hammer and give the mower a whack. Often, that's all it took to get it started. Pure luck! Dad wasn't mechanically minded. Orville, the yardman, generally took care of the mowers, but when he wasn't around and one broke down, Dad often drove twenty or thirty miles to get a part. What a relief when a reliable mower repair man was found with a pick-up and delivery service. He liked Dad and made a special effort to give him quick and reliable service.

There was also the yard around the perimeter of the house to care for, to which Orville tended. When it came to the fields, Dad wouldn't let anyone use the big Toro mower, not even Orville. Well, a funny thing happened one day. It was a Saturday, and for a change of pace, Dad happened to be out mowing the fairway near the road. He looked like hired help in his bib overalls and straw hat.

A car slowed down, then stopped. Honking and waving to get Dad's attention, the driver called out from his car. Dad had to turn the mower off to hear him.

"Is this where Chester Gould lives?" called the driver.

"Yes," responded Dad, then started mowing again. The man seemed satisfied and drove off. Dad had to chuckle to himself.

Many things grow out of proportion from their original idea, and Dad found the golf course had done the same. But he also found that the beauty and enjoyment it offered couldn't be measured. During the summer, almost every Sunday morning, one of Dad's dear friends, Ken Fiske, came over, and he, Dad and Ray would play something called Bingo Bango Bongo. The first nearest the green, the first on the green and the first in the hole won points, which translated into money. If my family and Dick Gauger were out for the weekend, the two Dicks and Tracy, who was in junior high school, joined them, too. Coming into the screened-in area at the pool after the game, they always made us laugh as we watched and listened to them figure out what seemed to be complicated scorecards. "You owe me $2.50." "I lost $1.75." "I won $1.25." "No, you owe me $1.25." "I won $.75." It was just a lot of foolishness.

As the House Took Shape

The French doors that had opened onto the patio from the conference room would now be replaced with splendid new double doors. These new doors would open into the large new foyer, the beginning of the new part of the house. Here a graceful freestanding cast cement stairway would curve its way to the second floor, to the rotunda. Beneath this stairway, a lighted sunken garden of greenery was planned, and this was where the old horse-drawn hand plow (the first piece of farm equipment Dad bought in 1935) would be placed. Standing among luscious greenery and painted gold, it looked charming.

The large living room to the south of the foyer would have an oversized fireplace on the east wall, flanked by French doors. These doors would open to the lower terrace to the east. Another set of French doors on the south would open to the sprawling lawn and gold course beyond. Just to the west of the living room was the swimming pool, divided by a wide wall of glass and a set of sliding glass doors. The living room would overlook the pool's sparkling aquamarine water. The low lannon stone walls built along the perimeter of the pool in 1947 would now have lannon stone buttresses added to support the poolroom roof. Between the buttresses, sliding glass windows would run atop the stone walls the full length of the pool area on the north and south side, following the walls and turning at right angles into the screened in area. Here they would become sliding glass doors to completely enclose the pool from the screened-in area during the winter months. (I could just see Sue and Tracy, then 9 and 10 years old, when winter snowdrifts built up outside those windows; they would no doubt want to hop over the wall and through the opened window into the snowdrifts, squealing, to roll over and over in the snow in their swim suits, then scurry back and jump into the pool water, which would feel so warm. Sure enough, this turned out to be a winter ritual.)

Panes of clear Plexiglas on a large portion of the south side of the pool roof would welcome added sunlight and warmth to the room, creating a perfect atmosphere for Mother's green thumb. I remember some of her climbing vines grew up to the roof, displaying leaves the size of place mats. They loved the warm, humid atmosphere.

All of the downstairs floors in the new house addition, save for the dining room and kitchen, were laid with Indiana blue stone, including the pool area (where new blue stone concealed radiant heat piping in the floors).

From the east end of the pool, against the lannon stone covering the house, a circular stairway would wind its way down to the men's dressing room, if you turned left, and to the two basements, if you turned right. One basement had all the equipment for the pool and the other basement housed the furnace for the new part of the house. (The women's dressing room was to be on the pool level.) This same stairway spiraled up to the second floor balcony off the master bedroom. Looking at the drawing, I noticed how the balcony almost extended over the deep end of the pool, and I thought of how daring it would be to jump off the balcony into the pool water. No one ever did.

During all this construction, I wondered how Mother would get to the grocery story and Dad to the post office, with all the hassle and the trucks and workmen blocking the way. But they never had a problem. A funny thing about Dad going to the post office: For years, ever since I can remember, each morning at 9:30 sharp, he would put his pen down, cap his ink bottle, push away from his drawing board and drive into Woodstock to the post office. Though he always wore a hat to tip as a good morning gesture to people he saw, he never took off his bedroom slippers. Carrying a big brown grocery bag, he would head for Box #191, where he would carefully transfer the mass of mail from this large post office box to the bag. If I happened to be at the house, Dad would have me go in for the mail with explicit instructions to take a grocery bag with me. I couldn't help thinking that this was the kind of thing that B.O. Plenty would do—carry a big empty grocery bag emblazoned with "A&P" or "National Tea."

Pouring the mail out onto his cleared-off drawing board, Dad would methodically go through each piece, setting aside categories and making immediate phone calls concerning business letters if Dad had a question. By the time he was finished, he had organized stacks of mail to be answered, bills to be paid, the investments to take care of, fan letters that needed answering and an ocean of opened envelopes and junk mail scattered on the floor around his drawing board to be tossed out. As business letters were answered they were stacked on the bookshelf. Each day, Dad tackled the mail in this fashion, never getting behind. As he said, "Tomorrow there's a whole new batch of responsibilities. You can't get behind in anything."

During the months and months of building, there were plenty of interruptions in Dad's routine. Sometimes awakening in the night, thinking of a idea or question he wanted to ask the electrician, he would make a phone call—even if it was 2:00 in the morning. Not until the house was complete did the electrician, Dean Mishler, say laughingly under his breath, "When the phone rang in the middle of the night, I knew that could only be Chet, and I finally told him I'd gone to Africa." This same electrician's father had wired the 1935 house when it was built, so there was sentiment in all the guffawing.

The architect had masterfully worked his plan around the courtyard, the lower garden and the pool, which had been built in 1947. These areas went undisturbed throughout the whole construction process. The split rail fence along the driveway just at the front gate had been removed, and a temporary pathway for the trucks veered off the driveway onto part of the golf course, so as not to have them driving on the courtyard's paving bricks with their heavy loads.

By 1967, the plastic barrier was removed and Mother and Dad moved across to the south wing of the newly completed house. Then the plastic was replaced, again dividing the two house sections. A guest room and their master bedroom with two baths awaited them. Their bedroom, right over the living room, overlooked the beautiful swimming pool. Opening the sliding glass doors on this wall, one could walk out onto a small balcony and sit and have a cup of coffee in the pool area or walk down the spiral stairway that led to the pool. Two other balconies off the bedroom had south and east views offering spectacular views of the countryside.

One of the final pieces to be built was a massive, solid oak dining room table, four feet wide by ten feet long, built right on the spot. It must have weighed three hundred pounds when completed and easily seated twelve people. A huge gold chandelier with English gothic glair was a focal point, and it complemented the table. The electrician worked for days converting it from candles to electricity.

It took over one year to complete the work on the house down to the final decorating. Privacy, peace and quiet finally reigned. I marveled at how Mother and Dad, who were now in their later sixties, were filled with the excitement of a young married couple building their first house.

The back of the finished house, showing the covered swimming pool. 1967. (Photograph courtesy Richard Pietrzyk.)

In a windowed corner of the dining room overlooking the lower garden and golf course, two comfortable upholstered high-backed chairs sharing a small table invited one to sit and enjoy the view. That's where Dad and Mother enjoyed a cocktail and conversation each day before their main meal of the day.

Every night like clockwork, before turning in, Dad would make the rounds, checking the two basements behind the pool and the basement in the older part of the house, making sure all was operating to his satisfaction. It boggled my mind to think of all the mechanical paraphernalia in that house. The largest circuit breaker box I had ever seen had been placed in the old basement. I think even Dad was a little awed by the equipment. He didn't want anything to get "off-kilter." A feeling of well-being was a great comfort to Dad at the end of the day.

Finally, before dark, arm-in-arm, he and Mother leisurely took their late afternoon walk with the dogs, taking in the aroma of the clean country air, which included walking around the perimeter of the house to see that all was well.

All the laughter and happy times our family had around the beautiful dining room table at meal time created many treasured memories. We all pitched in, wanting to help Mother with everything. Finally, Dad, the flamboyant meat carver, took his place at the cutting board where he knew he would have an audience. Everyone wanted to watch his culinary flair, and samples were always handed out.

For Father's Day one year, my husband gave Dad a wooden shingle he had made for the hobby/pro shop, where golf clubs and the golf cart were stored. This 20" × 30" shingle read, "GOULD'S GOLF." Dad hung it from an iron strap at the corner of the building. The raised bright red letters and curved border were a handsome contrast against the dark stained background, all carefully carved away from the lettering border. Dad always took pride in this shingle and even created a golf scorecard for the golf course from the shingle design. The scorecard read, "In the Heart of BEAUTIFUL BULL VALLEY, GOULD'S GOLF." The rest was silly humor — "The Only No-Par Course. Don't Call Us We'll Call You," and it included a choice of scorekeeper's remarks on the back. It was just all in fun, because Dad never took golf too seriously.

Like Dad's golf game, his scorecard was never to be taken seriously.

"What's That Doing Here?"

By 1976, Mother could see Dad taking more time away from his drawing board to stretch out and ease his lower back pain. He wasn't sleeping well at night and was unable to find a mattress that helped him. Goodness knows they tried everything. Then an idea popped into Mother's head.

A few days before Christmas, a furniture truck drove in. Dad was working at his drawing board when he heard the driveway bell ring. He looked up and saw a truck heading into the courtyard. In his usual way he said, "Who in tarnation is that?" He never liked to be disturbed by an unexpected car or truck while he was working.

Mother hurried to the door and the delivery man brought in a recliner chair and put it in the spot in Dad's studio where he usually sat. His other chair was quickly moved out of the way.

Pushing back from his drawing board to see what was going on, he exclaimed in rather a harsh tone, "What's that doing here?"

"That's your Christmas present from me," said Mother.

"I don't want a chair like that. I don't even like it."

"Just try it. It might help ease your back pain," Mother said, holding back tears and hurt feelings.

Dad looked at it almost in disdain. He sat down in the chair. "We don't need this."

"Just lean back and push it into a reclining position. Just try it," Mother pleaded.

Dad did and didn't say much. The delivery man left.

The rest of the day, every time Dad left his drawing board, he tried the chair. By evening, he said to Mother, "You know, this is a terrific little chair. I think I'll try sleeping here tonight."

Well, that was a change of heart, Mother thought, and was delighted. She knew it was hard for Dad to admit that she was right.

The first thing Dad said in the morning after his good morning kiss for Mother was, "You've got to get one of these chairs, it's great for the back." Mother smiled with an inner satisfaction and that very day ordered another chair just like the one she had given Dad. Whether it was to keep Dad company or whether she really loved its comfort, she slept there with him in the studio, each in their own recliner every night.

A Turning Point

By 1977, Dad was feeling more and more pressure in turning out six strips and a Sunday page each week. For forty-six years he had leaned over that drawing board, knowing that the pressure of a deadline for *Dick Tracy* loomed over him each week, and it was catching up with him. When you consider that a comic strip appears 365 days a year in the newspaper, it's amazing to think of the thousands of panels of artwork a cartoonist creates over the years. Yet for Dad, it was something he was born to do, a love that ran deep.

Was it time to retire? That was a big decision. Retiring meant relinquishing his strip to the *Chicago Tribune*, who had owned the *Dick Tracy* copyright since its inception in 1931. The *Chicago Tribune* had always owned the copyright to its comic strips—*Gasoline Alley*, *Little Orphan Annie*, *Terry and the Pirates*, *Harold Teen*, *Brenda Starr*, *Smiling Jack*, *Winnie Winkle*, and *Smitty*, to name a few.

Dad finally made the heart-rending decision. He would retire by the end of the year. He set up talks with the *Chicago Tribune* people, who gave him a choice of a lifetime retirement agreement or the *Dick Tracy* copyright. Knowing that the *Dick Tracy* copyright would not ensure financial security, Dad chose the lifetime retirement agreement. That agreement would provide financial security for Mother and Dad. His last strip, a Sunday page, appeared in the newspaper on December 25, 1977, when he was seventy-seven years of age.

(It wasn't until after Dad's death that I came across his lifetime retirement agreement with the *Chicago Tribune* signed September 6, 1977. That dear, proud Dad of mine never told me that the *Chicago Tribune* had asked him to retire.)

The Pains of Retirement

The *Chicago Tribune* hired two people to take over the *Dick Tracy* strip. Rick Fletcher, Dad's assistant, would continue on as the artist for the strip and Max Collins would be hired as the writer.

Thinking back over the impossible situations that he put Tracy in over the years, never knowing how he would get him out of dire situations, Dad wondered if others would give his strip the thought he had given it. The transition was painful. Some very difficult days lay ahead, and there wasn't anything any of us could do. When the advance copies of the black and white Sunday pages, the proofs, arrived in the mail each week, Dad found he couldn't open the manila envelopes that contained them. He didn't want to. It was almost like tearing his heart out to know someone else had taken over a creation that had been his life's effort.

It should have been a time to rest and enjoy life, but it wasn't. Not for such a driven man. Fortunately, the drawing board still beckoned to him. That was a blessing. Never a day passed that Dad didn't sit down at his board to keep his hand and mind agile by translating new ideas into cartoon form — this time without the pressure. One of these ideas grew out of his own experience. It was called *Check-Out-Chickie,* a fresh and delightful strip filled with Dad's natural humor and inspired by the days he would go to the grocery store for Mother. Because he never seemed to know where anything was, the clerks just clamored to help him. He was so charming and appreciative of their help and would laugh at himself for his awkwardness in the art of grocery shopping. He was always greeted with, "Hello, Mr. Gould. What could we help you find today?"

Then Dad accepted the position of honorary chairman of the campaign for the Woodstock Community Hospital. Using a drawing of Tracy, he emphasized the importance of reaching the hospital's campaign goal to raise the money for their continued expansion. He and Mother contributed to this campaign as well as to the Easter Seals for McHenry County, which was one of their favorite organizations. They contributed to Northwestern University every year through the John Evans Club, an alumni association. As a member of the Lake Zurich Golf Club in Lake Zurich, Illinois, since 1960, Dad designed notices about the coming programs each month and caricatured each new club president. He kept himself busy.

A Feeling of Still Belonging

Dad retained his office at the Tribune Tower, and he made it a point to take the train into the city every Monday, just as he had done for years. Taking a cab from the Chicago Northwestern Railroad Station in Chicago to the Tribune Tower, he would enter the lobby feeling exhilarated, and would exchange casual remarks with the guards and elevator operator, who had all grown to know him over the years. On the twenty-second floor, he transferred to a smaller elevator taking him to the twenty-sixth. There in the small area of the hallway (because this was in the tower of the building), he opened his office door marked "Chester Gould." The office was long and curved, conforming to the shape of the tower, with floor-to-ceiling French doors tucked between heavy Gothic architectural turrets. The doors opened to a small balcony overlooking the Michigan Avenue Bridge to the south, a beautiful sight.

Seeing everything as he had left it — his drawing boards, the taborets (where inks, pens, pencils and art gum erasers are kept), the large worktable and chairs, all gave him a feeling of comfort, almost as if nothing had changed. Even mail and business newspapers were still stacked on his large worktable, just as they had always been every Monday for years.

Sitting down at his drawing board each Monday, he would begin by going through his mail. He still had fan letters to open. Then he would make a few phone calls or thumb through his newspapers. Often he held interviews, something he could never do without time constraints before retirement. In fact, two FBI men came one Monday to interview him and compliment him on his years of faithful representation of law enforcement in his strip. Occasions like this were a terrific boost for Dad, and often times ended over lunch at the Tavern Club (the club that Dad had been so impressed with in 1923, when his boss at the *Evening American* took him there for lunch, and with which he was still impressed).

Otherwise, lunching weekly with a friend or business associate kept Dad up to date with what was going on. Dick Locher, who had assisted Dad on his strip for several years in the

In 1978, the Tavern Club, Chicago, Illinois, had a one-man show honoring Dad and *Dick Tracy*. As you stepped off the elevator, Tracy's image and message greeted you.

Tavern Club exhibit, 1978. Mother and Dad proudly pose.

late 1950s, went on to become an editorial cartoonist for the *Chicago Tribune* and received the Pulitzer Prize for his editorial cartoons. He was a close friend and one of Dad's favorite lunch partners. They had much in common and were both optimists.

One Monday in 1980, Dad's trip into Chicago would be different. Even at eighty years of age, he had made it a routine to walk from the Tribune Tower to the Chicago Northwestern Railroad Station when heading for home. It was well over a mile, he enjoyed the walk. This particular Monday, Dad left the building and crossed Michigan Avenue just opposite the Tribune entrance, just as he had done hundreds of times. Walking over the Michigan Avenue Bridge, he waited at Wacker Drive for the "walk" light to signal his safe crossing, while a cab waited to turn right on a red light. As the "walk" light came on, the driver, not seeing Dad, turned right and hit him. Dad fell to the street. Paramedics rushed him to the Northwestern Memorial Hospital. X-rays were taken and by some miracle, Dad hadn't broken any bones. As he began to come out of the sedation, Dad mumbled to the doctor, "I have to get home. Edna expects me on that 3:30 train." The second miracle was that Dr. Fischer, a friend who lived out near us, was tending Dad, and though he felt Dad should spend the night for observation, he knew he wouldn't. Having called Mother and broken the news to her as gently as he could, Dr. Fischer took Dad home. Mother called me the minute she knew what happened. By the time I arrived at the house, Dr. Fischer was gone and Dad lay on the couch in the studio, still somewhat groggy. When I saw Mother, I held her close, trying to hide my tears while

The whole family from left to right: My son, Tracy; Mother and Dad; my daughter, Sue; my husband, Dick; and me. At the Tavern Club 1978.

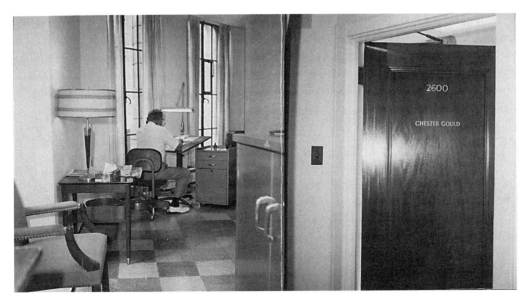

After his retirement, Dad retained this office on the 26th floor of the Tribune Tower.

imagining the anguish she must have gone through waiting at home alone. Then I fell down on my knees and hugged Dad, letting the tears that I had held back roll freely down my face. Before long, with some help, Dad sat up as the grogginess wore off. He seemed more like himself, especially when he said with a bit of a nonchalant chuckle, "They told me at the hospital that I was hit by a cab. I don't remember a thing." I could only think how thankful we were that he was all right.

The next day, the owner of the cab company called, extending his apologies for the accident and inquiring as to whether Dad was going to instigate a lawsuit.

"I want you to do one thing for me," said Dad.

"What is that?" asked the cab company owner nervously.

"All I want you to do is make a contribution [and Dad told him the amount] to the Salvation Army in my name. That's all."

The owner of the cab company must have been relieved and thankful. As for Dad, his right shoulder was never the same. He wouldn't see a doctor about it and lived the rest of his life probably with a torn rotator cuff, which caused some pain and restriction.

Forever Optimistic Last Years

Dad continued to go into Chicago to his office for almost another year. Then, due to a growing hearing loss, he decided to cancel his office rental space in the Tribune Tower. He had grown to accept his retirement. He was eighty-one years old.

Though his hearing disability made it difficult for him, he still accepted a few dinner speaking engagements that were related to law enforcement. He could still capture an audience's attention with his humor, talking about his strip, his beliefs in law enforcement, and his childhood that led him from Pawnee, Oklahoma to Chicago.

I can remember his making light of changing the battery in his hearing aid, as it usually whistled while putting it back in his ear. With a chuckle he would say, "I'm getting Cincinnati." He never lost his sense of humor.

Around 1983, Dad felt as if he was sometimes having trouble breathing, not always, but enough to cause him to want to see a doctor. Mother and I were alarmed when we heard this, because he never wanted to go to the doctor. He already had a pacemaker. After a thorough exam Dr. Simpson told Dad that he had the beginning of congestive heart failure. He recommended that Dad rent a portable oxygen tank to use at home when he felt the need of it, and suggested that he might, in the future, feel more comfortable having a nurse at home.

It was a great shock to the whole family to learn what was causing his discomfort. All I could think was, how could this happen to one who loved life as much as my father, one who was always in control of his life? It just couldn't be. But it was.

Dad's attitude was remarkable. He had always had that God-given strength within him. Now it seemed to form an aura around him. We could all feel it, and it made us stronger as the days and months passed.

That same year, I asked Dad if he would sit with me and talk about his childhood, his life growing up, his memories and his beliefs. We would talk each day just as long as he felt comfortable. Those talks provided an important framework for this book. At the end of our final session, I asked Dad, who was then eighty-three years of age, some rather profound questions, which I have included here.

How did you learn to stand on your own two feet?
Well, if somebody's trying to knock you down, you stand up. I never was a guy to run away from anything.
How do you overcome your fears?
Fear of what? I had no fear. That you take and hide under the bed. If you're going into a new phase of your life you never go in with fear. You go in with the idea that you can't miss.
What do you think is the best way for us to conduct our lives?
Well, basically, you must have an ingrained religious view, which implies utter honesty, as well as perseverance. Treating your friends and neighbors as you would want them to treat you. That's the Golden Rule, I believe. Those values to me are just as important and new as they were when they were recorded in the Bible.
If you were to give advice to me or my children today or even to the children to come in our family in the future generations, what would it be?
That has many classifications of advice, but if it's the case of a young man or girl wanting to go out on her own and be self-supporting and get a job, well, the idea is never be disappointed. Nothing is important enough that you have to give up your career or your point of view. Just keep trying. That's an old, old bit of advice, but it will be new a hundred or a thousand years from now.

By 1984 and 1985, I was driving to Woodstock three times a week, leaving Geneva early in the morning. It was almost an hour's drive, but I knew those were precious times for me, and I didn't know how long they might last. Dad was able to sit up in a wheelchair for several hours at a time, but then he welcomed the comfort of his hospital bed with the oxygen to help his breathing.

While I was there, I would go into the post office for the mail, have Dad look over everything, get some instructions from him, pay the bills and so forth. Then Mother and I would go into Woodstock and grocery shop. Each Sunday, my family and I drove together to Mother and Dad's. I brought the Sunday noon meal. How well I remember those unforgettable days gathered around Dad's hospital bed with Mother sitting right next to him. We laughed as we related some of the funny, newsy happenings that were going on. It was a happy time for everyone, especially seeing Dad laughing and chiming in. At mealtime, the nurse helped him into his wheelchair and we all went into the dining room and enjoyed our Sunday meal.

Top: Dad sitting at the dining room table autographing a book for a friend. We took this picture without his wheelchair or oxygen tank in sight. This was in November 1984, six months before Dad died. *Bottom*: Dad, Mom and me with Cissygirl, one of their beloved schnauzers.

Shortly before Dad passed on, our daughter, Sue, shared some happy news. "Baba, you and Gram are going to have a great-grandchild," she said proudly. Sue always remembered what "Baba" said when his brother Ray died in 1974. "Just remember, life goes on. We live for the living." I knew just what Sue was thinking. We were going to lose a precious life in our family — a father, a husband, a grandfather, who had touched each of us so deeply with his caring love. A new blessed baby would soon enter our lives to carry on. It was very important that Sue's grandfather know about this new life.

In the weeks to come, Dad's health declined rapidly. Daily, Mother sat next to him, and, holding hands, they would say the Twenty-Third Psalm together. If Dad couldn't finish it due to lack of oxygen, she would finish the prayer. It was a beautiful sight to see Mother's strength and such devotion that had spanned fifty-eight years.

Dad needed the oxygen more and more. I remember one day when I was there, the phone rang and it was for Dad. He wanted to know who it was. I told him. He signaled "just a minute" from his bed. The nurse helped him sit up on the side of the bed as I brought the phone over to him. Taking a deep breath, he assumed an upbeat manner and said, "Hello, Bill." Then, undoubtedly responding to Bill's inquiry as to how he felt, he took another deep breath and said, "I just have the flu." I couldn't believe my ears. Then I thought about Dad's pride. Of course, he would say something like that.

On May 22–23, 1985, the McHenry County Crime Stoppers was going to host the Mid-America Crime Stoppers Conference. Months before, they had asked Dad to be their honorary chairman. He was honored and accepted. But now, things were different. When I told them a few weeks before the conference that Dad was very ill, they asked to come to the house just to get a few words from him to take back to the conference.

When they arrived, Dad was sitting in his wheelchair. He was thin and weak, but like a miracle, he rose to the occasion. He listened to their remarkable accomplishments with pride, then mustered up enough energy to say, "I want you to ... know that the ... Crime Stoppers is really important ... in my life. ... because ... it's the best ... living thing ... from *Dick Tracy*. Thank you ... for the honor of ... being part of ... this conference."

Knowing his time on earth was growing short, Dad asked his nurse if she would take him around to the windows of his home. He took his time studying the view from each window, taking in the beauty of the country he so loved for one last time. Two days later, that dear father of mine who could climb any mountain, ford any stream, passed on peacefully, knowing how much his dear family loved him. On May 11, 1985, we said goodbye.

Dad was laid to rest on May 14, 1985, in the Oaklawn Cemetery in Woodstock. Mother joined him nine years later on March 27, 1993.

Chester Gould's signature

12

Honoring Chester Gould's Legacy

About a year after Dad's death in 1985, I received a phone call from the mayor of Woodstock. He spoke about how much Dad had meant to Woodstock, not only as a cartoonist, but as a man who cared about his community. "Can we do something to honor Chester Gould, with maybe a plaque, a statue or a library?" he asked.

This was a complete surprise to me. I hardly knew the mayor, having only met him at an Easter Seals dinner honoring Dad in 1979. And I knew very few Woodstock people after being away from Woodstock for so many years. Before the mayor continued, I said to him that I hoped he would understand when I said this was too soon for me to think about a memorial for my father. It was as if I had built a high, protective wall around Dad since his death. I wanted to keep the world out. Right now his precious memory was just mine. Mayor Shoemaker seemed to understand and thanked me, saying he would like to call again in a year if that was all right. "Of course," I said, and thanked him.

After Dad's death, I felt compelled to open his black trunk that had stood off in a dark corner of the basement, ignored for years. Dad said it just contained "stuff" from years ago. Having set up a long table, I pulled the trunk out from its dark corner into the open. My heart was beating faster than usual as I unlocked the two latches that had safely held the box's contents all of these years and lifted the top, laying it back carefully. I could see Dad had saved so much from the past. Nothing had been disturbed since he had placed it in there.

I felt emotion and tears build up as I began to go through his treasured memorabilia — — these were some of the most heartrending and beautiful moments I can ever remember. I felt so close to Dad. During those hours, I pictured him as a young boy winning his first drawing contest; then I could almost see him in college in Oklahoma. Then coming to Chicago full of ambition — there were many rejection letters, and so much rejected artwork, over ten years' worth, showing how he tried to get the attention of the *Chicago Tribune*. There were many newspapers and the newspaper clippings of his own work as it appeared in Oklahoma as well as in Chicago newspapers before *Dick Tracy*. It was all here. I was looking at a remarkable history of a man coming from a humble beginning in Oklahoma and working his way to the top, attaining his childhood dream in spite of rejection after rejection. He just never gave up. It was sheer determination and belief in himself that sustained him through those ten years.

I was overwhelmed at seeing all of this. Looking up from the basement toward Dad's studio, I saw the telegram that hung on the wall next to his first *Dick Tracy* Sunday page dated October 11, 1931. I knew the telegram by heart: "Believe Plain Clothes Tracy has possibilities. Would like to see you when I go to Chicago. Please call *Tribune* office Monday about noon for an appointment. J.M. Patterson." The contents within this trunk laid the groundwork for that telegram. After Dad received it, he closed the trunk. A new day had dawned. Seeing these ten years of work laid out before me, all the work that Dad had put forth throughout those years, touched me deeply. That telegram would be the beginning of a legacy that Dad would create in the years to come.

When Mayor Shoemaker called a year later, he again spoke about a memorial for Dad. This time, he revealed that Woodstock was already thinking about a Chester Gould Memorial Library.

"A library?" I said. There was a hesitation on both our parts. "What about a small museum?" I said, thinking about all the visual insight I had gained since our first conversation. Another hesitation — then, "Yes, a small museum." We almost said it together.

"How do you start a museum?" I asked. There was another hesitation as we thought about it. "Well," I said, "I could put together a pictorial display with my dad's early Oklahoma beginning, and go from there with text and comic strip rejection examples, and his first *Dick Tracy* strips to start with. There is some great correspondence and photographs, depending on the space. I also have Dad's original drawing board and taboret that he bought when he first arrived in Chicago in 1921, the same drawing board that he created *Dick Tracy* on and used throughout his life."

By the time we finished talking, Mayor Shoemaker was thrilled with the idea, but he must have also been in turmoil because he supported Woodstock's memorial library idea that the community had been planning. He said, "I will get back to you soon. A museum sounds like a wonderful idea." And we said goodbye.

The next time Mayor Shoemaker contacted me, he had met with Don Peasley, a well known Woodstock writer and journalist, who had been a strong advocate in establishing a memorial for Chester Gould. He was enthusiastic about the museum. Then the mayor met with Cav Peterson's committee. When he called me, his voice was upbeat. "Yes, they would certainly be interested in a small museum." He went on to say that Cav and her committee had already created an idea for a festival that they had been planning to kick off for the summer of 1989. They were going to call it "Dick Tracy Days." Cav undoubtedly was a woman full of ideas.

By the summer of 1989, Cav and her committee, with the help of many people in the community, put on their first Dick Tracy Days celebration, held during the third week in June. Starting on a Wednesday night with an old fashioned ice cream social and band concert in the park square, it branched out into other festivities during the week, and ended with a parade on Sunday afternoon. The response was enthusiastic.

That same year in Hollywood, Warren Beatty was making what he and Disney were calling a blockbuster *Dick Tracy* movie. Warren Beatty was starring as Dick Tracy, and they were pulling out all the stops to make it an Oscar winner. It would premiere at Disney World in Orlando in 1990. Cav Peterson had some ideas "up her sleeve" for Woodstock.

Over the winter of 1990 Cav and her committee not only organized the second Dick Tracy Days, but a special committee within this group organized to draw up the bylaws and get the necessary legal work in founding the Chester Gould–*Dick Tracy* Museum Foundation. The costs were gratefully donated by one of the original founders of the museum. Meanwhile, Cav and her group were looking for a place to locate the museum, preferably somewhere on the square. Beverly and Cliff Ganchow had purchased the old McHenry County courthouse on the town square when the county found it necessary to rebuild elsewhere to enlarge their facilities. The Ganchows turned this building into a wonderful arts center. That's where a small room was found for the museum, in the old courthouse on the square.

Cav and her committee continued forging ahead. She knew they needed a good fundraiser. Her brother, who was in the movie industry, was able to direct her toward the right people to hear her story about Woodstock, Chester Gould, Dick Tracy Days and the founding of the Chester Gould–*Dick Tracy* Museum Foundation. What a fund raiser it would be to have the *Dick Tracy* premiere on the last day of Dick Tracy Days! It was a shot in the dark, but she had to try.

Cav knew that Orlando's (Hollywood style) premiere was the night of June 14, Monday night. She wanted the movie for June 13, on Sunday night. After what seemed like months of waiting for a response from her contact, Cav finally received an answer. Her long wait had paid off. Woodstock would get the *Dick Tracy* movie on June 13! Warren Beatty and Disney had a big heart.

In a June 6, 1990, issue of the *Woodstock Independent* newspaper, reporter Don Peasley listed the plans building up to the premiere:

*"Voice of America" plans to broadcast the June 6 band concert to servicemen around the world.

Life magazine plans to attend the preview concentrating on the angle of Chet Gould's hometown and how Woodstock is honoring this artistic genius.

*Fox TV 32 in Chicago has told Mayor Shoemaker the station wants to telecast the arrival of dignitaries and the accompanying preview festivities.

*Channels 2 and 5, and possibly Channel 9, have indicated plans to "do something" during the week. Live coverage is anticipated and Chief of Police Herb Pitzman is setting up crowd and traffic control as he awaits last-minute requests for newspaper, radio and TV invasion.

*Shel Dorf is coming from San Diego to represent Disney Productions. He's a longtime Dick Tracy collector and Chet Gould fan.

*Max Collins and Dick Locher, current artists on the strip, will be here for the preview and reception.

*Larry Doucet is coming from his home at Yorktown Heights, N.Y. He's considered a collector extraordinaire of Tracy souvenirs, strips and memorabilia.

*John Iltis, Disney Midwest distributor, says, "This event is just the kind *People* magazine wants."

*Leslie McLeer reports both Crime Stoppers breakfasts for youngsters are booked solid.

*Joyce Gentile says all seats for the Mystery Dinner at the Old Court House Inn have been reserved.

*Chamber Executive Director Jean Saidler late Friday reports burgeoning interest in the window display contest sponsored by the Chamber of Commerce. The theme: "Dick Tracy and Woodstock" or something related to Chester Gould.

*Tom Loizzo reports nearly 100 units for the parade on Sunday, June 10, including the Chicago Vanguards, one of the nation's leading drum and bugle corps."

Not mentioned was the colorful *Dick Tracy* shoot-out performed by professional actors, which the TV people loved filming.

Cav had lit a fire under the town of Woodstock. She planned to dress up during Dick Tracy Days in her Keystone Cop uniform and sell Dick Tracy T-shirts and other Dick Tracy items around town to help the fund raiser for the coming celebration. The Woodstock movie theater was going to show free movies on Saturday for children, and

McDonald's was donating 300 Egg McMuffins for the children's breakfast before the movie. The VFW was donating the use of their space for the breakfast. The community was really pulling together.

The night of the premiere in Woodstock, the marquee on the Woodstock Movie theater, which had been freshly painted, was all lit up announcing "Dick Tracy is on his way." Floodlights were crossing each other in the sky. It was Main Street, Woodstock, Illinois, but it looked like Hollywood. All the excitement was there. People were everywhere. The television news media seemed to have been everywhere too, but most obviously during the premiere of the movie. This was a unique situation and even the news media felt important. How often had a community had the privilege of showing a premiere just to help benefit a man and a comic strip character? Cav and the Woodstock community had made this an unforgettable Dick Tracy Days, and certainly a most memorable fund raiser. That night Woodstock found itself on many Chicago television news channels.

The Chester Gould–Dick Tracy Museum

With the ground work having been laid, the next step was to develop the museum. From the black trunk, I chose a few of Dad's rejected comic strip ideas and several letters to represent the sixty different rejected pieces that he had tried to sell J.M. Patterson from 1921 to 1931. These were monumental years for him. The 1931 telegram was the key to those ten years and opened the door to the *Dick Tracy* comic strip, so I put the telegram with the first ten episodes of the *Dick Tracy* strip that appeared in the newspaper in 1931.

With text and photographs, I was ready to set up the display in the museum. Though small, it would touch on Oklahoma, Chicago, Wilmette, and Woodstock. With the drawing board, chair, and artist's floor lamp, the small museum would look full and very interesting. One large 3' × 5' photograph of Chester Gould sitting at his drawing board would hang on the wall facing the door to welcome visitors.

The following year, 1991, Mayor Shoemaker picked up Dad's drawing board, his taboret, chair, and floor lamp from my home. They were put in place in what would soon be the Chester Gould–Dick Tracy Museum in the Arts Center. It was a cheerful room facing the street, measuring only about 12' by 18'—all we could afford to begin with. The displays I had brought were in place. The room looked cozy but pretty impressive, chock full of illustrations, photographs and text. The drawing board is what stood out in that little room.

Jim Pearson, the high school art teacher, had even cut out a wonderful life-size plywood free-standing figure of Dick Tracy and Junior, which he also beautifully painted. Standing just inside the door with his arm outstretched as if welcoming visitors, this plywood figure of Tracy in his yellow trench coat and fedora looked dazzling, along with Junior next to him. There was even a decal on the glass door denoting that this was the Dick Tracy Museum. Was this really happening?

Cav Peterson and her committee had worked so very hard behind the scenes since 1987, seeing that a memorial for Chester Gould became a reality. I only hoped that on June 12, 1991, when the ribbon cutting ceremony opened the door to The Chester Gould–Dick Tracy Museum, that the City of Woodstock and the Woodstock citizens weren't disappointed that it wasn't a Chester Gould Memorial Library. I prayed they would look on it as an asset to their community. Only time would tell.

An exciting day for the Chester Gould–Dick Tracy Museum: the ribbon cutting ceremony in 1991. From left to right: First museum president and co-founder Cav Peterson, Dick Tracy artist Dick Locher, Beverly Fletcher (wife of the late *Dick Tracy* artist Rick Fletcher), me, *Dick Tracy* writer Max Allan Collins, Woodstock *Independent* editor Cheryl Wormley, avid *Dick Tracy* fan and Woodstock citizen Jeff Kersten, and Mayor James Shoemaker.

The Spokes in the Wheel

To bring the museum to life was an enormous job. All the technicalities one faces, all the behind the scenes problems that one does not know about until faced with them, all the unexpected things that arise, not to mention the manpower needed, the hours and imagination it takes to raise money, the talent put forth, the means to achieve this—well, it is just overwhelming, and yet, so very amazing to see what we as human beings accomplished in founding the Chester Gould–Dick Tracy Museum in 1991. For this reason I want to list the original committee and supporters who made this possible: Mayor Shoemaker, Cav Peterson, Don Peasley, Police Chief Joe Marvin, Tom and Linda Loizzo, Farlin and Claris Caufield, Joyce and Bob Gentile, Beverly Fletcher, Virginia Peschke, Scott Connell, Barbara Britt, John and Cathy Cole, Mary and Dave Roberts, Tom Menge, George Pete Corson, Ross Fletcher, Cathy Werrbach, Herb Pitzman and Leslie McLeer. Other vital participants were Peter Gill, Diane Branstram, John Trione, Doug Wilbrandt, Jean Saidler, Greg and Deb Beglinger, Jack Darby, Don Puzo, and Jim and Lorna Fleming. They are all important and I am truly sorry if I missed any others.

Board Members at Work

We found the museum was a work in progress and its evolution was gradual, for there was so much to learn. Slowly, with the help of some professional board members, an important mission statement was established, which read:

The Chester Gould-Dick Tracy Museum, a not-for-profit organization, is established to display, promote and honor the work, achievements and life of Chester Gould, creator of the Dick Tracy *comic strip and character. The Museum perpetuates the legacy of* Dick Tracy *and the heritage of the comic strip for this and future generations.*

In the year 2000, the board made an addition to the mission statement, whose last sentence now reads:

The museum perpetuates the legacy of Dick Tracy *and the heritage of the comic strip, and Crime Stoppers, through the development of the "Crime Stoppers Youth Program," developed in 2000.*

We knew we had to develop fundraisers to sustain the museum and continue our work. This proved, and will continue to prove, to be our biggest challenge. We learned that soliciting grants for operating funds for a museum is extremely difficult, if not impossible. Through the years we were able to obtain grants for small projects and even received several museum awards, but none of these helped pay for the day-to-day operation of the museum. One of the grants we did receive enabled us to open the Crime Stoppers Club Room, a hands-on room filled with exhibits for young people.

Everything I contributed to the growth of the museum was done out of love and pride for my father and his accomplishments. Even though the *Chicago Tribune* has owned the Dick Tracy copyright since its inception, it has nothing to do with the museum — including support.

Golf outings and other fund raisers, including membership drives, have been a great help, but like every organization, we always need more to make ends meet, so the Chester Gould family has contributed much to keep the museum doors open since it was founded in 1991.

As the museum grew, it moved into larger quarters within the old courthouse. Displays took on a wider scope as Chester Gould's life and his *Dick Tracy* comic strip could be further developed. Much was added around the perimeter of the room showing the growth of *Dick Tracy* in various displays.

These displays took hours of time and were a labor of love. I do not have many original strips to work from, at least the ones I seem to need; most of them had been given away before Dad died and the remainder were willed to the Museum of Cartoon Art. Lacking originals, I needed to copy from Dad's library of bound newsprint books that date back to 1931. One of our displays, for example, illustrated the first invention that came out of *Dick Tracy*, the 2-Way Wrist Radio in 1946. Copying the newsprint from that year, I found that because of its age, the solid blacks and some of the whites reproduced very poorly. I had to take a sable paint brush and India ink and ink in the solid blacks; then I had to brush white acrylic paint where the white areas had become spotty from age. It was a time consuming job, but I loved going over what Dad had drawn. The next step was to enlarge each strip to its display size, trim it and set it aside for dry mounting.

Sometimes it took several *Dick Tracy* strips to describe an invention idea in the story. I would arrange these along with a newspaper article referring to the story inventions, then text concerning its current application, such as the teleguard camera that later became the surveillance camera, the telephone number pick-up that became caller ID, and so forth. I would lay it all out on the living room floor on a sheet of black foam core. When it was arranged to my liking, I would take a close-up Polaroid photo of the arrangement. Then, being careful to pick up the artwork and text in the position in which it was laid, I would carefully paper clip it together between a folded sheet of paper with the Polaroid picture. All that was left was to have it dry mounted on black foam core. I'll admit, it was a rather homespun way

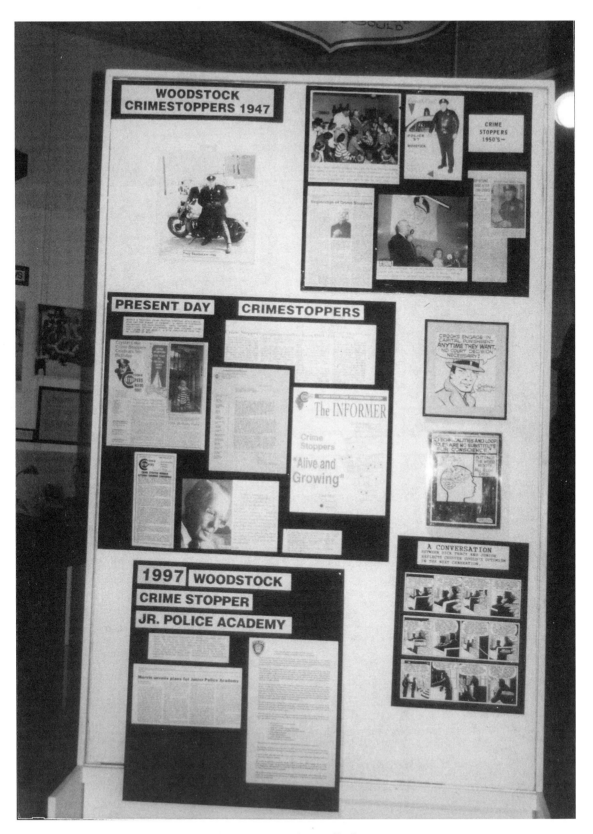

Crime Stoppers History display.

Top: An early display in the Chester Gould–Dick Tracy museum. *Bottom*: Jean Gould O'Connell (Greenbrier Photography)

of accomplishing the end result, but it worked. As I was doing all of this, I marveled at Dad's remarkable imagination. Even articles that came out in the newspapers attested to it.

The new displays provided more extensive photographs of Dad's childhood and youth in Pawnee, Oklahoma; more examples of his rejection ideas and rejection letters; police technology; the beginning of the Crime Stoppers; the *Crimestoppers Textbook* tips, *Dick Tracy* inventions; police recognition; government recognition; celebrity recognition; community service; Chester Gould at home; and games and toys of the past and from the *Dick Tracy* movie. There is also a *Dick Tracy* gift shop.

It has never fails to amaze our museum board how many visitors come from everywhere in the United States and many different parts of the world. It seems that the museum and its mission to promote and perpetuate the work of my father is accomplishing what it set out to do. At the time of this writing, the museum's mission continues.

In recent years, a new board member created a web site for the museum. We are most grateful to announce to the world that you can now find us at www.chestergould.org.

13

Afterwords

How did three children discover Dick Tracy? Well, of course, they are grown now, but their accounts are delightful to read. They encompass many memories of the past, and as adults, their professional comments on Gould's work and opinions of Gould as a writer and cartoonist are quite remarkable. These three people were true fans and enthusiasts of the *Dick Tracy* comic strip. Through their correspondence over many years, they each became friends with Gould and had a chance to spend some time with him at his home.

Shel Dorf

Sheldon, better known as "Shel," and *Dick Tracy* both got their start in Detroit, Michigan: Tracy on October 4, 1931, and Shel on July 5, 1933. Shel grew up an avid comic strip fan, starting to collect newspaper cuttings of *Dick Tracy* in 1944 with the episode of the Brow. These cuttings he put in a scrap book, thus beginning a hobby that lasted over 60 years.

Showing artistic talent, Shel took commercial art at Call Technical High School and the School of the Chicago Art Institute (Fine Art). His hobby of comics collecting was enriched when he met other local collectors and formed one of the country's first comic conventions, the Detroit Triple Fan Fair, in 1965. Over the years, he corresponded with Chester Gould and Milton Caniff, his two favorite comic strip creators. Dad always responded to Shel's letters of praise with handwritten letters of thanks, and over the years Shel became a very good friend of our family.

After a brief stint in New York, Shel followed his family to San Diego, California. Shortly after arriving, he met a group of young comic book collectors in 1970 and created the now world famous San Diego Comic-Con.

Another cartoonist friendship blossomed when Milton Caniff (*Terry and the Pirates, Steve Canyon*) moved to Palm Springs in 1970. Caniff's longtime lettering man took ill and in 1974, Shel took on the job of lettering *Steve Canyon* until 1988 when Mr. Caniff died and the strip ended. Dad respected Mr. Caniff and was very proud that Shel had worked for him.

Shel's longtime interest in the comic strip field resulted in his interviewing many cartoonists. These think-pieces appeared in publications such as *Cartoonist Profiles, Comic*

Buyers Guide, Comic Interview, Amazing Heroes, The Menomonee Falls Gazette, and *Comic Book Marketplace.*

In 1984, Shel joined forces with a San Diego publisher to produce a long series of *Dick Tracy* comic book reprints in black and white. Shel was still cutting and pasting Tracy stories, but this time on a professional level. Our family helped him get the finest reproduction possible, along with family photos. Milton Caniff had drawn a beautiful portrait of Dad for one of the issues. Shel reproduced some of those *Dick Tracy* strips, first as a monthly comic book, then as a weekly. It sold very well. Although it was a small print run — just 5,000 copies, compared to a 2,000,000 print run for Spiderman — Shel was very proud that he at last had a chance to reproduce *Dick Tracy* in comic books. *Dick Tracy* had a small audience but a loyal one. To this day Shel is proud of those books. He published ninety-nine issues of the comic book and twenty-four graphic novels — little square-bound, high quality books that sold for about $6 each (the comic books sold for about $2). Anyway, it was full circle. Shel was able to bring Tracy out to another generation.

This line of Tracy comics was used as reference for Warren Beatty's *Dick Tracy* movie in 1989. Warren eventually invited Shel and our family to Hollywood to watch the filming. Shel, in turn, represented Disney at the Woodstock premier of the movie.

A lifetime of exciting events was the result of a day in 1944 when a Sunday page of *Dick Tracy* attracted Shel's attention, an experience Shel describes here:

I remember the drug store at the corner of my neighborhood had the national edition of the *New York News,* which was printed a week ahead of time, and *Dick Tracy* was always on the

Taken in the makeup trailer on the Touchstone Pictures set of Warren Beatty's 1990 *Dick Tracy* movie. From left to right: Ed O'Ross (as "Itchy"), Shel Dorf, and William Forsythe (as "Flattop").

front page. I was 11 years old when I first saw Dick Tracy and I remember the page exactly. It was where the Brow was escaping Tracy. He had just thrown a lightning rod into Tracy's shoulder up in the attic and he slid down the side of the barn and made his escape in a hail of bullets, with drops of blood coming down the sides of his horrible face. That Sunday page grabbed me like nothing else did. You can imagine a child, 11 years old, and the impact it must have had. At that point I became interested in *Dick Tracy*.

We didn't take the *Detroit Free Press* that carried the strip, but our next door neighbor did. They would put out their old newspapers on the back porch and I would rifle them for the comic section. I started clipping out *Dick Tracy*. When my stack became too big, I went to the dime store and bought a blank scrap book (one of many) and glue and started a project that would last over sixty years.

One of the things that made me kind of an oddball as a child in my own family was that they could not understand why I was clipping out comic strips, putting them in scrap books, and saving them instead of being outside playing baseball or doing other things that children do. But here I was, sitting at the bridge table clipping out comic strips, keeping these scrap books. Nobody had heard of such a thing. They'd heard of saving comic books but not keeping scrap books of strips. So I guess I was just ahead of our time. Economically, it was cheaper than buying comics. A comic book was ten cents, but even at that, we were just

coming out of the Depression and I think my whole weekly allowance was twenty-five cents. Buying the *New York Sunday News* national edition was ten cents and you'd get a beautiful rotogravure section with a movie star's picture on the front, and then the wonderful comic section, which I clipped. Later on I ran into dealers and other comic fans at used book stores on Saturdays, sometimes. Most of them collected comic books. A few of them clipped out strips as well, and of course years later, I discovered there were actual dealers selling old newspaper comics in mail-order businesses. I filled in some of my gaps by buying strips from some of these people. As I grew older, I became a *Dick Tracy* historian because I used to love to talk about Gould and his work. Eventually I created a slide show that I showed before different groups including the Chicago Comic Convention.

Getting back to my childhood, I became so involved with Chester Gould's story telling because he had so many cliff hangers. You could never tell what was going to happen in the strip. It took me about two years to convince my dad to subscribe to the *Detroit Free Press*. We

Sheldon Lee Dorf.   took the evening paper, and I would wait on the porch knowing when the newsboy would turn the corner. Then I'd run up to the corner to get the paper. I couldn't wait to see what happened in *Dick Tracy*.

Shel's classmates and friends read *Dick Tracy*, but that's as far as it went. They had other interests, other hobbies. But for Shel, passion for the *Dick Tracy* strip ran deep. He studied Chester Gould's two-dimensional artwork, especially his use of blacks and whites— how they lent direction, leading the reader from one panel to the next into the exciting story.

As I filled my scrap books, I knew I had to write the artist and tell him how much I loved his work. Coming home from school, which I did not like at all, and rereading my Tracy scrap books where I submerged myself in Dick Tracy, was the highlight of my school week. Actually, in my young life, those scrap books and the Saturday afternoon movies were the two highlights in my week.

I was absolutely passionate about finding out what Tracy stories came before 1944. I found the strip had actually started in 1931 and, much to my surprise, in the *Detroit Mirror* [Shel's hometown paper, owned by the *Tribune*]. Well, I'd go to the library and ask to see the micro-film, and here's this kid tying up the micro-film machine just to read the comics, and more than once the librarian came over to me and said, "Oh, you can't occupy the machine just to read the funnies. This is a serious library." Anytime from then on, I would feel the librarian approach and would quickly turn the crank and hit the editorial page or something like that, and pretend I was doing research. But I was there to read the ten years of Tracy that I had missed.

I found moral lessons; I think it helped without my knowing it. It made me become a better person, a better citizen. Stressing public service, good character, and starting the Crime Stoppers— these elements came out of *Dick Tracy*. Anyone going back and reading Chester's stuff sees an underlying love of family, his relationship with Junior for instance, where Tracy took an orphan who was being led astray by a criminal and adopted him. All these elements influenced my life in a moral way. I don't think I ever told Chester that.

During World War II we had newspaper drives at our schools. Kids were also very patriotic about buying war stamps. For ten cents I would buy a little war bond stamp and keep it in a book until it was filled, then turn it in and get a war bond. Newspapers were used somehow in the war effort, so school children would take their wagons and go from door to door on the weekends. On Mondays, we'd bring in bundles of newspapers that we had collected. I've got to be honest: When I found that some people had kept their newspapers for years and found a bonanza like that, I'd bring them home and go through each copy and tear out the dailies and the Sundays, then take the rest of the papers back to school on Monday. To this day, some of those strips are in my *Dick Tracy* scrap books which I donated to the Chester Gould–Dick Tracy Museum. They have all my scrap books now. I feel pretty good about that.

Shel shared a bedroom with his brother, which also meant sharing a closet where Shel's collection of scrap books was kept. The day Shel's brother broke out with scarlet fever was a day Shel will never forget:

There was a warning sticker put on our front door. Our whole house was quarantined. Everything in our room had to be burned, and of course that included all of my *Dick Tracy* scrap books in our closet. I was able to sneak a few of them to the basement where I hoped the germs would eventually disappear on them. But, sad to say, I lost most of them. That was a devastating thing to have happened in my young life. It was like losing a part of me. My brother felt such guilt for so many years, though of course it wasn't his fault.

Eventually Shel started collecting *Dick Tracy* dailies and Sundays all over again. From neighbors and neighborhoods around the area, he collected old newspapers. He even found some used book stores in Detroit that had old newspapers for sale. Eventually, he was clipping and creating scrap books again. It took patience and time, but he accumulated five times as much as he had lost.

Shel remembers the excitement he felt one day in 1949 when he finally met Chester Gould:

My dad was on a business trip to Chicago and he drove that extra sixty miles out to Wood-stock. A man in the grocery store gave us the directions to the house. I just wanted to drive by the house, but I guess we decided to drive a little closer. We parked in front and his dog, Mugg, came out. Then Chet came out in a robe. We were totally unannounced and it was an imposition. Chet and his family were out by the pool. At that time, the swimming pool was not attached to the house. It was an outdoor pool. I had done a watercolor in school and I presented it to Chet and told him what a fan I was. He remembered my name from some of my letters. We took pictures and it was a wonderful experience. We went back to Detroit and I was absolutely floating on air. If he had been a top movie star, I couldn't have gotten more pleasure out of shaking his hand and meeting my hero. The irony was that I was so tongue tied my brother and Dad had to do all the talking for me. Years later of course, when I was grown up and entered the profession myself as a lettering man for cartoonist Milton Caniff (creator of *Steve Canyon*), I was in a more professional plane with Chester Gould.

Over the years Shel tried to analyze why Gould's Tracy had such an impact on him:

The only thing I can come up with is his story telling ability. I loved his artwork ability. His design quality in each panel was so well done. It's a lesson for any cartoonist, the way he laid out the point of view of the action. Once I told him, "Every Sunday in the last panel you have such a cliff hanger that I can't wait to see what was going to happen on Monday." Chet said, "Well, if you see some of those last panels, you would see a lot of erasures where I kept trying to make that panel more and more dynamic. That was my job. My job was to sell tomorrow's paper, and if I succeeded, I was doing my job."

I found Chet to be a very modest man, very down to earth, both feet anchored on the ground, such a friendly man. There was a sense of camaraderie about Chet and his work. He was devoted to his career. No one could stay on the front of hundreds of major Sunday comic sections of newspapers like Tracy, and that was a sign of popularity. It was later that *Peanuts* was on the front page, but Tracy, for forty-five years, had that position.

My friends, when I was a kid, accused me of being a little sadistic with my love for *Dick Tracy* and the ugly characters because I picked up on the gore and the violence, which was just a dramatic effect, the way Chet held readers. It wasn't sadistic at all. Chet made the statement many times that he wanted to distinguish between the good guys and the bad guys. Crime is ugly. That's why he made the villains so ugly. You could tell by looking at the strip who the bad guys were.

Most of the other cartoonists of the day would criticize Gould's artwork, which I could never understand. It wasn't until years later that scholars decided that he was such a unique stylist that he more than earned his place in the arts as a cartoonist. Gould described his style as a sort of "shorthand" and he got everything down to a graphic essence. Scholars since those early days have since analyzed his strip. I guess he was just before his time. I don't think it bothered him, because he had such an enormous success in popularity.

There was also the touch of humor in his strip. Most people overlook the fact that Chet was a great humorist. It wasn't corny jokes or joke situations. It was a creation of personalities. I am told that B.O. Plenty had a real-life counterpart somewhere. There were characters like Yel-lowpony (named after Chet's grade school friend Moses Yellowhorse, a full blood American Indian) in Pawnee, Oklahoma. But I think basically, the strip was a combination of all of his influences. Here was a man who was such an incredibly alert and curious person about every facet of life, that he was just assimilating all kinds of information which he would then use to put his own spin on in the strip. He did things that no one seems to know the inspiration for, little inventions such as when Junior was on the back of Shaky's car and he wrote in the dust on the back car and Tracy followed him. Shaky drove into this garage, and I guess it had this motorized door, like today's remote control gadgets. The garage door opened, the car drove in and the door closed. Tracy drove right by. Junior got under the car because he didn't want to be discovered; then all of a sudden the door in the back opened and the car drove off and the electric eye closed the other door, leaving Junior trapped in this sort of phony garage that enabled Shaky to make his getaway. These little bits and pieces were so fascinating and added so much to the story. That's what Chester Gould was all about, as far as I'm concerned. You could never predict what was going to happen in the strip.

To go back to when I first discovered *Dick Tracy*, the Brow was escaping the police and got shot up. Bloodied, he drove his car off the edge of the road and into a gravel pit and was discovered by this old hermit, witch-like character, Gravel Gertie, who was man crazy and deprived of any social contact. She lived in a shack on the gravel pit, saw this wrecked car and rescued the Brow and tried to nurse him back to health. That's how she came into the strip. Then later on B.O Plenty came into the strip in the Breathless story. He was introduced as this smelly old farmer plowing the field and Breathless was escaping the law and wanted B.O. to plow her under. She was hiding out from Tracy. She lay down in the field and with the tractor he plowed her under. This is how B.O. Plenty came into the strip. Several months later, B.O. Plenty and Gravel Gertie met, which was an incredible chemistry that these two grotesque weirdoes were capable of falling in love. A lot of that was humorously done, but also very touching. Well, they decided that they would get married, which was probably quite inspirational to middle-aged people, showing them that there was still hope no matter what. Of course several months later, to everyone's surprise, Gravel Gertie was pregnant. There was so much speculation about those ugly people and what kind of a baby they would create. Well, it turned out to be a most pleasant surprise because the baby was beautiful. This led to probably the most incredible marketing doll since the Shirley Temple doll, the Sparkle Plenty doll, an enormous best seller.

All these little elements in the strip and the way Chester Gould's mind worked were just fascinating to all of us. He was totally unpredictable and always focused. He gave everything he had and then some. Anyone who read the strip for any length of time would realize that this was a really unique story teller. We were his audience for life. He even killed a few of the lead characters, which touched a nerve in a lot of people. He brought some lead characters near death. B.O. Plenty was shot and hovered between life and death, and at one time, little Sparkle Plenty was kidnapped.

There was one thing that tickled me: when this adorable Sparkle Plenty, who hadn't been seen in the story for a long time, then came back in an adventure at Sunny Dell Acres one year. She was a teenager and had gotten really fat. We see the Plentys' house and there she is in the back, playing a bow fiddle, this really fat girl. We were horrified that our beautiful Sparkle Plenty was now a fat kid. Tracy asked B.O. how things were going, and B.O really didn't want to say anything. It turned out to get that bow fiddle, they had to send in so many box tops of this breakfast cereal, and Sparkle always ate the breakfast cereal. That's what made her fat. Each little touch of humor in the strip I would say rounded out the violence. It was a perfect balance. (I can talk about it now; I just felt it in those days. I wasn't able to write about it. Thinking back over those times, what in school could compare? Certainly not geography! I liked reading and library; they were nice. But I just couldn't wait to get home to read my Tracy scrap books.)

Another fascinating angle to the strip is the scientific inventions, the first one being the 2-Way Wrist Radio that B.O. Plenty discovered at the scene of a murder in 1946. This was an unheard of electronic gizmo. Now we have microscopic chips to create something that tiny, but in those days, everybody knows how big a radio was. They didn't even have these little miniature radios, let alone a thing you could strap to your wrist. Well, the 2-Way Wrist Radio was such a publicity-getter that people all over the world were just fascinated by this little device, and I'm sure scientists were inspired to try to create their version. I think a company came out with some kind of a toy of that sort.

Also, he followed that invention with the atom light, the mini–TV camera, the police television show-up, the camera ring, the Dick Tracy Teleguard, which was closed circuit television (he was way ahead of his time) surveying jewelry stores, bank vaults, the telephone number pick-up, and so on. All of these things are familiar to us now, but they didn't exist when Chester Gould dreamed them up for his comic strip. So his impact on real life was tremendous. I don't know any other cartoonist that can say that. There is a little slang expression, like the word "hot dog," that came out of a comic strip. The word "Jeep" also came out, and of course Walt Kelly also created that famous environmental slogan, "We have met the enemy and it is us," and he was talking about pollution. When Chet came out with the Magnetic Space Coupe he made the statement, "The nation that controls magnetism controls the earth." Now here our scientists of today are making some very heavy-duty discoveries about magnetism. How did Chet know that? Was it just a guess? Did he talk to scientists? All of these elements he put into the strip. He never rested on his laurels. He was always looking for the next thing to excite his readership.

People make such a fuss over Arthur Conan Doyle and Sherlock Holmes. He wrote a limited amount of stories, but Chester Gould wrote forty-five years of stories and his stories were incredible, far superior to anything of Sherlock Holmes. There is a connection because Chet always said that Tracy was a sort of reincarnation of Sherlock Holmes. Instead of a deerstalker cap, he would have a snap-brim fedora. Holmes was an inspiration for Chet. But he far exceeds, in my opinion, and I am sure history will prove that Chester Gould was a much greater story teller than Arthur Conan Doyle.

There is something about playing to the masses in the newspaper that people put on a lower plane, and I don't think that is true at all. I think the point is, when you have a hundred million readers a day as Chester had for *Dick Tracy*, that's an enormous indication of success, because people are very discerning. If they don't like what they read they won't read it the next week, and he held his audience in suspense for forty-five years.

Chet struggled for ten years trying to land a strip before he hit on *Dick Tracy*, and when he won that prize, he put his all into it. He never forgot how grateful he was to have that job and have the attention of the whole nation and the world. His strip was translated into a number of different languages—French, Italian, Spanish and some others. I don't think he ever took having the strip for granted. He felt responsibility to his readership that a lot of artists today just don't feel. He was paid back threefold for his years of popularity.

To this day I have a beautiful framed portrait profile of Tracy on my wall. It's the first thing you see when you come into my studio. It says, "To Shel Dorf with best wishes, Chester Gould." Well, it has been a treasure that I have had for years. You asked the right guy when you asked me to get excited about Chester Gould and Dick Tracy. I never stopped collecting until Chester Gould wrote and drew his last strip on December 25, 1977, and that's where my scrap books ends.

Richard Pietrzyk

Born in Oak Park, Illinois, Richard Pietrzyk worked on comic strips *Brenda Starr* and *Dick Tracy*. He scripted stories for comic book characters Katie Keene and Archie.

He is an avid photographer and has photographed such Hollywood stars as Elizabeth Taylor, Paul Newman and Bob Hope. Pietrzyk's photograph of Chester Gould, which appears on the cover of this book, has also appeared in many books, both in the states and internationally.

I remember when I started reading *Dick Tracy*. I was ten years old. It was Saturday morning and I was being particularly pesty. My mother was trying to get some housework done and she said, "Richard, find something to do!" I was bored with TV and my toys, and I said, "Like what?" Since I had an interest in art, she said, "How about doing something with the comics. Maybe make a scrap book."

It sounded like an okay idea, but which comic strip? For a small boy with an attention span of a cocker spaniel, only a story strip brimming with adventure could meet the challenge. *Terry and the Pirates*? Too sophisticated. *Brenda Starr*? For girls. *Dick Tracy*? Hmm!

When I picked up the previous Sunday's comic section, I discovered Dick Tracy to be a tall, square jawed detective. The black suit and the yellow fedora just grabbed my eye, as did the supporting characters. There was uniqueness about them. A bramble-haired farmer named B.O. Plenty appeared to be giving Tracy a hard time, and Miss Egghead, the villain in the story, was peering through the window, eavesdropping. She had evil written all over her. What was she up to? Though the characters engaged in conversation with one another, and no action was depicted, I knew I liked the style of the artwork and wanted to see more.

We kept a stack of Sunday papers in the cellar, so I went through them, piecing together the beginning of the Miss Egghead story. Not only did this one project interest me on that one Saturday morning, but it kept me busy for many days thereafter. This story took turn after exciting turn, like when Tracy trailed Miss Egghead to Cuba and was then stranded on a lost Caribbean Island, only to wind up in the path of a raging hurricane.

Richard Pietrzyk.

I could barely wait until 7:00 P.M. each evening when the *Chicago Tribune* released the next day's paper. On summer evenings, I was allowed to walk to the local grocery store for a box of Good and Plenty candy or a Three Musketeers bar and my daily dose of *Dick Tracy*. This was a summer routine.

As I followed the adventures of the great detective, I became a part of the story. Tracy's concerns were my concerns. Tracy's dangers were my dangers. Sam Catchem officially may have been Tracy's partner on the force, but I was Dick Tracy's true partner in crime, or rather, in crime fighting.

Sunday mornings could be a challenge for a ten year old because there were church services to attend before we bought the Sunday paper. The newsstand was set up just outside the church, and as far as I was concerned, Dick Tracy was fighting crime just ten feet from the front door. It was very difficult to sit through hymns, silent meditation and the lengthy sermon and stay focused on church, especially on those days when Dick Tracy was in danger. How could a small boy listen to excerpts from St. Paul's letters to the Corinthians while the great detective was fighting off starvation on a lost desert island or about to close in on a ruthless slot machine gang?

Not only did I enjoy reading *Dick Tracy*, but with my interest in art, I wanted to draw *Dick Tracy*. I would look at people and wonder how Chester Gould would depict them. This was another pastime I engaged in during church services, when I wasn't pondering Dick Tracy's fate: to glance at parishioners, noting their similarities to a *Dick Tracy* character. One church usher had hair like Nothing Yonson. A woman wore her hair down to the waist like Gravel Gertie. At one early morning service, a man, head thrown back, mouth open and asleep, looked just like Gargles gargling. I would also study my fellow worshipers' faces, exaggerating an eye here, a nose there, and create an original character. After all, what better place to study people than at church?

Being completely focused on *Dick Tracy* in church had its own reward. Once, two boys in the pew behind me were laughing and talking when their mother shushed them, saying, "Why can't you be quiet and pray like this little boy in front of you?"

What fascinated me about Chester Gould's work was that each story was utterly different. It was impossible to guess what would come next, let alone the outcome of the story. Certain sequences made each tale memorable: Mumbles and Cinn searching for treasure on a bleak marshy shore, while a dark sky descends like a guillotine on them. Little girl Sarah Crystal searching for ice cream bars in the cavernous walk-in freezer of her home, as the frozen body of a dead man sits in the shadows. Tracy being stalked through rain-swept city streets by the silhouetted form of Mrs. Pruneface. These and so many other sequences are still in my memory today.

The characters themselves were always a treat to behold. Characters in other comic strips had a similarity to one another, but Chester Gould's characters were different. Each one looked like he or she was drawn by a different artist. Their only similarity was that they were so dissimilar. A character could be winsome and cute like Popsie (1958), followed by a hideous Rhodent (1959).

As I created characters, I began to write my own *Dick Tracy* stories. Some of my school mates joined in the fun. We used a comic book format. Everybody liked to create the cover. The cover always showed Dick Tracy in some cliff hanging predicament or fighting with a criminal. The hard part was writing the story based on the cover. While I enjoyed the character portion of the story, some of my friends were more interested in detailing a crime or a car chase. My cousin, Tom (who later became an architect), was interested in location and backgrounds. Occasionally, we would take the El into Chicago, clattering through various neighborhoods, from residential to industrial, speculating on whether a passing auto repair garage or a boarded-up El station would make a good hideout for our story.

Inspirations for characters developed as my cartooning skills developed. After running through an overgrown prairie near my home, I found my socks and shoe laces covered with little burrs, inspiring me to create Burface. After suffering through my attempt to wear contact lenses, I created Onionhead, a man with an onion-shaped head who constantly weeps due to ill fitting contact lenses. Chester Gould's story featuring Spots and Ogden fascinated me, so for two villains, I created daughters, Dots and Shelly.

I originally drew my comic strips on typing paper with colored pencils. As time passed, my interest in cartooning grew. My fellow cartoonists fell by the wayside to pursue other interests, like baseball and model airplanes. Meanwhile, I tried to copy Gould's style by using the materials he did, 3-ply Strathmore paper with a Gillott pen point and India ink.

As my interest in Chester Gould's art intensified, I ventured to send a fan letter, followed by some drawings, and even a story. I had heard that Gould was hesitant in accepting story ideas by mail, but he was always complimentary and positive in his response to my submissions. A positive critique by Chester Gould of my art validated my efforts in a way none of my art teachers could.

In time I got to know Chester Gould, having some enlightening and memorable conversations with him about his work. I even had the opportunity to work on the comic strip with Gould's longtime assistant, Rick Fletcher. Over the years, I have read and reread the stories. I have never lost the thrill of excitement when seeing Gould's art. It's my "Rosebud." Whenever I see Dick Tracy investigating a crime scene, hot in pursuit of a fleeing felon or facing a notorious Flattop, I am ten years old again.

Matt Masterson

Matt Masterson was born on April 1, 1935. He graduated from Malden High School in Massachusetts, where he was named Class Artist for his work as a sports cartoonist and illustrator on the school newspaper. Matt won a four-year scholarship to the Massachusetts College of Art, where he received a B.A. in commercial art and design.

Matt worked as a greeting card designer and art director at a Boston publishing company for thirty years while doing free lance artwork, including some *Dick Tracy* projects for my father. Dad and Matt formed a strong and lasting friendship over the years, often spending weekends at the farm, discussing forty-six plus years of *Dick Tracy*.

Now retired, Matt enjoys spending time adding to his *Dick Tracy* comic art collection, which is often displayed in museum galleries, and devoting time to volunteer work in local animal shelters.

It was great being a kid in the 1940s. I had a paper route and delivered six or seven different Boston newspapers in my hometown of Malden, Massachusetts, a small town eight miles north of Boston. On Sundays, as I made my deliveries, I got to read *Mutt and Jeff* in the *Globe*; *Flash Gordon*, *Blondie* and *Bringing up Father* in the *Advertiser*; and *Tarzan* in *The Post*. My personal favorite comic section was in the *Herald*. It featured the comic strips syndicated by the *Chicago Tribune* such as *Terry and the Pirates*, *Little Orphan Annie*, *Gasoline Alley*, *Smilin' Jack*, *Gumps*, *Smokey Stover*, *Moon Mullins*, *Harold Teen*, *Winnie Winkle* and the strip that had the greatest impact on me ... *Dick Tracy*!

Chester Gould's masterpiece appeared on the front page of the *Boston Sunday Herald*, and I can still remember the riveting effect the artwork had on me. I had never seen such beautiful cartoons. I would study them for hours. And then there were those villains that gave Dick Tracy such a hard time in the early 1940s: unforgettable names such as Littleface, Mole, B-B Eyes, Pruneface, Brow, Shaky and Flattop. A passion for drawing was born, and I started creating my own drawings of *Dick Tracy* characters. It wasn't long before I would be called to the blackboard by my grammar school teacher to draw those *Dick Tracy* characters, much to the delight of my school mates, who especially enjoyed my interpretations of Gravel Gertie

Matt Masterson

in 1944 (third grade) and B.O. Plenty in 1945 (fourth grade). It was a great boost to my self confidence and popularity. I earned the nickname "Dick Tracy"!

I recall going to my neighborhood movie theater with my mother on Saturday afternoon when a school chum I knew passed us on his bike yelling, "Hey, Dick Tracy! Is that Gravel Gertie with you?" My mother, whose name was Gertrude, wondered how he knew her name.

The year 1946 was a great one! The war in the Pacific was over, and Chester Gould created the 2-Way Wrist Radio in January, adding an even greater dimension to the strip. I was in the fifth grade and still being besieged for drawings of *Dick Tracy* characters. In the summer of 1946, the artwork in *Dick Tracy* seemed even more exciting to me, with designs of black and white contrasting areas, exquisite crosshatched shading, thick and thin pen and ink lines to die for, and an imaginative "Crime does not pay" storyline. Those ingredients, plus the appearance of a new villain named "Shoulders"—a real bad guy with a massive upper body, cold, steely eyes and a deformed ear, who in the conclusion of his story crashes a stolen plane into a huge overhead gasoline storage tank—just added to the excitement. The drama and artwork in the Sunday pages from July 1946 was so exciting, I pinned them to the wall in my bedroom.

On August 18, 1946, Gould devoted the entire Sunday page to B.O. Plenty and Gravel Gertie's wedding. That page was filled with yet another magic touch—Gould's unique and wonderful sense of humor. Who could not adore this comic strip?

Next up was the villain "Gargles," a constantly gargling germophobe who distributed phony mouthwash. He wore an eye-catching herringbone jacket and diamond stick pin. In what is still my favorite chase sequence in *Dick Tracy* history, Gargles escapes a shoot-out with Tracy (amid giant bottles of phony mouthwash) by hiding inside a flower box outside of his hideout window. He eventually confronts Dick Tracy in a glass factory and comes out on the short end by tumbling down a stairwell as huge shards of broken glass pierce his body! It was that Sunday page from November 19, 1946, that convinced me that I should cut out *Dick Tracy* from the newspapers and preserve it in scrap books. Wishing I had started clipping *Tracy* earlier, I went hunting for back issues. I got chased out of a few apartment buildings by janitors who did not appreciate an uninvited, crazed eleven year old lurking in the stairways and going through old newspapers that had been piled up for months in the basement. To me, however, it only added to the excitement.

In the summer of 1947, I was rushed to the hospital with appendicitis caused, no doubt, by eating large amounts of grapes (seeds and all!) which my friends and I would rob in nightly raids from neighborhood grapevines. Back in those days, one was required to spend *ten* days in the hospital for an appendectomy. Those ten days of confinement and the weeks of recuperation that followed were my first lesson in "Crime does not pay" as well as in the function of the appendix. I would have gone stir crazy had it not been for *Dick Tracy*. Chester Gould was wrapping up the "Coffyhead" and "Autumn Hews" sequence in the *Daily Newspaper*, and as a double treat, a monthly comic book entitled "Super Comics" was reprinting a *Dick Tracy* adventure from 1943, which contained the ultimate "death trap" and revenge-seeking villainess, Mrs. Pruneface. My imagination just soared as I read how Mrs. Pruneface stalked and overpowered Tracy with her Amazon size and trusty bullwhip. Her plan was to chain Tracy to the floor in her kitchen between two huge blocks of ice on which rested a wooden plank with a metal spike driven through it and placed directly over Tracy's heart. A refrigerator was placed on top of the spiked plank for weight, and the oven was turned on to melt the ice so that the spike would be driven slowly through Tracy's chest.

Yes, you can say that reading Dick Tracy was just what the doctor ordered.

When I was forty years old, I was to meet my idol, Chester Gould, in person. Over the years, I had written him numerous fan letters commenting on the endless array of imaginative storytelling and colorful villains. I always received an enthusiastic and encouraging reply, but the best was yet to come in 1975. "Chet" invited me to visit with him at his studio on the 26th floor of the *Chicago Tribune*.

That day I spent with Chester Gould was better than winning a billion dollars. A warm and friendly gentleman, full of exuberance and loaded with energy, with a generous smile that never left his face, he reminded me of my favorite Sunday school teacher rather than the creator of the hard-driven, tough as nails, crime fighting detective *Dick Tracy*. Lunch with him that day led to invitations to spend weekends with him and his equally wonderful wife, Edna, at their home in Woodstock, Illinois.

So there we were, sharing a breakfast of peanut butter and honey on toast, myself being taken for a joy ride around Chet's golf course in his Cadillac and, best of all, kneeling beside his drawing board and watching him create a special drawing of Dick Tracy just for me. Watching the magic unfold before my eyes as he slashed the ink with his pen upon the Strathmore drawing paper, I marveled that here was the genius who had created an American icon, *Dick Tracy*, a comic strip that became an instant classic almost upon conception.

In my estimation, *Dick Tracy* remains the greatest comic strip ever created. Not only for its unique storylines and larger than life characters, but especially for the artwork, which held me spellbound with each daily installment. Not overly illustrative and not a mere cartoon, it was a perfect blend somewhere between the two, masterfully crafted to grab and hold your attention.

Today, Chester Gould's powerful *Dick Tracy* original art is displayed in numerous museums and galleries and in the homes of lucky collectors, including myself.

Chester Gould once told me that his main job was to sell newspapers. While doing that, he became not only one of the all-time great American success stories but the greatest cartoonist of them all!

Appendix A.
The Grandchildren Remember

Sue O'Connell Sanders

I remember my grandfather, Chester Gould, not as the creator of *Dick Tracy*, but as a man who was full of love, great stories of the "olden days" and non-stop fun! I grew up calling him "Baba," my special name for this very special man.

My memories of my grandfather are forever merged with those of my grandmother, most likely because, to me, the two of them seemed to be so emotionally connected. My grandmother, a petite but strong, intelligent, and gracious woman who adored my grandfather, always praised and supported him in all areas of life. I think she was his rock.

As a little girl, I knew that going to Baba and Gram's meant fun and adventure. We might spend an afternoon being pulled on sleds behind Baba's jeep in the winter, or perform acrobatic shows on the trampoline in the summer or be in awe of his magic tricks, usually done after dinner. There was never a shortage of laughter around him.

Baba could sit at their baby grand piano and play anything — all by ear. He never took a lesson. Baba didn't always play alone, however. Rocky and Cissy Girl, two of the family dogs, would usually accompany him, howling off-key. Ironically, it was Cissy Girl who was the baritone. Gram played the piano too, having studied it as a young girl, and she and I would sometimes sit and play together. Baba loved to listen and watch the two of us "tickle the ivories." That piano now sits in our living room, and our daughter, Megan, plays it.

My brother, Tracy, and I used to spend hours with Baba making silly tape recordings on his tape recorder. This was a new piece of

Sue O'Connell Sanders

equipment back in the 1960s and it absolutely fascinated us. Baba would interview us by introducing us as funny characters and we would ad lib some nonsense. As we played it back, we would laugh uncontrollably and want to do another "interview" right away. This was one of the many pastimes we enjoyed while spending a week with Gram and Baba, which we did every summer.

In addition to all the fun, we also had jobs we were expected to complete during our stay. Baba would make up a job chart for us and we would work out a schedule for each day. Even though these were "jobs," there was always an element of fun or silliness involved; after all, we were at Baba and Gram's! The jobs usually included things like helping Gram clean out closets (filled with treasures), watering the abundant plants (Gram had a very green thumb), sweeping the blue stone around the swimming pool area, pulling weeds, and so forth. At the end of the week Gram and Baba would take us out for a wonderful dinner.

When we stayed with Gram and Baba for a week, we knew that Baba had to work at his drawing board in the studio. He started very early in the morning and would finish up around 2:00 P.M. After that he would sometimes mow his vast acreage, something he loved to do. However, no matter how busy he was while drawing *Dick Tracy*, whenever I happened to stroll up to his drawing board to take a peek, he would stop what he was doing, put his arm around me and say, "What do you think, Sue doll?" He always had the time to make us feel important. After sharing a hug, I would be on my way. I suppose that is why the fact that he drew *Dick Tracy* was nothing extraordinary to me at that age. Baba was always a grandfather first.

My grandfather was always the one to say grace before each meal. They were beautiful graces, though nothing structured. He just spoke from his heart, thanking God for "bringing us together." It left a lasting impression on me. As he got older, there would sometimes be tears of gratefulness within his prayers, tears he never tried to hide.

Mom, Pop, Tracy and I would visit Baba and Gram almost every Sunday to have Sunday dinner (held at noon). After Sunday dinner, in the summertime, the men would play golf on the course, which surrounded the house. Tracy and I would be hired to caddy for them. We would make fifty cents or so, and when we were done, we would generally change into our bathing suits and jump in the pool for a swim or have a diving competition. In later years, after the pool was enclosed, in the wintertime we would roll around in the snow and then jump into the heated pool. The whole family had many fun afternoons in the pool, which Baba kept impeccably clean. It was crystal blue and always beckoning. Gram kept live geraniums in each corner of the pool gutters for a splash of color. I was fascinated by the way Gram could float on her back without moving a muscle. She would just lie there, looking totally relaxed. Although I am a good swimmer and diver, that is something I never was able to achieve.

The swimming pool, built in 1947 and enclosed in 1967, was a blessing for Baba. He used to swim laps each morning to keep his back limber. It had grown stiff over the years of leaning over the drawing board. He did a slow, steady stroke, back and forth and back and forth. I only saw him do this if I got up really early, as he did this before beginning his day at the drawing board.

When my husband, Brett, and I were married in 1981, Baba and Gram were with us. I was so glad that through our years of dating, Brett had gotten to know these two special people in my life, and they him. In April of 1985, just before Baba passed away, Brett and I were able to share the news that we were expecting a baby. I was so happy that Baba knew that "life was going on," and his family was growing.

I didn't realize until I was grown what a vital part of his life the *Dick Tracy* comic strip was. To me, Baba was this remarkable grandfather who knew how to create fun out of nothing. His wisdom knew no bounds in my eyes. I was twenty-eight years old when Baba passed away, but his positive influence on my life is eternal. He was a loving grandfather, talented artist, creative story-teller and brilliant businessman, a man who truly loved life. His humble beginnings never lacked for love nor discouraged this man's perseverance in accomplishing his dream.

I am very proud of my mother for writing this book about my grandfather's life. It was her love for him that fueled her ambition to accomplish the writing of his story. It was her admiration and pride for Baba that made her want to share his story with others. Thanks, Mom!

Tracy Richard O'Connell

My grandfather was quite a man — really one of a kind. As a friend of mine put it at his funeral, "They broke the mold when he was born." That they did! Here was a man who grew up poor, in a dirt-floor log cabin, and went to the top in his field. Despite his fame and success, he never forgot where he came from.

Visiting Gram and Gramp was anything but routine. There was fun and laughter with every visit. In my earliest memories of my grandfather, my sister and I are riding in his surplus World War II jeep. We must have been four or five at the time. As we got older, we did many other things, from being pulled on the toboggan behind the jeep to clowning around using the tape recorder. Gramp had an endless supply of fun things to do. For instance, he and I would work on the golf course or tend to maintenance items in and around the house. I remember one spring break from high school he wanted to trim a willow tree that was getting a little too big on one of the fairways. So we cut halfway through this limb using a hand saw and then hooked up a log chain around the branch and attached it to the back of the jeep. It actually lifted the back of the jeep off the ground until the branch eventually broke. Talk about funny!

I remember going into his studio at their home to watch him draw *Dick Tracy*. He sometimes would let me erase the pencil marks on the inked daily strips or a Sunday page. Little did I think about the millions of people reading those strips, holding their breath to find out if Dick Tracy was going to make it through another day of crime fighting.

In my office at home, I have an original Sunday page that featured a fire engine I drew as a kid. I used to draw a lot when I was little, and I especially liked to draw fire engines. One that I drew kind of looked like a crane with a big boom that sprayed water along with sprinklers all over the fire engine. Gramp saw this drawing one Sunday when he and Gram visited us. Little did I know that that fire engine would appear in a Sunday page in the *Dick Tracy* strip. In one of the panels of this Sunday page, Diet Smith is showing Tracy his latest mammoth machine. "Engineered by T.R. O'Connell, my head designer, this steel jacketed brute contains thousands

Tracy Richard O'Connell

of perforations through which water is atomized at 2,000 pounds pressure," he said. "With its 200-ton hammer swinging, as well as shooting water, it goes directly into the heart of the inferno in a mist of water and chemicals. Steel beams, stones, all, are like matchwood. Inside the machine, men breathe fresh clean air and press buttons." This Sunday page appeared April 3, 1966, when I was in fourth grade, and what a thrill! As young as I was, I felt this was Gramp's way of seeing whether I might have a future interest in working with him on the strip. As it turned out, I did not—but I did become a degreed engineer.

When I told Gramp that I had joined the Lambda Chi Alpha fraternity at Florida Institute of Technology, to my surprise, he said he was a Lambda Chi at Oklahoma A & M and at Northwestern University. We were not only grandson and grandfather; we were brothers. What are the chances of that happening?

In his later years, I would drive him to the Lake Zurich Golf Club, where he was a member, and into the Tribune Tower to take care of business. For lunch, we would eat at the Tavern Club where the bartender referred to us as Dick Tracy and Junior. I told my grandfather many times that just being around him recharged my batteries. He had that kind of charisma and outlook.

In 1985 Gramps' health was failing. He passed away in May. I lost not only my grandfather, but also my best friend. What a legacy this one man left. A master story teller and an artisst who created a world re-known icon—Dick Tracy!

This book that my mother has written is a blueprint of this man's success, persistence and non-stop determination.

Appendix B. Awards and Honors Received by Chester Gould

1953   Northwestern University's Award of Merit

1957   American Institute of Men and Boys Wear

1959   The Reuben Award for Outstanding Cartoonist of the Year

1976   The Tavern Club: extensive one-man show of Gould's *Dick Tracy*

1977   The Reuben Award for Outstanding Cartoonist of the Year

1979   Illinois Service Organizations (USO) of Chicago, American Armed Forces Recognition Dinner and award

1979   The Ninety-Sixth *Congressional Record* recognition of Chester Gould and Dick Tracy as American heroes

1979   Easter Seals Benefit of Woodstock honoring Chester Gould

1979   The Inkpot Award (San Diego Comic-Con voted *Dick Tracy* the most popular comic strip of all time.)

1980   Press Veterans of the Year

1980   The Edgar Allan Poe Award (For the first time in their thirty-four year history, the Mystery Writers of America presented a special award to a cartoonist and comic strip. Said mystery writer Donald E. Westlake, "When Gould created *Dick Tracy* in 1931, the American procedural detective story was born.")

1981   Chicago Journalism Hall of Fame induction

1981   Northwestern University Alumni Medal

1983   Bonifex Maximus Award (Tavern Club Recognition Dinner)

Posthumous Honors

1985   Personal letter from President Reagan

1985   General Assembly of the State of Ohio's 116th General Assembly proclamation in memory of Chester Gould

1990   Northwestern University's night school (University College) Alumni Association development of *The Chester Gould Society*

1990   Award of Achievement from Lambda Chi Alpha's 55th General Assembly and Leadership

1993   State of Oklahoma proclamation in memory of Chester Gould; "Chester Gould Street" named in Pawnee, Oklahoma

Recognitions from Presidents

1973   President Richard Nixon

1979   President Jimmy Carter

1983   President Ronald Reagan

Other Recognitions

1949   Police Athletic Leagues

1953   Associated Police Communications Officers, Inc.

1958   National Police Officers Association

1968   The Honor Legion of the Police Department of the City of New York

1973   The FBI (Clarence M. Kelley)

1975   Special Agents Association

1976   Illinois Crime Prevention Officers Association

1979   Illinois Crime Prevention Officers Association (in recognition of Crime Stoppers): Proclamation for Outstanding Contributions in the Area of Crime Prevention

1980   Chicago Police Department

1982   The Illinois Police Federation

1985   Crimestoppers for McHenry County

Index

DATE DUE
